Also by Luc Sante

Low Life: Lures and Snares of Old New York

Evidence

The Factory of Facts

Kill All Your Darlings: Pieces, 1990–2005

Folk Photography: The American Real-Photo Postcard, 1905–1930

EDITOR AND TRANSLATOR

Novels in Three Lines, by Félix Fénéon

The Other Paris

Farrar, Straus and Giroux   *New York*

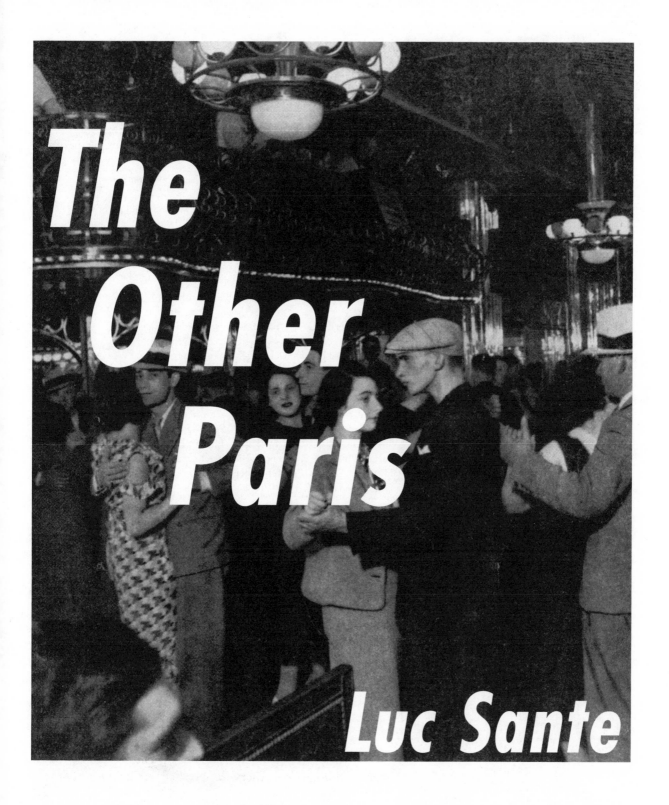

The Other Paris

Luc Sante

Farrar, Straus and Giroux
18 West 18th Street, New York 10011

Printed in the United States of America
First edition, 2015

Grateful acknowledgment is made for permission to reprint the following
images:
Page 27 (bottom): *Guide psychogéographique de Paris*, by kind permission of Greil
Marcus.
Page 78: Rally in support of the United Front, copyright © Corbis.
Pages 270 and 271: Stills from *Le Pont du Nord*, with thanks to Jacques Rivette and
Les Films du Losange, and special thanks to Jake Perlin.

Library of Congress Cataloging-in-Publication Data
Sante, Luc.
    The other Paris / Luc Sante. — First edition.
        pages   cm
    Includes bibliographical references and index.
    ISBN 978-0-374-29932-3 (hardback) — ISBN 978-1-4299-4458-8
(e-book)
    1. Paris (France)—Social life and customs—19th century.   2. Paris
(France)—Social life and customs—20th century.   3. City and town
life—France—Paris—History.   4. Poor—France—Paris—History.
5. Working class—France—Paris—History.   6. Criminals—France—
Paris—History.   7. Eccentrics and eccentricities—France—Paris—
History.   8. Paris (France)—Social conditions.   9. Paris (France)—
Description and travel.   I. Title.

DC715 .S3125 2015
944'.36106—dc23
                                                                    2015004988

Designed by Jonathan D. Lippincott

Our books may be purchased in bulk for promotional, educational, or business
use. Please contact your local bookseller or the Macmillan Corporate and
Premium Sales Department at 1-800-221-7945, extension 5442, or by
e-mail at MacmillanSpecialMarkets@macmillan.com.

www.fsgbooks.com
www.twitter.com/fsgbooks • www.facebook.com/fsgbooks

10   9   8   7   6   5   4   3   2   1

All translations, unless otherwise specified, are by the author.

For Mimi

Sire, I am from the other country.
                    —Ivan Chtcheglov

Contents

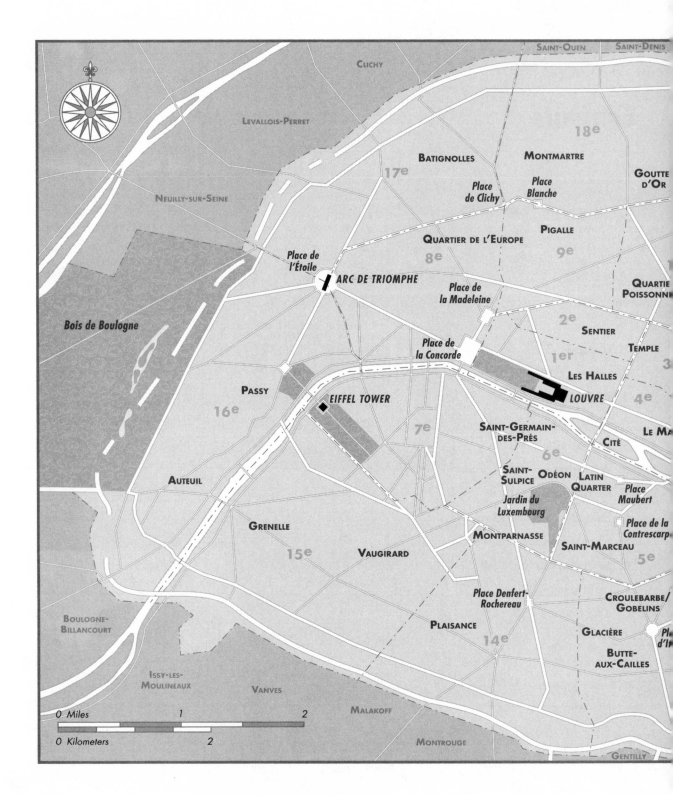

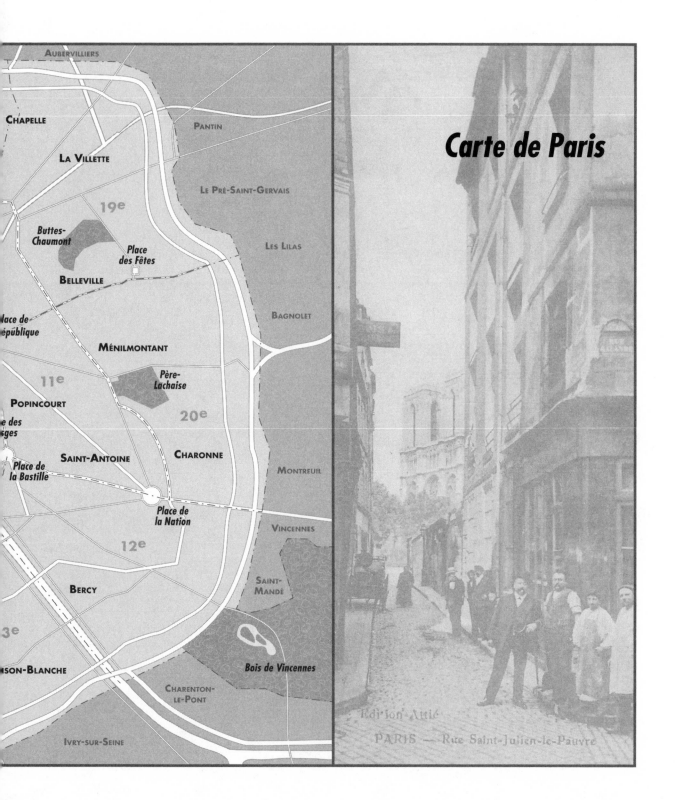

Carte de Paris

AUBERVILLIERS

CHAPELLE

PANTIN

LA VILLETTE

LE PRÉ-SAINT-GERVAIS

19e

Buttes-
Chaumont

Place
des Fêtes

LES LILAS

BELLEVILLE

lace de
épublique

BAGNOLET

MÉNILMONTANT

11e

Père-
Lachaise

POPINCOURT

20e

e des
ges

SAINT-ANTOINE

CHARONNE

Place de
la Bastille

MONTREUIL

Place de
la Nation

VINCENNES

12e

SAINT-
MANDÉ

BERCY

3e

SON-BLANCHE

Bois de Vincennes

CHARENTON-
LE-PONT

IVRY-SUR-SEINE

The Other Paris

1

Capital

In Julien Duvivier's 1937 film *Pépé le Moko*, set in the Algiers casbah, the two leading characters are waxing nostalgic about their native city. Gaby (Mireille Balin) was gently reared, while Pépé (Jean Gabin) is working-class.

> Gaby: Do you know Paris?
> Pépé: It's my village, Rue Saint-Martin.
> Gaby: The Champs-Élysées.
> Pépé: The Gare du Nord.
> Gaby: The Opéra, Boulevard des Capucines.
> Pépé: Barbès, La Chapelle.
> Gaby: Rue Montmartre.
> Pépé: Boulevard Rochechouart.
> Gaby: Rue Fontaine.
> Both: Place Blanche!

She names places in her city, he names places in his, and then they both agree on a square that straddles the border—the site of the Moulin Rouge and the place where the honky-tonk of Pigalle locks eyes with the gentility of the Quartier de l'Europe. Gaby's list defines the top edge of the pie slice of western Paris, a quarter of the whole at most, that then housed the gentry: the northwesterly course of Rue Montmartre that is picked up by Rue Notre-Dame-de-Lorette and then Rue Fontaine, and then

Mireille Balin and Jean Gabin in *Pépé le Moko*, 1937

Fireworks. Illustration by Félix Vallotton, 1902

goes on to merge into Avenue de Clichy. If she had been thorough she might have mentioned the other leg, on the Left Bank: Boulevard Saint-Germain, Rue de Sèvres, Avenue de Suffren. Pépé's list is far less comprehensive, but that's at least in part because in 1937 there was still so much more of his city than of hers.

This book will not be much concerned with Gaby's city. It has changed far less, for one thing. It retains the greatest concentration of money and power, and in that way common to old-money neighborhoods in many cities, it has probably preserved more of those small businesses, cafés, and such than have the more vulnerable neighborhoods elsewhere, because the rich have the power to save the things they love. That wedge of western Paris has changed primarily in that its composition now includes not just the old families and the nouveaux riches but also a significant number of foreign and often absentee property owners who invest in a Paris flat the way they might buy art and warehouse it. That attitude might almost make you think fondly of the old families, who at least are or were connected to the city's soil and history. But then you might recall how consistently inimical the western districts have been to the rest of the city over time, how they made common cause with the Prussians against the Commune in 1871; called for the extermination of the Communards, including women and children, during the Bloody Week in May of that year; and in 1938, after the Popular Front, "acclaimed Hitler in the cinemas of the Champs-Élysées at twenty francs a seat," while even fashionable ladies joined in shouting the slogan "Communists, get your bags; Jews, off to Jerusalem." It is no coincidence that the Gestapo office on Rue des Saussaies and the headquarters on Rue Lauriston of its French counterpart, the Carlingue, were both situated within that triangle.

But if Gaby's city was all demure white façades, discreet traffic, and well-mannered exchanges, Pépé's was undeniably rougher. The marketplace of the street brought all types to the fore, and they did not necessarily speak correctly or measure their tones or clean themselves up; they might not have wished you well. And the streets themselves held as many gaping eyesores as they did the sort of charmingly weathered houses you admire in Atget's pictures. You can read Georges Cain's description of the Marché des Patriarches, the now long-gone flea market around the church of Saint-Médard in the Fifth Arrondissement, and judge that it reflects the author's class bias, as an antiquarian and museum curator slumming around while looking for forgotten architectural treasures: "Tumbledown hovels sheltering miserable enterprises: resellers of nameless objects, dealers in rags, vendors of dust. A side of beef is being butchered alongside a big factory wall that looks like a prison. And everywhere the air is poisonous with sulfuric acid, kippered herring, and cauliflower." But nearly the same tone appears thirty years later, in a description of the area near Place des Fêtes, in the Nineteenth, by Eugène Dabit, the most self-consciously proletarian of writers:

> A shoelace vendor, his face ravaged, looks as if he's wearing a mask with a fake beard and red cloth lips. At the market on Rue du Télégraphe a woman selling thyme repeats in a piercing voice, "Give work to the blind." People drag themselves from job site to job site, picking up wood, and from street to street, picking up rags; others are trusties or nightwatchmen. On their days out, the guys from the shelters, in their rough blue uniforms, tentatively hold out their hands, hoping to pick up enough for a package of decent tobacco.

So, you might ask, why should we care that those people or their contemporary avatars have vanished from the city? Isn't it pleasant that Saint-Médard has been so nicely cleaned up and aired out that now it looks like the parish church in Anyville? And isn't it at least sanitary that Place des Fêtes has been so artfully landscaped? And if it is surrounded by monolithic high-rises with all the charm of industrial air-conditioning units, doesn't that at least mean they are designated for low-income housing? Because, after all, if the low houses that ringed the square before urban renewal claimed it had been cleaned and repaired instead of being razed, no one living there could today afford the neighborhood. There are indeed a few places in Paris where the poor can live, but the requirement is that those places be inhuman, soulless, windswept. In the past the poor were left to hustle on their own, which might mean accommodating themselves to squalor, with accompanying vermin; the bargain

The flea market called Marché des Patriarches, Rue Saint-Médard, circa 1910

they are offered today assures them of well-lit, dust-free environs with up-to-date fixtures, but it relieves them of the ability to improvise, to carve out their own spaces, to conduct slap-up business in the public arena if that is what they wish to do. They are corralled and regulated in ways no nineteenth-century social engineer could have imagined.

The relative intimacy of a city, any city, of a hundred or more years ago is as hard to overstate as it is to convey. There may have been nearly as many people, but they were more highly concentrated, in neighborhoods that were as delimited and self-sufficient as country villages, and where the absence of voice- and image-bearing devices in the home caused people to spend much more of their time in the street. There were no commuters to speak of, at least before the 1920s; everyone you saw, barring the occasional tourist or trader, lived right there in town, usually in the very neighborhood in which you spotted them. Every parish had its eccentrics, its indigents, its clerics, its savants, its brawlers, its widows, its fixers, its elders, its hustlers, its busybodies. Most of them had known one another all their lives. The income spectrum may not have been excessively wide, but on the other hand, the rich were right over there, in the next street.

Before Haussmann's reconfiguration of the center, the neighborhoods were tightly interwoven; afterward they were more separated, but the classes still met on common ground: on the squares and the boulevards. It was said that when cafés began to feature open terraces, the poor discovered what and how to eat from passing by and observing the diners as they ate. And the rich always had the opportunity to absorb the culture of the poor from their markets and entertainments. For that matter, the practice of *mixité* flourished for at least a century: a house of six or seven stories would feature a shop on the ground floor; the shopkeeper's dwelling on the mezzanine level; a bourgeois family upstairs from the mezzanine, on the "noble floor"; then each succeeding story would house people of progressively lesser income. People trudged up as few flights of stairs as they could afford, and as a result, every such house was itself a microcosm of society as a whole.

This is not to imply that society was just or kindly; it was brutal, generally. Nevertheless, there was room for the full range

A café. Illustration by J. J. Grandville, from *Scènes de la vie privée et publique des animaux*, 1842

of classes, and everyone was somehow equally involved in the common task of constituting a city. It was an ecosystem in which every aspect of the physical fabric was employed and drained and periodically revitalized, in which everything from rags and bones to ideas and fads was recycled and where nothing was disposed of until it was completely spent. So much of life was conducted in public that an entire education could be procured just by walking around, from riverbank to market to square to boulevard, from "the great poem of display" (Balzac) to the performances of the mountebanks, from the dance halls to the public executions, from the news vendors to the dandies, from the prostitutes to the bill posters, from the east to the west.

Rue Érard, circa 1910

The geography and topography were critical. The city grew in concentric circles as determined by its successive walls: under Philippe-Auguste, around the turn of the thirteenth century; Charles V, in the fourteenth; the Farmers-General, just before the revolution; Adolphe Thiers, in the 1840s; and, on the footprint of the latter, the Périphérique highway, completed in 1973. With every succeeding wall, some more of the surrounding countryside and its villages were absorbed into the city; what had once been periphery was directed toward the middle. Meanwhile, the center gradually moved. It did not go all that far, maybe a couple of miles over four or five centuries, but it entailed a larger movement of fashion. That began with the Louvre when it was a royal residence, slid east to the Marais in the seventeenth century, and then moved west again, serially along Rue de Rivoli and Rue Saint-Honoré and their parallel boulevards higher up, while the center of modish residence, by that time removing itself from commerce, glided northwest toward the Plaine Monceau and then farther, to Auteuil and Passy. Much of the center was shared and then disputed; even after Haussmann's reconfiguration, the gentry could not claim Saint-Denis or the Plateau Beaubourg or Les Halles. The rocky heights of Montmartre and Belleville and Ménilmontant were firmly of the people, as was the nebulous south: Maison-Blanche, Croulebarbe, Glacière, Butte-aux-Cailles, Grenelle, Montrouge.

Boulevard de Bonne-Nouvelle, circa 1910

The past, whatever its drawbacks, was wild. By contrast, the present is farmed. The exigencies of money and the proclivities of bureaucrats—as terrified of anomalies as of germs, chaos,

Rue de la Glacière, circa 1910

dissipation, laughter, unanswerable questions—have conspired to create the conditions for stasis, to sanitize the city to the point where there will be no surprises, no hazards, no spontaneous outbreaks, no weeds. The reformers and social activists of the past, faced with the urgent task of feeding the hungry and housing the unsheltered, failed to anticipate that the poor would, in exchange, be surrendering the riches they actually possessed: their neighborhoods as well as their use of time, their scavenger economy, their cooperative defenses, their refusal to behave, their ability to drop out of sight, their key to the unclaimed, the scorned, the common property of the streets. As a consequence of these and other changes, we have forgotten what a city was. There was a flavor to the city that has now been eradicated. It had a fugitive lyricism almost impossible to recapture. The young Verlaine affords a taste:

> The noise of the bars, the grit of the sidewalks,
> The decaying plane trees shedding leaves in the dark,
> The omnibus a hurricane of rattling iron and mud,
> That screeches, badly aligned on its wheels,
> And slowly rolls its green and yellow eyes,
> Workers going to their club, smoking clay pipes
> Under the noses of the police officers,
> Dripping roofs, sweating walls, slippery pavement,
> Cracked asphalt, streams filling the gutter,
> That's my road—with heaven at the end.

And sixty years later Francis Carco, a flâneur with a gift for verbal photography:

> I walked as far as the Pacra concert hall, on the corner of a boulevard and a street, turned onto the boulevard, entered a bar, read the papers. Night was falling. A pharmacy spread its green and yellow lights on the asphalt. From some dive came the ragged sound of an accordion. I noticed people as they passed: a fat man in a cap, a cop, three young girls with umbrellas, a whistling kid, a family of workers, two soldiers, an old woman selling papers shouting "*L'Intran*!," an Arab, a widower holding his little boy's hand . . . The blueish and bright orange lights of a cinema

Rue du Commerce, with elevated Métro and the Grande Roue, the 328-foot-tall Ferris wheel built for the Exposition of 1900

and the pink lights and huge arrow of a Dupont-tout-est-bon sign stretched their blurry electric trails along the façades, and the street was shaken by the taxis, the streetcars, the Métro that emerges from the ground at that point. At the corner of Barbès and Rochechouart, under an arcade, itinerant singers drew a crowd some evenings. Women milled around, pretended to listen, and walked off newly partnered.

Street singers, 1920s

All of Paris radiated out from Les Halles, the great central marketplace that dated back to the twelfth century, when the king, Philippe-Auguste, consolidated a number of smaller markets, and which was given its final form between 1852 and 1870, when Victor Baltard built the enormous cast-iron pavilions that covered most of the array. It comprised a number of major markets—*halles* for meat; for saltwater and freshwater fish; for butter, eggs, and cheese; for fruits, vegetables, and herbs; for flowers. It was immense. Zola describes "a strange city, with its distinct neighborhoods, its suburbs, its villages, its paths and its roads, its squares and its intersections, all sheltered under a hangar one rainy day on some cyclopean whim." Inside, in the early morning, the "river of greenery" gave way to the "the vivid stains of the carrots, the pure stains of the turnips . . . illuminating the market with the motley of their two colors," and "the reddish-brown varnish of a basket of onions, the bleeding red of a heap of tomatoes, the yellowish effacement of a pile of cucumbers, the dark violet of a cluster of eggplants lighting up here and there, while big black radishes, arrayed like mourning cloths, left a few shadowy holes amid the vibrant joys of the awakening."

But Les Halles wasn't just a market, it was the *rus in urbe*, not only connecting the city to the country but rendering the city in the light of the country, its population as varieties of fauna—it seems hardly coincidental that the market lay adjacent to the sempiternal flesh market of Rue Saint-Denis, where until not long ago the whores aligned themselves along the house fronts for blocks on end. Sherwood Anderson wrote in 1921:

The splendid horses of Paris pulling the great wheeled carts. Great hogsheads of wine, grain piled high in brown sacks.

The fish market at Les Halles, circa 1910

The vegetable market at Les Halles, circa 1910

The wheels of some of the carts are as high as the door of a church. Often the great horses are hitched tandem—three, four, six, ten. The horses are not castrated. There is fire and life in them . . . [The] men love the great breasted stallions as do I. They are not afraid. They do not castrate. Here life is more noble than anything machinery has yet achieved.

Les Halles was a biosphere, a living embodiment of the chain of production and consumption, an exchange where commerce remained as personal and sensual as it had been before advertising and marketing were invented, a tremendous social equalizer, a place where the jobless could always find pickup work and the hungry could scrounge for discarded but acceptable food, a hub with its own culture and customs varnished by nearly a millennium of use. It wasn't just the stomach of Paris but its soul. It was doomed by administrative decree in 1960 and demolished beginning in 1969, in favor of a wholesale-only market in distant suburban Rungis, and replaced by a hellish subterranean shopping mall that is nowadays topped by that urbanist cure-all, an *espace vert*.

Marco Ferreri's 1974 film *Don't Touch the White Woman!* belongs to a subgenre peculiar to that time, the farcical revisionist Western. It stars Marcello Mastroianni as a dim George A. Custer, Michel Piccoli as a mincing Buffalo Bill, and Catherine Deneuve as the titular white woman. Much of it takes place in a vast expanse of yellow that looks convincingly like the desert of the southwestern United States—until the camera draws back and you realize that it is instead the great pit dug out under the emplacement of Les Halles, the future site of the shopping mall and of the Châtelet–Les Halles RER station. Cavalry charges thunder down Rue Rambuteau, troops mass in front of the Bourse du Commerce, and then there is the poignant spectacle of hundreds of Native Americans, played by black-haired Parisians, being forced to march away from their lands along the deep flank of the pit, their Trail of Tears apparently endless even though it cannot be more than about five blocks long.

A still from Marco Ferreri's *Don't Touch the White Woman!* (1974)

There is a perennially recurrent Parisian identification with Native Americans, dating back to the 1820s and '30s and the furor caused by Fenimore Cooper's *Leatherstocking Tales*, cited as a primary influence by Balzac and Hugo, among others. That is perhaps what prompted Alexandre Privat d'Anglemont, the nineteenth century's consummate flâneur, and himself a mixed-race native of Guadeloupe, to mourn the decline of Belleville in the 1850s by writing, "Civilization has acted here as in North America; in moving forward it has cast out all the savages in its path." The Belleville he regrets was the one then outside the city limits, a rustic site of outdoor drinking places, dance halls, and the apparently enchanting Île d'Amour, "where so many fleeting liaisons began." Very soon after that, Belleville became the bastion of the city's working class, the heart of the Commune, sufficiently militant and volatile that nervous bureaucrats split it up among four separate arrondissements. It was "an ardent plebeian capital, as indigent and leveled as an anthill," according to the revolutionary and novelist Victor Serge, who moved there in 1909, while the British historian Richard Cobb called it the "high citadel of l'esprit parisien," which had emigrated from its former locus in the center, in the Cité and Rue Saint-Denis, having been relocated by the vast surgical enterprises of Baron Haussmann. In addition, Belleville over time became famous for taking in immigrants and refugees: provincials from the south and middle of the country; eastern European Jews crowded out of the ancient Jewish district in the Marais; North Africans, primarily from Algeria; West Africans from Senegal, Guinea, Gabon, the Ivory Coast; and Vietnamese and Cambodians, especially

"Stand still!"—Rue de Belleville, circa 1910

The cooperative La Bellevilloise, on Rue Boyer, circa 1910

Under the *métro aérien* on Boulevard de la Chapelle, circa 1910

ethnic Chinese from those nations. To some degree it remains so, the only part of the city to which the term *melting pot* could be applied.

The photographs by Willy Ronis of Belleville and Ménilmontant from the 1940s and '50s look like the photographs of Montmartre from fifty years earlier, only more crowded: houses spilling down the hill, piled on top of one another; gardens and vacant lots and even patches of woods tucked into any available niches; streets turning into stairs and back again; bars tucked away in alleys; artisans' workshops in tiny courtyards; lookouts from which you could see the whole city. The place was modest, a consequence of adaptation and making do; money and grand plans had never come anywhere near. One of the newest of the neighborhoods, historically, it kept faith with the spirit of the old city, and managed its limitations with maximum panache, as if it were a community of tree houses. A lot of this was regularized and normalized under urban renewal in the 1960s, and whole streets of ancient houses were razed, to be replaced by high-rise housing projects. You can still see the hammer and sickle on the entablature of the former cooperative La Bellevilloise, now a rock club, on Rue Boyer; and at the western end of that street, on Rue de Ménilmontant, observe the location of Prosper Enfantin's Saint-Simonian cenacle, where members of the community in the 1830s wore garments that buttoned in the back, so that even dressing would be a communal enterprise.

Above Belleville was La Chapelle, "a kingdom rather than an arrondissement," wrote Léon-Paul Fargue in the 1930s.

This kingdom, one of the richest in Paris in public baths where you wait as at the dentist's, is dominated by the aerial line of the Métro, which crowns it like the frontlet on a harness. Toward the north, Rue d'Aubervilliers shoots off like a long jamboree, filled to bursting with shops. Vendors of pigs' feet, of lace by the pound, of caps, of cheese, of lettuce, of slumgullions, of cooked spinach, of rooms with secondhand air that sit atop one another, astride one another, inside one another, like a nightmare construction toy.

La Chapelle and its neighbor La Villette—and other such liminal areas to the northwest, the east, and all along the south—

constituted the city's backside, the parts you weren't really supposed to see, although you couldn't help doing so when you entered or left: factories, gasometers, slaughterhouses, and the cheapest jerry-built housing, wedged between canals and railroad lines headed north and east out of the train stations bearing the names of those directions. Beyond them, until 1919, was the last military wall, and beyond that in turn was the no-man's-land called the Zone. Unlike most modern cities, sprawling in all directions, Paris was defined by its edges, where it set the limits of acceptability in utilities and the people who lived around them, propelling them out with a centrifugal force that has only increased over time but was already fully visible as early as 1850:

Boulevard de la Villette, circa 1910

> As a result of the transformation of the old Paris, the opening of new streets, the widening of narrow ones, the high price of land, the extension of commerce and industry, with the old slums giving way each day to apartment houses, vast stores and workshops, the poor and working population finds itself, and will find itself more and more, forced out to the extremities of Paris, which means that the center is destined to be inhabited in the future only by the well-to-do.

Thus you could say that Paris now is not only a creation of today's economic and cultural imperatives, but was also willed into being by people who have been dead for more than a century. Haussmann himself might as well have built the Bastille Opéra and the arch of La Défense. When Victor Hugo was writing *The Hunchback of Notre Dame* in 1830, he did not have to stretch to describe its fifteenth-century setting, since it still lay all around him. When he wrote *Les misérables* around 1860, evoking the Paris of thirty years earlier, he was peering across a gulf—a literal one, as he had been in exile for nearly a decade, but also a vast gulf of change. When Jean Valjean and Cosette arrive in Paris from the provinces, the neighborhood where their wanderings temporarily cease,

> located between Faubourg Saint-Antoine and La Râpée, is one that recent construction has transformed from top to bottom, disfiguring them according to some, transfig-

A still from *The Hunchback of Notre Dame* (1923), starring Lon Chaney

Edmond and Jules de Goncourt. Illustration by Gavarni, 1853

uring them according to others. The market gardens, the work yards, and the old buildings are gone. Today there are new broad avenues, amphitheaters, circuses, racetracks, train stations, and the prison of Mazas: progress, as you can see, and also its corrective.

From his seat in Guernsey, Hugo could really only surmise how deeply those recent constructions had altered Paris. The Second Empire had more than a few points in common with our own time: the heady displacements of capital, its muscular display in architectural form, its frenetic display in mercantile form, the desperate embrace of entertainment as an analgesic, the pervasive collective distrust. A way of life was disappearing, and what was replacing it was easily grasped in its outer manifestations, much harder to pin down in its inner essence. A generalized anxiety gripped not only the bottom tiers of society, ejected from the neighborhoods that had been their family seat for centuries, but also people in the middle and even the top echelons. "I understand very well that the purebred Parisian misses all those old and noisy customs of his city, which are progressively disappearing every day," wrote Privat d'Anglemont in the 1850s, around the same time that Baudelaire, in his poem "The Swan," wrote, "The old Paris is no more (the form of a city / Changes faster, alas, than the heart of a mortal)." The Goncourt brothers knew their time was up as they gauged the noisy disruptions of the new middle class, who had too much money for their own good and not enough in the way of manners. Visiting the enormous new Eldorado café-concert in 1860, they experienced the vertigo that comes to all, even snobs, when they note that no place at the table has been set for them. (Although their works were joint, each brother wrote in the first-person singular.)

My Paris, where I was born, the Paris of life as it stood between 1830 and 1848, is passing away. Social life is undergoing a great evolution. I see women, children, households, families in this café. The interior is doomed. Life threatens to become public. The club for the top rank, the café for the bottom: that is where society and the crowd will end up . . . I have a sensation of passing through, as if I were a traveler. I am a stranger to what is coming, to what is, as I am to those new boulevards, implacably straight, that no longer exude the world of Balzac, that conjure some American Babylon of the future.

But their own Balzac had already foreseen as much: "The ruins of the bourgeoisie will be an ignoble detritus of pasteboard, plaster, and pigment," he had written fifteen years earlier. And a decade before that, when Louis-Philippe installed Napoléon's Egyptian trophy on the site that had held the guillotine during the revolution, Chateaubriand felt apocalyptic intimations: "The time will come when the obelisk of the desert will once again know, in that place of murder, the silence and solitude of Luxor."

Everything is always going away, every way of life is continually subject to disappearance, all who reach their middle years have lost the landscape of their childhood, everyone given to introspection feels threatened. Everything was always better before—and in many ways it probably was, since there were, among other things, fewer people, which made for more space and less competition for scraps, gave more room to chance and to nature. Eugène Dabit wrote in 1933 that "our time is hard, without beauty. We can no longer contemplate the sky, now hidden by tall buildings. We can no longer listen in silence to the delicate call of the wind. Our trees are strangled by iron grilles, planted in the earth as if in pots, prisoners in squares as dusty as museums." But despite various fantasies by the likes of Le Corbusier, the depredations of technocrats over the decades after Haussmann were relatively small-scale and could be regarded as anomalous—until the 1960s. That was when the trio of Charles de Gaulle, Georges Pompidou, and André Malraux (the onetime novelist become minister of culture) gave their *nihil obstat* to ambitious young men, graduates of the top schools, who liked to imagine things on a grand scale, who liked acronyms and right angles, who wanted to make Paris into a power city keyed to the growth of modern money and the free flow of modern traffic.

It was then that the fate of Les Halles was decided, that La Défense and the road tunnels under the Right Bank were planned, that the destruction of the Montparnasse train station was ap-

"Paris in the Future: The Panthéon," circa 1910

The Halle aux Vins—the wine depot—circa 1910

proved and the city's first skyscraper was designated to replace it, a giant upended turd purposelessly dominating the Left Bank. Those managers cleaved and sectioned Belleville-Ménilmontant; chased the natives out of the Marais and the Latin Quarter and rezoned those areas for the convenience of money; razed La Glacière; eliminated the Halle aux Vins and the wine depots at Bercy, consented to the aggressively repellent Pompidou Center, and stopped just short of putting multilane highways through the center of the city—they were playing Haussmann, only with motor vehicles and mechanized means of destruction. And their successors have continued, erecting the Bastille Opéra, which looks like a parking garage, and the chilling Mitterand library, which looks like a housing project on the moon. The story is told, furiously, knowingly, and in great detail, in Louis Chevalier's *The Assassination of Paris* (1977). Summing up the toll of destruction, he notes:

> Not one of these places, and so many others of which these are only a sample—theaters, streets, alleys, passageways, intersections, cafés, the quays of the Seine and those of the Saint-Martin canal [. . .]—not one of these places, and other even more insignificant places, bewildering in their banality, failed to have its place in some great chapter of the history of literature, of performance, of art, of beauty. Not so much because beauty was created there as if it could have been created anywhere, but because it could have been created nowhere else, above all not in the places designated for its creation, where it is allegedly manufactured . . . no more than on the symbolic mountain where Hugo wants to make us think he sought inspiration, whereas he tells us plainly in *Choses vues* how he found his ideas by chance in the street.

At the other end of the political spectrum from Chevalier, something of a conservative, was Guy Debord, who ended up making common cause, having a hand in reprinting Chevalier's book after its first publisher dumped it, and who expressed similar views in similar terms: "Paris, a city then so beautiful that many people preferred to be poor there than to be rich some-

A magazine advertisement, 1890s, offering the collected works of Victor Hugo on an easy-payment plan, with either a set of dishes or a Gladstone bag with a rack for toiletries thrown in absolutely free

where else." Since the early 1950s, the Lettrist International and its successor, the Situationist International, had been engaged in, among other things, reimagining the city. In 1955, for example, the Lettrist newsletter, *Potlatch*, featured a "Project for the Rational Beautification of the City of Paris," which included such propositions as arranging, with ladders and footbridges, a promenade along the roofs of the city; putting switches on lampposts so that lighting decisions could be made by the public; redistributing works of art currently held in museums among local bars; and turning churches into either romantic ruins or haunted houses. By 1978, in the bitterly elegiac narration of his last film, Debord was moved to write, "We were, more than anybody, the people of change, in a changing time. The owners of society were obliged, in order to maintain their control, to desire a change that was the opposite of ours. We wanted to rebuild everything, and so did they, but in diametrically opposed ways. What they have done illustrates our project, in negative form."

The Lettrists' propositions were in the interest of laughter, of poetry, of ambiguity, of menace, of release, of intoxication. The plans that have been carried out are equally as radical, but they are in the interest of control and manipulation.

•

This book is not intended as a polemic, for which it's much too late anyway. It might be something of a cenotaph—or catacomb, since it contains the skulls of vast numbers of people who lived and died in Paris but would be unlikely to find a home there nowadays. Instead, I mean it mostly as a reminder of what life was like in cities when they were as vivid and savage and uncontrollable as they were for many centuries, as expressed by Paris, the most sublime of the world's great cities. Life was of course not all fun and games; the expression of every sort of behavior inevitably included a great deal that was unpleasant if not inimical and even murderous.

It was a city composed of myriad small undertakings, momentary decisions, fluctuations of enthusiasm, accommodations to fortune, which accrued and weathered and developed a patina, and were built on top of and next to and around in an endless process of layering. Even now, the layout of streets in some

Rue Saint-Antoine, circa 1910

"When I feel down, I change eras": Fréhel in *Pépé le Moko*, 1937

parts of town derives from ancient and forgotten circumstances—some course of water or farmer's field or half-whimsical decision made in the Middle Ages or even earlier—and over time this curve and that angle, having no evident logical sense, developed, as it were, personalities. They colored the ideas and habits of those who lived on the street or used it every day, allowed for dark corners in which dark thoughts could be stored, and created off-kilter rhythms that prevented monotony. And then those subtle turns and nudges slowly and invisibly engendered all sorts of things: beauty, curiosity, ambition, skepticism, discontent.

Until not so long ago it was always possible to find a place in the city. There were cheap neighborhoods, and failing that there were places to roost, to hide away, places left unattended long enough to allow squatting and repurposing. Until not long ago, except in the most extreme circumstances, there existed the option, for those who wanted it badly enough, to thumb one's nose at the directives of fashion and progress and authority and carve out an eccentric path of one's own—this more so in Paris than anywhere else, because there willful eccentricity was respected if not necessarily understood. Perhaps that remains an option, but it has been driven indoors, out of the social realm, and is progressively more difficult to pursue as the controlling interests of society have become ever more adept at shape-shifting and assuming the semblance of forces once opposed to them. Nowadays "anarchy" means conformity, "rebellion" means compliance, "revolution" is the seasonal rotation of dry goods, and "freedom" is the exercise of license by the powerful. Perhaps under the circumstances it's asking too much to continue to believe or at least hope that the stubborn and perverse human capacity for disobedience will prevail in the end, the way worms can undermine a wall, but for now that's all we have.

2

Ghosts

Paris is sufficiently compact that you can cross it with ease, in a few hours, and it has no grid, forestalling monotony. It virtually demands that you walk its length and breadth; once you get started it's hard to stop. As you stride along you are not merely a pedestrian in a city—you are a reader negotiating a vast text spanning centuries and the traces of a billion hands, and like a narrative it pulls you along, continually luring you with the mystery of the next corner.

Paris contains some 3,195 streets, 330 *passages* (a term that encompasses both arcades and alleys), 314 avenues, 293 impasses, 189 villas (an enclosed mansion, or a grouping of houses not unlike a mews), 142 *cités* (a contained development, sometimes carefully designed and sometimes a slum), 139 squares, 108 boulevards, 64 courts, 52 quays, 30 bridges, 27 *ports*, 22 *galeries* (arcades), 13 *allées*, 7 *hameaux* (literally "hamlets"), 7 lanes, 7 paths, 5 ways, 5 peristyles, 5 roundabouts, 3 courses, three *sentes* (another variation on "path" or "way"), 2 *chaussées* (an ancient term more or less cognate with "highway"), 2 *couloirs* (literally "hallways"), 1 parvis (an open space in front of a church, in this case Notre-Dame), 1 *chemin de ronde* (a raised walkway behind the battlement of a castle), and 11 small, undefined passageways. At least those were the figures in 1957; since then quite a number of the smaller entities have been obliterated by urban renewal, while others have been confected by those or other means. A count

The frontispiece, by Célestin Nanteuil, for *Les rues de Paris* (G. Kugelmann, 1844)

19

Boulevard de Ménilmontant, circa 1910

Rue Cloche-Perce. Photograph by Suzanne Beaumé, circa 1900

made in 1992 gives the total number of Parisian thoroughfares as 5,414, which is 133 more than there were twenty years earlier and nearly 1,700 more than in 1865, when the city's present limits were fixed.

Sometimes the histories of streets are inscribed in their names: Rue des Petites-Écuries because it once contained small stables, Rue des Filles-du-Calvaire (Daughters of Calvary) after a religious order that once was cloistered there, Rue du Télégraphe marking the emplacement during the revolution of a long-distance communication device that functioned through relays of poles with semaphore extensions. Sometimes streets named by long-ago committees take on a certain swagger from their imposed labels: the once-lively, nowadays flavorless Rue de Pâli-Kao given a touch of the exotic (the name is that of a battle in the Second Opium War, in 1860), the stark and drab (and once extraordinarily bleak, owing to the presence of enormous gas tanks) Rue de l'Évangile endowed with the gravity of the Gospels, the already ancient Rue Maître-Albert made to seem even more archaic in the nineteenth century by being renamed after the medieval alchemist Albertus Magnus, who once lived nearby.

Among the oldest thoroughfares in Paris are the streets of the Grande and Petite Truanderie, which is to say the Big and Little Vagrancy Streets. There is the Street of Those Who Are Fasting (Rue des Jeûneurs), the Street of the Two Balls, the Street of the Three Crowns, the Street of the Four Winds, the Street of the Five Diamonds, the Street of the White Coats, the Street of the Pewter Dish, the Street of the Broken Loaf—one of a whole complex of streets around Saint-Merri church (near the Beaubourg center nowadays) that are named after various aspects of the distribution of bread to the poor. Many street names were cleaned up in the early nineteenth century: Rue Tire-Boudin (literally "pull sausage" but really meaning "yank penis") became Rue Marie-Stuart; Rue Trace-Putain (the "Whore's Track") became Trousse-Nonnain (Truss a Nun), then Transnonain, which doesn't really mean anything, and then became Rue Beaubourg. Many more streets disappeared altogether, then or a few decades later, during Haussmann's mop-up: Shitty, Shitter, Shitlet, Big Ass, Small Ass, Scratch Ass, Cunt Hair. Some that were less earthy and more poetic also disappeared: Street of Bad Words,

Street of Lost Time, Alley of Sighs, Impasse of the Three Faces. The Street Paved with Chitterling Sausages (Rue Pavée-d'Andouilles) became Rue Séguier; the Street of the Headless Woman became Rue le Regrattier.

Sometimes the streets come assorted in themes, such as the Quartier de l'Europe, which encircles the Saint-Lazare train station: Rues de Bucarest, Moscou, Édimbourg, Madrid, Rome, Athènes, and so on. The exterior boulevards are called *les boulevards des maréchaux* because they were all named after field marshals in Napoléon's army: Brune, Masséna, Poniatowski, Sérurier, Ney, Murat, Macdonald, etc. You'll note that the American names—Avenue du Président-Wilson, Avenue du Président-Kennedy, Avenue de New-York, Rue Washington—are clustered in the high-hat Sixteenth Arrondissement or the adjacent western edge of the Eighth. Names associated with the labor movement or left-wing motifs, on the other hand, tend to be restricted to the northeast of the city: Avenue Jean-Jaurès, for example, after the great Socialist leader assassinated in 1914 (and there is not a sizeable city or industrial suburb in France that lacks a thoroughfare named after him) or Place Léon-Blum, after the leader of the Popular Front in the 1930s, or Place de Stalingrad (officially renamed Place de la Bataille de Stalingrad in 1993, lest there be any confusion), or indeed Rue Marx-Dormoy, although it was named not for Karl but for the Socialist politician René Marx Dormoy, assassinated in 1941, who was no relation.

There is seldom a correspondence between a nominal theme and one of ambiance or architecture, and the disjunction can provide a sort of cognitive dissonance, frequently disappointing. If you expect a water tower on Rue du Château-d'Eau, for example, or think you might spot a knoll, let alone quails, on Rue de la Butte-aux-Cailles, you are more than a century too late. But the streets do develop their own thematic tendencies, not all of them imposed by architects or developers. Some of them have accrued through occupational necessity (all those large courtyards along the formerly artisan-intensive Rue Saint-Antoine) or topography (such as the tiered terraces that tumble down the hill in Ménilmontant, definitively spoiled by urban-renewal demolition and construction in the 1960s, but shown to advantage in

Rue Taille-Pain. Photograph by Paul Vouillemont, circa 1900

Porte Jean-Jaurès, leading to Pantin, probably 1914

Albert Lamorisse's lovely short film *The Red Balloon*, 1956), or sometimes they were founded in the mists and are perpetuated by custom, such as the eternally carnivalesque Rue de la Gaîté. You see the way a theme will establish itself along a given street—for example, the Egyptian motif on Rue du Caire (the exception that proves the rule) or the country village ambiance of Rue de Mouzaïa or the august academic procession of Rue d'Ulm—and then be contradicted, sometimes radically, with the simple turn of a corner. The city is not just a palimpsest—it is a mass of intersecting and overlapping palimpsests. Even as it becomes socially more homogeneous, many of its streets and houses continue to bear witness to former circumstances. The tone of the Marais is still determined by medieval walls and Renaissance *hôtels particuliers*, and while today these are employed and intermittently decorated by the fashion industry and its ancillary commerce, if you look above the storefront level you can here and there make out traces of the centuries of misery that prevailed between the era of their construction and ours. You can admire the tenacious way the Canal Saint-Martin still assumes the existence of barge traffic, Rue de la Lune seems to have been designed for prostitution, or Rue Volta folds together about seven centuries, not necessarily including the present one.

Walter Benjamin wrote, "Couldn't an exciting film be made from the map of Paris? From the compression of a centuries-

Rue des Immeubles-Industriels, Walter Benjamin's favorite street, circa 1910

long movement of streets, boulevards, arcades, and squares into the space of half an hour? And does the flâneur do anything different?" Paris invented the flâneur and continues to press all leisurely and attentive walkers into exercising that pursuit, which is an active and engaged form of interaction with the city, one that sharpens concentration and enlarges imaginative empathy and overrides mere tourism. The true flâneur takes in construction sites and dumps, exchanges greetings with bums and truck drivers and the women washing their sidewalks in the morning, consumes coffees and *gros rouge* at as many bus stop cafés as terrace-bedecked boulevard establishments, studies trash and graffiti and sidewalk displays and gutters and rooftops, devotes as much attention to the arcades filled with dentists' offices or Indian restaurants as to the ones lined with antique shops, spends more time in Monoprix than at the Louvre.

An illustration by José Belon for *Paris anecdote*, by Privat d'Anglemont, 1885 edition

The history of Paris, the active and engaged history of the streets, was written by flâneurs, and each conscious step you take follows their traces and continues their walk into a continuous walk across the centuries. The great text of the streets was given voice by those relentless walkers who were also writers: Louis-Sébastien Mercier and Nicolas-Edmé Restif de La Bretonne in the eighteenth century; Alexandre Privat d'Anglemont, Victor Fournel, Alfred Delvau, Joris-Karl Huysmans, and Victor Hugo in the nineteenth; in the twentieth, Georges Cain, André Warnod, Francis Carco, Léon-Paul Fargue, Walter Benjamin, Jacques Yonnet, Jean-Paul Clébert, Robert Giraud, Richard Cobb, Louis Chevalier, and the members of the Lettrist International, most notably Guy Debord and Ivan Chtcheglov; thus far at least Éric Hazan in the twenty-first.* This to name only the most significant and most committed—there have been hundreds of others. Of course there were also those who expressed themselves by different means. These would include the artists Constantin Guys, Célestin Nanteuil, Honoré Daumier, Gavarni, Édouard

---

* I don't have to tell you that the absence of women from this list is the sadly simple result of social conditions—until very recently it was impossible for women to walk around by themselves unobserved, and it is crucial for the flâneur to be functionally invisible. Among the numerous women of the past who might have been flâneurs had they had the opportunity, perhaps the most striking is Marie d'Agoult, the novelist and republican who wrote the most observant and detailed chronicle of the revolution of 1848; it and all her other work appeared under the byline "Daniel Stern."

Nicolas-Edmé Restif de La Bretonne

An illustration by Théophile Steinlen for *Barabbas: Paroles dans la vallée*, by Lucien Descaves, 1914

Manet, Gustave Caillebotte, Edgar Degas, Camille and Lucien Pissarro, Jean-François Raffaëlli, Georges Seurat, Théophile Steinlen, Félix Vallotton, André Dignimont, and the photographers Charles Marville, Gabriel Loppé, Eugène Atget, Brassaï, Germaine Krull, Eli Lotar, André Kertész, Henri Cartier-Bresson, Robert Doisneau, Willy Ronis, and Ed van der Elsken, among others, including some of the seldom-credited press photographers of the past and the anonymous makers of the very local postcards that were produced in Paris before World War I. Even those whose habits are unknown to us can be considered part of the company by virtue of the fact that they were observers who caught things on the fly—they moved through the streets, collected and preserved their impressions, and left us with valuable information about time and place, in addition to beauty.

Baudelaire most famously defined the flâneur: "The crowd is his domain, as air is that of a bird, as water is that of a fish. His passion and his profession is to *marry the crowd*. For the perfect flâneur, for the passionate observer, it is an immense pleasure to make a home in the multitude, in the flux, in the motion, in the fleeting and infinite." Richard Cobb, the British historian of France, specified further that the task requires going "into the streets, into the crowded restaurant, to the central criminal courts, to the *correctionnelles* . . . , to the market, to the café beside the Canal Saint-Martin . . . , to the jumble of marshalling yards beyond the Batignolles, to the back-yards of the semi-derelict workshops of the rue Saint-Charles, to the river ports of Bercy and Charenton . . ." It is imperative "to dawdle, to stop, to see, to notice small changes and to have one's attention caught by a drawn blind, by a closed shutter, by a shop-door without its handle, by the small square of a white notice, *Fermé pour cause de décès* [closed on account of death], or *fermé jusqu'au 1er septembre*, by a sign-painter painting out a familiar name, by a child's face at a window, by a geranium in flower."

The flâneur is not a reporter. Reporters are in the business of asking specific questions, to which they require specific answers. The flâneur may entertain questions in the course of things, but overall he or she is in the business of negative capability. The flâneur must be alive to the entire prospect, to the ephemeral and perishable as well as the immemorial, to things that ordinarily lie beneath notice, to minute changes and gradual shifts of fashion, to things that just disappear one day without anyone paying attention, to happenstance and accident and incongruity, to texture and flavor and the unnameable, to prevailing winds and countercurrents, to everything that is too subjective for professionals to credit. The flâneur must possess a sixth sense, possibly even a seventh and an eighth, must have an intuitive suss for things about to occur without warning and things that are subtly absent and things that are silently waving goodbye. The flâneur must be able to read the entire text of the streets, including its footnotes, interleavings, and marginal commentary. The flâneur must comprehend the city holistically, must understand it as a living being—on the order of, though infinitely more complex than, those mushroom colonies that may cover hundreds of square miles while remaining a single entity—and must constantly risk overidentifying with his or her subject.

"Who opens the door of my death chamber? I said that no one shall enter. Whoever you are, go away!" Plaque marking the house where Lautréamont died, 7 Rue du Faubourg-Montmartre

Among the intuitive stretches required of the flâneur is a lively belief in ghosts that does not particularly assume a belief in the supernatural. The past is always present, if sometimes in the way of those movie spirits who can be seen in the room but not in the mirror, or vice versa. All the tyrants and landowners and monopolists in vain set their shoulders to bulldoze the past out of existence, but it stubbornly remains, sometimes in the most indefinable and evanescent way and sometimes as a bad conscience. If you are properly attuned you can feel it even in the middle of the Passerelle Simone de Beauvoir, the footbridge across the Seine that links the Parc de Bercy with the Bibliothèque Nationale, a place from which it is nearly impossible to see anything much more than twenty years old—and yet in that formerly industrial location countless people labored and many died, from accidents and floods and wars, in the complex of wine depots on the one side and the vast railroad freight terminal on the other. A bit farther down, near Rue Watt, on the Left Bank side, under residential high-rises and the Diderot branch of the University of Paris, is the site of the municipal storehouses (Magasins Généraux), which beginning in November 1943 were employed as an internment camp for Jews.

The popular historian G. Lenotre, who arrived in Paris from Lorraine as a teenager at the outbreak of the Franco-Prussian

The corner of Rue de la Parcheminerie and Rue de la Harpe, circa 1910

War (and then, over the next sixty-five years, wrote more than fifty volumes of *petite histoire*, primarily about the city during the revolution), recalled that even as he was dazzled by the swarm of traffic that he could see from the windows of the modest hotel on Rue Montmartre where he first lodged, as well as by the masses of tall houses on every side, he could not help thinking about what those houses had witnessed and contained over the decades. "Each of those casements opened onto a room where how many comedies had transpired! And how many dramas, for that matter! Their shutters had been closed in times of mourning, they had been bedecked with bunting and hung with fairy lights on occasions of victory. For the first time there came to me the vague thought that houses have a soul, composed of the joys and sorrows and labors of those they have sheltered, and that all have their history: secret, romantic, or joyful."

The occult forces in the city are always at work, indifferent to rationality, scornful of politics, resentful of urban planning, only intermittently sympathetic to the wishes of the living. They operate with a glacial slowness that renders their processes imperceptible to the mortal eye, so that the results appear uncanny. But much like the way stalagmites and stalactites grow in caves, such forces are actually the result of vastly long passages of time, of buildup and wear-down so gradual that no time-lapse camera could ever record them, but also so incrementally powerful they could never be duplicated by technology or any other human intent. Over the course of time they have worn grooves like fingerprints in the fabric of the city, so that ghostly impressions can remain even of streets and corners and culs-de-sac obliterated by bureaucrats, and they have created zones of affinity that are independent of administrative divisions and cannot always be explained by ordinary means.

Guy Debord and his barfly friends in the early 1950s, who came to constitute the Lettrist International, were the first to attempt to chart what they called "ambience units" (*unités d'ambiance*), even if they were hardly the first to notice them. These units could be entire neighborhoods, could be described in a few words (for example, the Îlot Chalon, the first Chinese district in Paris, a tiny cluster hard by the Gare de Lyon now erased by urban renewal), could be determined by architecture (such as the extraordinary rotunda built by Claude-Nicolas Ledoux in 1785 as part of the wall of the Farmers-General and which now sits by itself in Place de Stalingrad, shadowed by the Métro overpass), could embody a forceful rebuke to their surroundings (such as the Lettrists' beloved and now long-gone Rue Sauvage, by all accounts an eerie blend of desolation and *rus in urbe*—"the most confounding nocturnal landscape in the capital," according to their newsletter, *Potlatch*—that plied a parallel course between the riverbank, edged with vacant lots, and the tracks leading to the Gare d'Austerlitz). Or the units could be fleetingly subjective, identifiable only by their familiars, an effect of light and shadow or an imbalance of scale or a pattern of commerce. A map Debord annotated in 1957, covering just the first six arrondissements, shows some seventy-five of those units, a few no more than a block long. That same year, he produced the exploded maps *The Naked City* and *Guide psychogéographique de Paris*, each of which isolates kernels of blocks in the center of the city, according respectively to their function as *plaques tournantes* ("turntables," in the railroad sense) and as "psychogeographic gradients," with arrows of varying thicknesses showing the involuntary tendencies of pedestrians to err this way or that when pursuing the determined wandering that Debord called *dérive*, or "drift."

Rue Saint-Julien-le-Pauvre, circa 1910

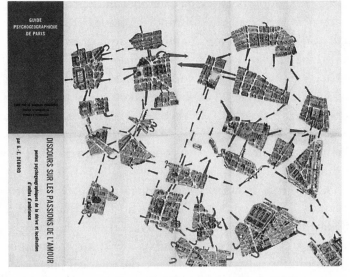

Guide psychogéographique de Paris, by Guy Debord, 1957

Rue Mouffetard, circa 1910

Home base for the Lettrists was the "Contrescarpe continent," a vaguely oval complex of blocks centering on the Place de la Contrescarpe, just southeast of the Panthéon in the Fifth Arrondissement. This area, a very old working-class district that shades into the Latin Quarter, was of interest to them not only for its proximity but because of the way it seemed to direct the steps of anyone venturing in. Owing to the turnings of streets and to the way edifices seem to abruptly block passage while artfully concealing narrow channels that wind around them, so that the pedestrian changes course without really thinking about it, the district presents only one smooth route of entry (which is nevertheless mined with attractive digressions), from the north, and only one reasonable exit track, toward the south. This remains the case and can be verified by visitors. As a consequence, the zone, according to Debord, "inclines toward atheism, oblivion, and the disorientation of habitual reflexes."

Ambience units are collective, anonymous works achieved over long passages of time through accretion, accident, habit, juxtaposition, improvisation, endurance, and one or more inexplicable X factors—a sort of blend of theater and sculpture enacted upon the city and adapted to the *longue durée*. Who knows how many of them came and went in the centuries before ours and especially before Baron Haussmann's depredations of 1853–70? In parts of the city without interfering large-scale landowners, where all building and alteration occurred through small-scale labor, the crop of ambience units was once so dense and profound that it seems incongruous to call them that. It is easy to imagine that every corner had its own distinct flavor, that such a thing would have been taken for granted the way every face is different. *Ambience units* begins to sound like a name given in an alienated time to the last isolated examples of a phenomenon that was once so widespread that it was the rule.

They were habitats in which generations spent their entire existences, happily or not. People who lived there naturally gravitated toward the local commerce, trade, or practice the place was known for—associations owed to circumstances often lost in the mists of time. Hence the mystical phenomenon of unexplained recurrence. "There is always a certain public square or a certain intersection that, through mysterious and providential forces, seems forever devoted to a single specialty," wrote a mid-nineteenth-century chronicler. "I don't know what secret instinct impels the same classes or the same professions always toward the same places. Thieves, pickpockets, beggars, streetwalkers, street performers have still not left the haunts they have inhabited since the Middle Ages." His subject was Rue Pierre-Lescot, which lay somewhere in the tangle of streets east of the Louvre, cleared by Haussmann a decade later. The name—that of the sixteenth-century architect responsible for the southwest wing of the Louvre and for the Fontaine des Innocents—was then reapplied to the street marking the eastern edge of Les Halles, formerly Rue du Cloître Saint-Jacques, so that, curiously, his observation applies today. The thieves, beggars, and streetwalkers may no longer live nearby, but they certainly exercise their trade on the block; shopping mall, fast food, fake Irish pubs, and cheap teenage clothing outlets have drawn their own sucker traffic.

The dog pound. Illustration by J. J. Grandville, from *Scènes de la vie publique et privée des animaux*, 1842

In the 1950s the historian and redoubtable flâneur Louis Chevalier noticed a local anomaly around Place de la Bastille, which was never "a particularly criminal district and . . . not even a place of prostitution, except for one side street, Rue Jean-Beausire, where prostitution thrives." There was no reasonable explanation, no matter of lighting or building stock or layout that could account for this street being set aside from all the others around it. Therefore, "from all the available evidence, circumstances beyond those of the present must be exercising an influence," since the material reality of the current era is shaped by the past—by "the force of interests, habits, and beliefs, particularly if those habits and beliefs are negative, which . . . are more ineradicable than their positive counterparts." And indeed, the street had been the site, long ago, of a *cour des miracles*, which was the name given in the Middle Ages to an encampment of beggars, whores, and thieves.

Today it is clean, neutral, and impersonal. But even now there remain streets and vicinities that draw prostitutes and their clients as they have for generations if not centuries. Rue Saint-Denis was until very recently the main stem, a virtually unbroken line of *filles publiques* on display at all hours, from Place du

A *cour des miracles* in the Middle Ages

Porte Saint-Denis, circa 1910

Châtelet to Porte Saint-Denis.* This had been the case since sometime during the Middle Ages, perhaps before. Rue Saint-Denis is one of the city's oldest streets, going back to Roman rule in the first century. Until the royal palace moved to Versailles under Louis XIV—arguably the pioneering instance of suburban flight—it was the custom for newly crowned kings to descend its length as they officially proceeded from the basilica of Saint-Denis, north of Paris, to their residence at the Louvre (and they departed in the reverse direction after death). Perhaps the royal procession and the procession of harlots are not unlinked. For that matter, excavations for the Métro in 1903 uncovered the skeleton of a woolly mammoth, leading to the discovery of the pachyderms' habitual path from their dwelling on the heights of Belleville down to the river to drink and bathe—their course descended obliquely via what is now Rue de la Grange-aux-Belles, then joined the future Rue Saint-Denis at about the height of the *porte*, which is to say the top of the street's miracle mile. Rue Saint-Denis remains to this day an unprepossessing, surprisingly narrow thoroughfare, but it was clearly consecrated to the pageantry of horizontal motion.

The city's principal constituent matter is accrued time. The place is lousy with it. Not everyone is happy about this, since the past is burdensome and ungovernable and never accords with totalizing ideologies or unified design theories or schemes for maximizing profit. The faceless residential and commercial units that conceal large parts of working-class northeastern and southeastern Paris were imposed over the past half century for reasons that include the wish to extinguish an unruly past. History is always in the gun sights of planners and developers, and of reactionaries, who in the absence of a convenient past are content to invent one, winding their fantasies around some factual nugget suitably distant and fogged by legend. Official appropriations of history, however ostensibly benevolent in intent and graced with accredited consultants, will always be chary of the

* In 2003, France passed an internal security law, put through by Nicolas Sarkozy, who then held a string of cabinet positions, including the charmingly named pair "internal security and local freedom." Solicitation was targeted, along with begging and vagrancy, and the hitherto undisguised display suddenly disappeared—although that doesn't mean the girls aren't still out and about.

The people of Les Halles, 1906

actual mess and stink of the past, and as a consequence they always gravitate toward the condition of the theme park. Those paddle-shaped markers planted here and there throughout Paris are very nice, but they are like historical multivitamins, meant to be ingested and immediately forgotten. They are nagging footnotes to your shopping and dining experience, good for you but starchily dutiful, so that you tend to avoid them and feel obscurely guilty about it. And of course they are far less evocative of lived time than the most derelict building in any chosen neighborhood.

What the flâneur sees while walking around is a tremendous expanse of time in compressed and vestigial form. The flâneur is in sympathy with time not from nostalgia but from an obligation to truth. The past is hardly a single era, after all, but the combined, composted layers of a thousand eras, and any given moment includes some proportionate blend of all those eras. The future is a threat or a sales pitch, the present flies around you like the landscape as seen from a moving car, but the past is what you stand on, lean against, breathe in. The very spark of the new that distinguishes an era will be fully visible only in retrospect. Each epoch may dream the next, in Jules Michelet's formulation, but that dream will come while it is digesting its predecessor. The past is always in flux, surviving not in icily dust-free façade restorations but as a dynamic undercurrent—in the slope of hills, shapes of streets, breadth of squares; in lintels, shutters,

Les Halles and Saint-Eustache, late nineteenth century

courtyards; in habits and associations and prejudices; among working people and recent immigrants and the aged and a lot of youths who didn't go through the career door; among what remain of vagrants and eccentrics and clochards; among a great many people lying low who remember things.

To experience Paris as an organic entity is to absorb that great undulating panorama down below and forget what year it is, like Francis Carco looking south from the heights of Montmartre:

> He bore to the right to get to Rue Lamarck and suddenly, under the vast sky, heavy with rain, the whole of Paris appeared. He took in its receding immensity. Smoke coming from different points wove together and fluttered in sharp chorus. The wind blew through the acacias, their jumble of foliage blending with the fog. In the distance, thousands of fires flickered. Black holes indicated neighborhoods hidden below, from which crowds of shadows emerged: Grenelle and Montrouge. A necklace of stars marked the Great Wheel. Things gradually revealed themselves. Diffuse glimmers shone and then dimmed. Successive strings of lights rose tier upon tier, followed by an opaque and swelling wave of clouds. The belfries of Notre-Dame looked as big as thimbles, but you could make them out, and you could also make out the fluid coil of the river that snaked behind them and stretched out toward the red glimmer of the train stations. What a world! It wasn't a city, but an ocean of swells and eddies. It was a living mass. It quivered, fluctuating like the sea, a rough gray sea barely heaved by the light wind, and he heard the acacias grinding drily above like rigging.

3

Pantruche

It was Lutèce, or Lutetia, under the Romans, and became Paris around 300 C.E. François Villon called it Parouart in his fifteenth-century thieves' cant; Rimbaud called it Parmerde in a letter written in 1872. Sometime in the early nineteenth century, people started referring to it as Pantin—ironically, since Pantin was then a rustic village on the plain northeast of the city (the word also means "puppet," which may have had something to do with its use)—and then around 1849 the name acquired an argot suffix and became Pantruche; the *-truche* may have derived from *autruche*, "ostrich." The moniker survived well into the twentieth century, although somewhere near that age's beginning it was overtaken in popular speech by Paname. Was that name inspired by the 1892 government swindle concerning the faltering Panama Canal project, described as the largest corruption scandal of the nineteenth century? That seems a likelier source than the Panama hat, cited by some, the object of a vogue after adorning the heads of workers returned from the isthmus. Paname stuck because it was sort of perfect: raffish, satirical, swaggering, and pointed all at once. Paname, like argot itself, has come to be most enduringly associated with *chanson réaliste* singers, midcentury crime fiction writers (Albert Simonin, Auguste le Breton, San-Antonio), and movie gangsters from Jean Gabin to Lino Ventura. Today it enjoys another life in hip-hop, employed by rappers as the local equivalent to the Rastafarians' Babylon: the root of all corruption, racism, and malice.

Sheet music for "Je revois Paname," 1928

The inhabitants, for somewhat more than a century, have been Parigots, with another pejorative suffix. (*Parisien*, meanwhile, was the slang term for an old horse about to be put down; it is also a loaf of bread.) Now and then you still hear the term *titi*, which comes from a word for street urchin (and ultimately from *tirailleur*, "sharpshooter") and denotes a working-class Parisian of old stock, someone whose family had lived in the neighborhood for a century or more. There aren't very many of those left. The *titi* was a creature of the city when it was composed of so many villages—quartiers with functional autonomy, ad hoc institutions, and unspoken codes; where everyone of a given age had been kids together and knew one another's virtues and foibles intimately. The quartier was for centuries the basic local entity. When the city was a world, the quartiers were nations, and they correspondingly drew all the fervent loyalty and instinctual identification that cities or countries usually inspire—the larger entities generally went without saying, except maybe in times of war. In 1943, A. J. Liebling encountered a tattooed casualty, with a tricolor wrapped around his waist, in a field hospital on the North African front. "When I asked him where he came from he didn't bother saying 'Paris'—just 'Nineteenth Arrondissement.' That's Belleville—the stockyards . . . He had a mouthful of gold teeth and a tough chin. I asked him, foolishly, what he had done in civil life. He said, 'I lived on my income.'"

Nowadays, while the quartier hasn't entirely disappeared, its cohesiveness has been destroyed. Administratively there are still eighty of them in Paris, four per arrondissement, but like the arrondissements themselves they were designated by bureaucrats armed with rulers and compasses. How many de facto quartiers were actually in place at any given time over the centuries is somewhat conjectural and elusive, but you might estimate that today there are somewhere between forty and fifty that continue to possess some kind of defining characteristic. The historian Éric Hazan divides these into three groupings, by age—which is to say, according to which of the successive walls of the city first contained them. The oldest, to which he assigns the name quartier, are the ones that were included within the first ring of boulevards, as established under Louis XIV. These include Les Halles, the Cité, the Sentier, the Marais,

An illustration by Théophile Steinlen for *Dans la rue*, vol. 2, by Aristide Bruant, 1889 and the boulevards running from the Madeleine church to what would become Place de la Bastille, on the Right Bank, and Saint-Germain-des-Prés, the Latin Quarter, the Odéon, and Saint-Sulpice on the Left. The next ring consists of the faubourgs, which occupy the space between the old boulevards and the wall of the Farmers-General, built in the late eighteenth century: the Temple, Saint-Denis and Saint-Martin, Saint-Antoine and Saint-Honoré, Popincourt, Quartiers Poissonnière and de l'Europe, and three now-vanished neighborhoods: Porcherons, Nouvelle-France, and Quartier de Bréda; and on the other bank, Saint-Marceau, Saint-Jacques, and Montparnasse.

The third ring, of *nouveaux villages*, dates from the later nineteenth century—the last batch of villages was annexed only in 1860. These include Grenelle, Montrouge, Vaugirard, Plaisance, Glacière, Maison-Blanche, and Butte-aux-Cailles on the Left Bank, and Passy, Auteuil, Clichy, Montmartre, the Goutte-d'Or, La Chapelle, La Villette, Belleville, Ménilmontant, Charonne, and Bercy on the Right. Within these at any given time might be smaller entities—for example, the district sometimes known as Croulebarbe and sometimes as Gobelins was often detached from Saint-Marceau; Notre-Dame-de-Lorette was once separate from both the boulevards and Montmartre; and in the southern portion of where the Buttes-Chaumont park was established in 1867 there were quarries called Mississippi, later called Amérique (perhaps because their product was exported across the ocean) around which a neighborhood by that name coalesced for a while.*

The neighborhoods were self-contained and independent, each with its church, graveyard, main street, central square, range of shops and ateliers, as well as its own culture and ambiance, its folkways and politics. They were like the country villages of their time not just in their particular mix of atmosphere and occupation but also in that most people remained within their

Passage Cottin, circa 1910

Rue des Panoyaux, circa 1910

* A quartier d'Amérique remains as an administrative division, although it is functionally and texturally indistinguishable from its neighbors, especially since urban renewal in the 1960s replaced most of the area's distinctive features with housing projects. There was also once an outlying district called Nouvelle-Californie, which seems to have been named after the 1849 Gold Rush and is now part of the southern suburb of Malakoff.

An ambulatory vegetable seller on Rue du Surmelin, circa 1910

borders from birth until death, and many seldom ventured outside for any reason less momentous than a fair or an execution. Most things you would be likely to need were available right there in your vicinity, maybe right on your street, in your impasse or courtyard. Not only were the butcher, the baker, the stationer, and the haberdasher likely to be close at hand, but the minor aristocrat lived on the second floor, the crank toiled at his biblical exegeses in his mansarded aerie, the Italian political exile and family maintained a discreet presence on the fourth, the beggar sheltered in a hut attached to the courtyard, and the mayhem artist was on call in the dive around the corner. There was originally little hierarchy among neighborhoods. Every one of them carried the whole spectrum of status below the highest aristocracy; all of them had their dark alleys and their *hôtels particuliers*, their theater, their nunnery, their knackers' yard, and their *cour des miracles*.

The quartiers may have been rough equivalents to one another, at least before 1860, but on the scale of particular streets or clusters of streets the contrasts could be dizzying.* Privat d'Anglemont noted in the 1850s that "you turn a corner and the appearance changes, as does the population. Tastes, ways of life, jobs, industries—nothing is alike." He cites Rue Mangin, in the Sentier, where the main industry was the fabrication of clocks and precision instruments—but just past the intersection at the end of the street was a maze of narrow lanes that twisted around, doubled back on themselves, seemed to have been cut through at random, and human activity there was correspondingly unbridled. He remarks that "the Parisian of Faubourg Saint-Antoine is no more like the Parisian of Faubourg Saint-Marceau than the Frenchman from Perpignan is like the Frenchman from Amiens." Walter Benjamin, anticipating the Lettrists' psychogeography, wrote that "the city is only apparently homogeneous. Even its name takes on a different sound from one district to the next. Nowhere, except perhaps in dreams, can the phenomenon of the boundary be experienced in a more originary way than in

---

* It is worth noting here that the block (*pâté de maisons*) is less the fundamental urban unit of measurement than is the *îlot*, literally an islet, which is a cluster of houses that may be broken up by side streets and alleys. Paris does not, after all, adhere to any sort of grid.

Rue du Faubourg-Montmartre, circa 1910

cities . . . As threshold, the boundary stretches across streets; a new precinct begins like a step into the void—as though one had unexpectedly cleared a low step on a flight of stairs."

The idea that Paris was a plurality, a coalition of villages that were not so much rivals as cousins and trading partners, each with its own boasts and weaknesses, reaches back well before a written record of such things began. The perceived threat to this happy state was the first thing people held against Haussmann's project. As Victor Fournel wrote in 1868, after celebrating the multiplicity of Paris, ". . . this is what is being obliterated . . . by the construction everywhere of the same geometrical and recti- linear street, with its unvarying mile-long perspective and its continuous rows of houses that are always the same house." He also noted that the light and air of the new city came at the expense of "almost all the courtyards and gardens—which moreover have been ruled out by the progressive rise in real estate." Then, too, a report prepared by the Chamber of Com- merce and the police prefect in 1855, at the time of Haussmann's changes, lamented the passing of leavening effects that were the result of the classes being jumbled together in the center: "A kind of solidarity developed among the tenants of a building. Small favors were exchanged and mutual aid given. In cases of illness or unemployment, workers received a great deal of assistance. Besides that, simply obtaining human respect imbued workers' habits with a certain regularity."

"You're quite right, those who live in expensive houses aren't the lucky ones." Illustration by J. J. Grandville, from *Les métamorphoses du jour*, 1829

On the other hand, you had the reformers and moralists and commission chairmen and preservers of the social order, who tended to confuse humans with the deleterious environment they were subjected to. Those voices were perhaps the loudest. The criminal turned cop Vidocq thought Paris was "a sewer and the emptying point of all sewers." The reformer Henri Lecouturier, for his part, tended to equate the lower classes with air pollution:

> If from the heights of Montmartre or any neighboring hill one contemplates that congestion of houses piled atop one another at every point of an immense horizon, what does one notice? Above, a sky that is always overcast, even on the most beautiful days. Clouds of smoke, like a vast floating curtain, hide it from view . . . One tends to wonder whether this is indeed Paris, and taken by a sudden fright one hesitates to venture into that vast maze where a million people jostle one another, and where the air, tainted with unwholesome effluvia, rising in a noisome cloud, threatens to obscure the sun. Most of the streets of this wonderful Paris are nothing but intestines, filthy and permanently wet with pestilential water. They are narrowly squeezed between two rows of tall houses, so that the sun never manages to reach them and only visits the tops of the chimneys that rise above them . . . A sallow, sickly population endlessly traverses those streets, one foot in the gutter, their noses plunged in the stench, their eyes assaulted at every turn by the most repellent garbage. Those are the intact streets of the old city.

It's a matter of emphasis, of course. Louis-Sébastien Mercier had observed those sunless streets, that permanent cloud ("the sweat of the city") some seventy years earlier, and though hardly a populist, he tended to sympathize with the victims rather than blame them. Lecouturier places the lower-class population in the center of a cycle of infection and rot—they may be victims, but they are also and more important carriers of the disease. In the same work, he wrote: "There is no such thing as Parisian society; there are no Parisians. Paris is nothing but an encampment of

nomads." This formulation was to echo through the urban re-
form rhetoric of his time (and beyond, if you recall that Margaret
Thatcher said something rather similar, although not in reference to Paris*). Haussmann, for example, wrote in his memoirs
that "Paris belongs to France and not to the Parisians who in-
habit it by birth or by choice, above all not to the floating population of its furnished rooms, who corrupt the significance of the
ballot through their unintelligent votes."

That was the basis of Haussmann's justification for treating
the city as undifferentiated matter in need of coldly rational
organizational engineering, rather than as the accumulation of
people's homes and workplaces. Georges-Eugène Haussmann
(1809–1891) was himself a native Parisian, but he did not hesitate
to raze the house where he was born, when it stood in the way of
what was to become Boulevard Haussmann. He was named prefect of the Seine, and awarded his mandate to remake the city,
by Napoléon III in 1853, and served in that capacity until the
Franco-Prussian War brought an end to the empire in 1870.
("Baron" was an assumed title; he was never actually ennobled.)
It should be said at this juncture that Haussmann was neither
the first prefect of the Seine nor the first to demolish neighborhoods in order to cut through streets. Gilbert Chabrol de Volvic,
prefect from 1812 to 1830, and Claude-Philibert Barthelot de
Rambuteau, who served from 1833 to 1848, made the initial
forays into urban planning: designating maximum heights of
buildings, laying out street patterns in parts of the city that had
hitherto been farmland, and other such projects. Rambuteau
undertook to recast Les Halles according to rational principles,
although his most significant achievement was the cutting through
of the street that today bears his name.

Haussmann's achievements were in any case remarkable.
He built or rebuilt all the bridges, remade and vastly expanded the
sewer system, established several of the world's great parks:
the Bois de Boulogne and the Bois de Vincennes, as well as Parc
Montsouris and the Buttes-Chaumont. He built a new morgue,
improved street lighting, doubled the number of trees in the city.
He installed public urinals and omnibus shelters, improved the

* "There is no such thing as society."

An illustration by Théophile Steinlen for *Dans la rue*,
vol. 2, by Aristide Bruant, 1889

"They're right to leave that tower standing—you'd
have to go up in a balloon to tear it down." Illustration by Honoré Daumier, from *Le Charivari*, 1852

The corner of Boulevard Arago and Boulevard de Port-Royal, circa 1910

Rue Saint-Martin and the Tour Saint-Jacques, 1840s

quality of tap water and built new aqueducts to bring it in. He laid out the circular railway line (the *chemin de fer de ceinture*) that served the outer arrondissements for three-quarters of a century. His hundred-foot-wide boulevards and drastically broadened streets may have been intended principally to serve the military in repressing popular uprisings, but you could almost think he foresaw the coming of the automobile, a mode of transport the old, chaotically arranged city could never have sustained (although whether that's a good or a bad thing is another matter).

He gave the city a shape, a dramatic reimagining of itself. Aside from the Eiffel Tower and a few other such details, most of what the tourist thinks of as the look of Paris is the work of Haussmann: the Champs-Élysées, the Étoile, the Avenue de l'Opéra, the Boul' Mich'—the "wall streets" (*rue-murs*) of identically scaled, continuously aligned six-story houses, with their ornate second-floor balconies, unadorned fifth-floor balconies, and mansarded forty-five-degree roofs. He spent two and a half billion francs on his massive projects, which caused a scandal and is why action on his plan was barely resumed by the Third Republic, otherwise not unsympathetic. The defense of his fiduciary integrity is by far the most impassioned aspect of his memoirs.

He was called Attila by the people, and eminent domain was his knout. His actions affected 60 percent of the edifices in the city; he condemned and demolished some twenty thousand houses. He wiped out entire neighborhoods, such as the Carrousel, just west of the Louvre, now only a name given to a square and an arch; Petite-Pologne, laid waste for the installation of Boulevard Malesherbes; Butte-des-Moulins, vaporized for the emplacement of the Avenue de l'Opéra; and Arcis, which once surrounded the Tour Saint-Jacques (the isolated remaining Gothic belfry of Saint-Jacques-de-la-Boucherie, burned down during the revolution). He eliminated not a specific neighborhood but several neighborhoods' worth of houses in cutting through his major north–south conduit, the axis formed by Boulevard de Sébastopol on the Right Bank and Boulevard Saint-Michel on the Right.

He was said by his contemporaries to be possessed by the *culte de l'axe*, the "religion of the straight line." The word that recurs the most in accounts of his activities is *percements* (piercings, in reference to the cutting through of thoroughfares), a word that sounds oddly delicate in its violence. He realigned Boulevard du Temple and imposed the charmless and windswept Place de la République to eliminate the "Boulevard du Crime," the popular entertainment district, so called not because it was particularly dangerous but because of the blood-and-thunder fare of its theaters. He quadrupled the Place de l'Hôtel-de-Ville by demolishing all the houses in the immediate vicinity of its central edifice. He cut down the Tree of Liberty in the Luxembourg Gardens, the last living testament of the revolution. He stopped short of widening Rue de Rivoli and plowing it straight through to Place du Trône (now Place de la Nation), primarily because the plan would have involved razing Saint-Germain-l'Auxerrois. He was a Protestant; the church's bells had allegedly given the signal for the massacre of Protestants on Saint Bartholomew's Night in 1572; he did not want to be accused of seeking revenge.

Saint-Germain-l'Auxerrois, 1840s

The most enduringly notorious of his actions was the destruction of the Cité, the very heart of the city, possibly dating back to before the Roman conquest. The island today mostly presents a collection of official and monumental edifices, not only Notre-Dame and the Sainte-Chapelle but also the ancient Conciergerie (a palace, then a prison, and now the Palais de Justice), the Hôtel-Dieu (the city's first hospital, dating back per tradition to 651, although the current version was planned by Haussmann and completed in 1878), and the Préfecture de Police, popularly known by its address, Quai des Orfèvres. The few remaining residential streets cluster at either end of the island. What was there before can now be seen only in the photographs of Charles Marville (1813–1879), who in the 1860s was commissioned by the city to take archival pictures of places that were slated for demolition. His 425 plates include 23 of the Cité, its narrow snaking alleys, its gutters in the middle of the street, its ancient houses with their undershot ground floors, their stumplike bollards, their medieval details: a doorway built into a Gothic curved recess sliced off from a corner, or an arch cut into the ground floor, making the house a bridge; Rue des Marmousets, Rue des Trois-Canettes, Rue Haute-des-Ursins, Rue Cocatrix.

Rue des Trois-Canettes. Photograph by Charles Marville, circa 1865–68

Rue de Venise. Photograph by Paul Vouillemont, circa 1900

Marville did not, unfortunately, photograph Rue aux Fèves, the dank and leprous criminals' redoubt in Eugène Sue's epochal *Mysteries of Paris*, or its nearby twin, Rue de Jérusalem, where stood the old police prefecture (Haussmann's new police headquarters pointedly engulfed both streets); or Rue de la Licorne, site of the Cabaret de la Pomme de Pin, frequented by Villon and Rabelais. There is a single photo of narrow Rue de Glatigny, its houses seeming to lean over as if unsteady on their pins, but there is little sign that it was known as Val d'Amour for its profusion of prostitutes. On the basis of what he did photograph it's tempting to think the Cité wasn't actually so bad. The trickling gutters convey their nose-pinching reek, and the streets are indeed dark—although not so dark as to defeat the long exposures required by Marville's equipment—but the overall impression is of piles of massive stone, with generously proportioned doorways and windows, and one or more delicately bracketed lanterns in every shot. We cannot, of course, see inside the houses; our only glimpses come from the often hyperbolic Sue: "Wretched houses, with scarcely a window, and those of worm-eaten frames, without any glass; dark, infectious-looking alleys led to still-darker-looking staircases, so steep that they could be ascended only by the aid of ropes fastened to the damp walls by iron hooks." But while most contemporaneous testimony appears secondhand or otherwise suspect—"these dark, muddy, pestilential streets, which one would believe inhabited by frogs, owls, and bats"—the exact same tone is sounded by more generally reliable and humane narrators, such as Privat d'Anglemont, who refers to the "hideous, filthy, squalid misery . . . in the inextricable entanglement of little winding streets that the hammer of the magistrature has just happily eliminated."

Those little winding streets are cited again and again, well before Haussmann began his project, their lack of direct sunlight leading to permanent dampness, leading to permanent mud, leading to scrofula, scurvy, dropsy, rickets, arthritis, rheumatism. And the Cité was hardly the only part of Paris so afflicted. Balzac, writing in 1830, describes Rue du Tourniquet-Saint-Jean,

the widest part of which was its issue into Rue de la Tixeranderie, where it was only five feet across. In rainy weather brackish waters bathed the feet of the old houses that lined the street, carrying along the garbage each household had deposited in a corner by a bollard. Since the ragpickers' carts couldn't get through, the inhabitants counted on rainstorms to cleanse their permanently muddy street—how could it have been clean? When in summer the sun beamed its rays straight down upon Paris, a sheet of gold, sharp as a saber blade, momentarily lit up the shadows of the street without being able to dry the permanent damp that dominated those black and silent houses from the ground floor to the second. The inhabitants, who in June lit their lamps at five in the afternoon, never blew them out at all in winter. Even today, any brave pedestrian who wants to go from the Marais to the quays, and so passes from Rue de Chaume to Rue de l'Homme-Armé, Rue des Billettes, and Rue des Deux-Portes to Rue du Tourniquet-Saint-Jean, will feel that he has been walking through cellars the whole way.

Not far away, around the other side of the Hôtel de Ville, was Rue de la Vieille-Lanterne—formerly Rue de l'Écorcherie ("Flaying Street") and Rue de la Tuerie ("Killing Street"), because the blood from the abattoir that once stood nearby had flowed down the street's gutter on the way to the Seine—which achieved immortality as the place where the poet Gérard de Nerval was found hanged from the grille of a cabinetmaker's stall, coatless on a frigid January morning in 1855. Halfway through its short course the street abruptly dropped six feet, its two parts linked by a set of slimy, disjointed steps, on which, around that time, hopped a tame crow, cawing, and under which ran the sewer. Just past the steps an opening in a wall turned into a tunnel (narrow, dark, poisonous) that ran downhill to the river. Meanwhile, at the head of the street, on Place du Châtelet, a dealer in paints and varnish had installed as a sign, under glass in a box, a bona fide Egyptian mummy.*

* A fashionable color then was "pulverized mummy," much abused by Géricault in particular. It is said to have really been a bitumen compound, but also said (by Blaise Cendrars) to have been a black pigment officially marketed upon the return of Napoléon's troops from Egypt—leaving open the question of its actual composition.

Rue des Blancs-Manteaux, 1840s

Rue Taille-Pain. Photograph by H. Stresser, circa 1900

We are so used to considering the urban experience of over-crowding and vertical pileup as a relatively recent phenomenon that it is a bit disorienting to consider that in the center of Paris such conditions dated back to the late Middle Ages. People were crammed into tenements at a time when the countryside began a quarter mile away, or less. The streets were so narrow because landlords wanted to extract profit from every available inch. What had been courtyards and gardens were built upon; ad hoc constructions took root wherever there was an available corner. It is just possible to put together a rough mental image of what life was like inside the houses—straw beds, some kind of brazier with a pipe out the window, water in jugs brought up from a pump or maybe the river, livestock coexisting with humans in the darkness and damp—although there is a paucity of eyewitness accounts. You can extrapolate from this bit in Villon, that bit in Restif, some pages by Privat, a drawing by Daumier, but few who were capable of description seem to have ever entered the houses. That is where the flâneur's task fell short. The poverty of Paris, as sensitively as it was often observed and portrayed, was almost always, until the late nineteenth century, observed from the outside.

When the adventurism of Napoléon III resulted in the disastrous Franco-Prussian War of 1870–71, which terminated his empire, Haussmann's work nominally ended. "Bismarck finished what Haussmann began," observed Victor Hugo acidly, although he rather overstated the case. The Third Republic picked up Haussmann's loose ends, but his project would wait nearly another century for Georges Pompidou and André Malraux to complete it in the heyday of urban renewal. In the interim, substantial areas of Paris remained much as they had been. Two areas of the city in particular managed to retain a medieval character well into the second half of the twentieth century: the combined Marais, Temple, and Saint-Antoine neighborhoods in the Third and Fourth Arrondissements, and

Cendrars furthermore notes a black tint sold to painters under the brand name Égalité, alleged to have been derived from a royal cadaver, perhaps that of Louis XV, exhumed from the crypt at Saint-Denis during the revolution. David may have employed it in his *Coronation of Napoléon* (1806) and Ingres in his portrait of Monsieur Bertin (1832).

the greater Latin Quarter, in the Fifth. That Haussmann failed to mop up those two sectors resulted in a considerable amount of notable architecture being saved, such as the Gallo-Roman amphitheater the Arènes de Lutèce, near the Jardin des Plantes, which had been slated for demolition but survives today. In both areas, ancient buildings, some of real distinction, continued to be inhabited by the poor, as they had for centuries, as late as the 1960s. The city had no money for much of that time, especially after two world wars, and there was little incentive for private developers to acquire properties, all owned by different and usually absentee landlords, that generally combined narrow street frontage with vast and sometimes lightless depths behind.

Paul Juillerat's sanitary commission, from 1894 to 1904, isolated sections of the Third and Fourth Arrondissements where the death rate from tuberculosis was particularly high, labeling them *îlots insalubres,* "unsanitary areas." These included Saint-Merri, Sainte-Avoye, and Gravilliers, which ring the present site of the Pompidou Center; Saint-Gervais, behind the Hôtel de Ville (on the site of Balzac's Rue du Tourniquet-Saint-Jean, in fact); and Saint-Paul, a bit farther east, at the head of Rue Saint-Antoine. These became prime exhibits for reformers of every stripe, from public health crusaders and charities with sundry agendas to Le Corbusier, for whom the area served as a textbook illustration of a problem that would be preemptively solved by his Ville Radieuse (1935; needless to say, it was never built). Even so, decades of hand-wringing and stirring pronouncements were unaccompanied by action.

Within the orbit of Saint-Merri was Rue de Venise, as narrow as any of the former alleys of La Cité, so that it was often photographed and became, at least in daylight, a magnet for slumming tourists. There as elsewhere in the area, seventeenth-century mansions had been turned into flophouses—with lanterns inscribed ICI ON LOGE LA NUIT ("lodging for the night"), exactly as in the 1830s—where a bed cost thirty centimes, which is to say, pennies. Georges Cain (1856–1919), a historical painter employed as curator at the Musée Carnavalet (the city's historical museum, itself lodged in a sixteenth-century mansion in the Marais), wrote many guidebooks, walking tours of old Paris at the turn of the twentieth century, painstakingly researched and

Rue de Venise. Photograph by Paul Vouillemont, circa 1900

Rue Simon-le-Franc. Photograph by Paul Vouillemont, circa 1900

documented. He was not inhumane in his treatment of the misery he witnessed, but the conservator in him could barely suppress his emotions when for example he contemplated the Hôtel Chalons-Luxembourg on Rue Geoffroy-l'Asnier: "a wreck from the Great Century [the seventeenth] that looms above a miserable neighborhood" and itself housed grim dives, or when, on Rue des Jardins (today Rue des Jardins Saint-Paul), he saw "women in camisoles, hair in their eyes, working and chatting in front of massive doorways from the seventeenth century." Around the church of Saint-Merri he noted "narrow Rue Taille-Pain, crisscrossed by blackened beams propping up dislocated hovels that otherwise would collapse one atop the other," which led to

> a strange spiderweb of alleys—baroque, sinuous, narrow, oxydized as if by fire—which tangle together and form the most picturesque décor . . . Handcarts are piled in courtyards from the sixteenth century; acrid, sulfurous fumes emerge through the thick bars concealing the windows of an ancient *hôtel* corroded by saltpeter and humidity. What weird trades are practiced in those casements made of stone of rebarbative aspect, enclosed by heavy doors bristling with rusty nails? Ragpickers and peddlers of dubious objects populate these shabby streets; lean, starving dogs wander about; an odor of wine dregs and burnt onion seizes the throat.

After World War I the list of *îlots insalubres* was expanded from six to seventeen. These included areas of Belleville, La Villette, Picpus, Glacière, Plaisance, and Les Épinettes (a neighborhood in the Seventeenth, west of Montmartre and south of Clichy), and a major portion of the most ancient part of the Fifth, a quartier once called Saint-Séverin, which comprised the area around Saint-Julien-le-Pauvre, directly across the river from Notre-Dame, and a large swath that more or less corresponds to the Lettrists' Continent Contrescarpe. Those places did not escape Cain's eye. He gained access to an old house on Rue Maître-Albert (formerly Rue Perdue, Lost Street), half a block from the Seine:

After climbing a rotting outdoor staircase to the third story, we enter the hovel, where an acrid odor seizes us by the throat. The present tenant is a dealer in cigarette butts collected on the public street. After frittering his merchandise he lays it out for drying on the bed, the chest of drawers, the floor, and also the small Louis XVI mantelpiece, which is still intact . . . After exiting that sad house we enter number 15, next door, where a fruit vendor has oddly set up shop in a courtyard indicated on the Turgot map of 1739 . . . Nearby, under the severe countenance of an old *hôtel* dating back to Louis XIV, a coffee vendor has disposed on trestles her stove, her bowls, and her mound of sugar cubes.

Such refined and informed observations of the slums eventually laid the ground for the urban renewal practice that was to succeed outright Haussmannization, an operation named, with a medical flavor, *curetage urbain*. This consisted in essence of retaining the façades of the buildings along a street while gutting their interiors, presumably salvaging any Louis XVI mantelpieces that might come along. Anglophones may be more familiar with the term *façadisme*, although that is retail where *curetage urbain* is wholesale.

How these once-fashionable neighborhoods—with their *hôtels*, their massive doorways, their courtyards, their friezes and cornices and architraves, their mantelpieces and balusters and bas-reliefs—wound up in the hands of the rabble is a complex tale having principally to do with fashion. The Marais in the sixteenth century was dominated by immense domains: complexes of buildings nearly village-like in their amplitude and surrounded by farmland. They included the Temple, the mother-house of the Knights Templar, the semimystical military order founded by crusaders in Jerusalem in the twelfth century; and a few significant holdings by royal personages. When those estates were broken up, mostly in the seventeenth century, for a variety of reasons (although the Templar order had been dissolved by the pope in the early fourteenth century, the domain endured in other hands, and its central edifice stood until it was demolished by order of Napoléon in 1808), the aristocracy vied with one another to buy the lots and erect their own *hôtels*. The Marais then

The *hôtel particulier* on Rue de Charonne where the inventor Jacques de Vaucanson died in 1782, seen here circa 1910

Rue des Francs-Bourgeois, circa 1910

became a suburb of the nobility, especially after Henry IV ordered construction of Place Royale, later Place des Vosges, in 1605. The grandeur of the square is still very evident; the figure it must have cut as the formal centerpiece of the aspirational ancestor of every gated community in the world can only be surmised. Even so, its arcades sheltered not only purveyors of silk brocades and other accoutrements of the rich, but also gambling dens and numerous prostitutes.

The idyll of the Marais as home of the elite was to last little more than a century. At the start of the eighteenth, the end of the reign of Louis XIV, the more adventurous or misanthropic or ultrafashionable of the nobles began to move out to the greener pastures of Saint-Honoré, near the Louvre, or Saint-Germain, across the river from it. The movement toward the west soon became inexorable, sweeping along any aristo with the slightest interest in social standing. Well before the revolution the Marais had already become the province of the irrelevant and reactionary. Balzac consistently housed his stubborn solitaries and ruined gentility there. It could only tumble further. Much the same sort of hegira consumed the eastern side of the Left Bank, which in any case was much more socially mixed. Before very long both areas had not merely been scorned by the upper class; the dictate of fashion was so terrible and absolute that they had been relegated to housing some of the most concentrated misery in the city.

The misery gradually faded from view over the decades, especially after the Depression and two wars reduced much of the city to an indigence that differed from one quartier to another mostly in its presentation: threadbare respectability, familial making-do, cultured scavenging, black market chicanery, or end-of-the-line dissipation. The Marais became a sort of inhabited ruin, its architectural splendors barely noticed by anyone but the odd specialist aesthete, to whom Richard Cobb posed the question of "what historical interest, and the fascinating jumble of ancient, narrow-framed plaster houses, may mean in terms of human misery to their inhabitants, often crowded a whole family to a room. The people who live in the rue Volta, the only street in Paris with fifteenth-century half-timbered houses, would not feel themselves particularly privileged." It was a dank, gray place, enlivened only by the shredded movie posters glued to its historic walls, its houses barely heated in winter, with primeval plumbing that usually amounted to a water pump at one end of each floor, adjacent to the communal Turkish toilet, if that utility had been moved in from the courtyard; baths were taken at the neighborhood *bains-douches*, assuming they were taken at all. Some historically significant buildings had already been gutted by entropy and landlord neglect—there were *hôtels* in which you could see the sky from the ground floor—and were more likely to be tenanted by rats and pigeons than by humans. For the people who lived in the sector, wartime privation very often lasted until 1965 or 1970, when they were evicted in favor of renovations. The last thing that would have occurred to those with the power to do something about it would have been to repair the houses for the benefit of those who lived in them.

Across the river, the area stretching from Quai de Montebello to Place Maubert, up Rue de la Montagne-Sainte-Geneviève and down Rue Mouffetard had over the decades become primarily known for its large, mostly unsheltered population of chronic alcoholics; it was the Bowery of Paris, you might say. It was quite a bit livelier than the Marais, if not always happier. During the Occupation the poet and painter Jacques Yonnet met an ancient bum called Danse-Toujours who traced a rectangle for him on a map, one end of it seeming to follow the contours of Philippe-Auguste's thirteenth-century wall. " 'There's the circuit,' he said. 'Inside it everything is serious.' " He went on: "Listen: *every seven years* there's a pitched battle or a bloodletting, and not just any little scratch; it's got to be serious and it's got to flow. And *every eleven years*—it's a fact, you can look it up—there has to be a murder, loss of life. There *has* to be at least one guy who winds up dead. It's the street, the place itself that demands it."

It was not left to elderly drunks alone to suspect predestination or the malign influence of the genius loci. The area may well have been the ancestral home of the clochard. Place de la Contrescarpe, for example, had been established from time immemorial as neutral ground where the bums from Place Maubert (la Maub', as they called it) could parley with those from Saint-Médard without friction, a division of territory that suggests a dynamic somewhat more entrenched than is usually the case

Hôtel de Sens, Rue du Figuier, about 1867

Clochards on Place Maubert, 1930s

Rue de la Montagne-Sainte-Geneviève, circa 1910

with vagrants. Privat d'Anglemont, writing of the 1840s, well before Haussmann, noted that the city had "abandoned" the quartier centuries before, and observed that "whenever the municipal hammer, as it demolishes old neighborhoods to make new streets, drives away the vagabonds and beggars from a spot, they go seek refuge on the Montagne Sainte-Geneviève."

Even more than in the Marais, the sheer age of the neighborhood, its housing stock and traditions, gave the most improvised and ephemeral matters a feeling of deep pedigree and imbued the area with the sense that it was another city altogether, a counter-Paris with its own counter-history, indifferent to such details of the wider world as war or politics. In his great memoir *Paris insolite*, Jean-Paul Clébert describes the dives of Rue Maître-Albert in the late 1940s or early '50s, perhaps located in the same houses visited by Georges Cain half a century earlier:

> The saloons of the Maubert aren't the three modern bars that draw the rubes and the concierges of adjacent houses, the nightwatchmen and the sleepwalkers who go slumming in Rue des Anglais, but rather the kitchens of Rue Maître-Albert, that doglegged alley avoided by strangers, which are invisible from the street and are entered from the side, by way of the common hall, and you have to push open a door at random, the first one you come to, only to fall a step down into a room as big as a henhouse, the whole family assembled there, the counter barely wide enough for a couple of lovers, the table with its oilcloth cover on which the boss's wife is chopping vegetables for soup or feeding their youngest, and the double row of five bottles, wine and apéritifs including raki, which constitute their entire stock. There are more kids than customers. And if it happens that you're drinking with your ragpicker pal you whistled down to and who takes the occasion of knocking one back to get his liter bottle filled up for the night, the boss inevitably puts it off, and when it comes time to pay, you haul out the coin, twenty- or forty- or ten-sou pieces, a pinch will do and never mind about the francs. For that price you have another, and it's black night when you come out, knocking your head on the ceiling beam,

it's too late to go on to the next, which has already locked up, and the street is empty. The drinking goes on upstairs. You go up to have a look. And wind up having a quick fuck with the lady next door. Because sometimes it comes to that.

It will not come as a surprise that today Rue Maître-Albert presents a succession of demure white façades. The medieval city lives on in maybe a doorway here, a pedestal there, as well as on the map—that dogleg, the local narrowness of streets, the overall seeming randomness of layout.

Although the layout and the corresponding narrowness are obsolete by the standards of contemporary efficiency and its corresponding technology, that obsolescence is the very thing that accords it its picturesque charm, makes it a desirable place to live for prosperous and cultured Parisians. The city today is as divided on the matter of the picturesque versus the efficient as it was a century and a half ago. It should not be forgotten that among Haussmann's enemies were thoroughgoing reactionaries who didn't give a toss about the inhabitants of Arcis or the Cité or their misery but who wanted to hold on to the old buildings because they were remnants of the past and the past was perforce glorious. Today the Haussmanns want to erect as many

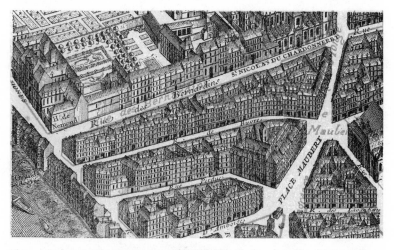

Place Maubert on the Turgot map of 1739. Rue Perdue, later Rue Maître-Albert, is the second street up from the bottom at left.

An illustration by Théophile Steinlen for *Dans la rue*, vol. 1, by Aristide Bruant, 1889

high-rises as possible within the city limits—there are probably fewer of them than in any other major city on the planet, barring special cases such as Venice—while their enemies include people eager to apply the curette to whatever remains of the unreconstructed past, saving its shell for romantic delectation.

Preservation may be better than amnesia, but certain apparently permanent and absolute changes in the human use of the world have forever altered the nature of city dwelling. One of these is the automobile, the ever-increasing traffic of which even Haussmann's boulevards are ill equipped to sustain. The older neighborhoods, meanwhile, might as well be so many cliffside villages in the Dolomites, planned for nothing bigger than a donkey. The American novelist Elliot Paul, who for several decades on and off lived on Rue de la Huchette, in the Fifth, not far from Saint-Julien-le-Pauvre, observed the daily employment of his street in the 1920s:

> Most of the traffic moved through the little street in an easterly direction, entering from place Saint-Michel. This consisted mainly of delivery wagons, make-shift vehicles propelled by pedaling boys, pushcarts of itinerant vendors, knife-grinders, a herd of milch-goats and the neighborhood pedestrians. The residents could sit in doorways or on curbstones, stroll up and down the middle of the way, and use the street as a communal front yard, in daylight hours or in the evening, without risk of life and limb from careening taxis.

Elements of this scene may have persisted here and there as late as the 1970s, but they will very likely never be seen again.

4

Zone

Paris was a fortified city from at least around 1200, when Philippe-Auguste's wall was erected (there may well have been earlier, unrecorded walls), until 1670, when Louis XIV, in the fullness of his royal self-confidence, decided to tear down the fortifications and lay boulevards in their place. The word itself reflects this step, since *boulevard* derives from the same root as *bulwark*. Before a century had elapsed, however, the open-city plan had revealed its weakness. The lack of a wall made it difficult to enforce collection of the *octroi*, the much-hated tax levied upon goods entering the city for immediate local consumption, wine in particular. To that end the Farmers-General (who were not farmers but rich and powerful tax collectors), beginning in 1785, built a new wall that had no military purpose, was only about ten feet high, and was meant to be breached by sixty toll-gates. Only fifty-four were built, because the architect was the visionary Claude-Nicolas Ledoux, whose vivid if rather super-erogatory *propylaea* were ridiculously expensive to build.*

The wall did not prevent smugglers from tunneling beneath it, nor did the decree stipulating that nothing could be built within three hundred feet of the wall on the far side preclude a

The *barrière* Montmartre, future site of Place Pigalle, in 1855

* Only four survived the revolution and still exist: the rotundas of La Villette and Monceau and the gates of the Trône, on Avenue de Vincennes, and d'Enfer, on Place Denfert-Rochereau.

"On more than one occasion, as he left the masked ball, M. de ** was arrested by the guards." Illustration by J. J. Grandville, from *Scènes de la vie publique et privée des animaux*, 1842

lively, free-flowing commerce flourishing in *guinguettes* (a name given to slap-up wineshops, generally outdoor and rusticated) as close to the boundary as was practicable. The *octroi*, which lasted until 1943, during the Occupation, and was formally repealed after the war, created a semipermanent black market economy, with housewives purchasing their soap and salt and flour in the *banlieue*, where such things were considerably cheaper, and sneaking through the contraband dissimulated in heaps of rags and the like. As with so many laws of its type, the *octroi* pushed masses of otherwise blameless citizens to petty criminality, and arguably did much to foster and perpetuate the famously defiant attitude of the Parisian proletariat with regard to the constabulary and its servants.

The tollgates, known as *barrières*, remained functioning long after many of their Ledoux structures had been demolished by the revolutionary masses. On the Left Bank, where construction south of the Latin Quarter and Saint-Germain was still haphazard at best in the early nineteenth century, the *barrières* were incongruous outposts of officialdom in the depopulated and anarchic wilderness. Victor Hugo, writing of the 1820s, noted that

> Forty years ago, the solitary walker who ventured into the wasteland of the Salpêtrière and descended the boulevard toward the Barrière d'Italie came upon places where you could say that Paris had disappeared. It wasn't empty, since there were passersby; it wasn't the countryside, since there were houses and streets; it wasn't a city, since the streets had ruts where grass grew, as on rural turnpikes; it wasn't a village, since the houses were too tall. What was it, then? It was an inhabited location where there was nobody, it was a deserted place where there was somebody; it was a boulevard in the big city, a street in Paris, that was wilder at night than a forest, gloomier in daylight than a graveyard.

The southern *barrières* became a byword for menace, obscurity, obscure menace. The term *rôdeur de barrières* (*rôdeur* means "prowler") came to designate a sort of urban highwayman, leaping out from behind the vegetation to accost passersby and relieve them of their negotiable goods, and it remained in the language as a generalized epithet long after urbanization had rendered this sort of banditry impracticable. Various sensational murders occurred around the *barrières*, with psychopaths taking advantage of the absence of potential eyewitnesses to kill by chance and at random. In the Parisian imaginary, place-names such as Glacière, Grenelle, Montsouris, even Montparnasse, and perhaps especially the Tombe-Issoire (an ancient if murky sepulchral title, now attached to a long, nondescript street in the Fourteenth, coincidentally near the Catacombs) became a sort of *in partibus infidelium*, a vague landscape of gnarled trees and blasted heaths, populated by beings whose heads grew below their shoulders.

Furthermore, in 1832 the guillotine was moved from its long-time emplacement on Place de Grève (now Place de l'Hôtel-de-Ville) to the *barrière* Saint-Jacques (now the site of the Saint-Jacques Métro station). It was a convenient location, since prisoners condemned to death were then kept at Bicêtre, just a few miles southeast. Hugo complained of it as an "expedient of philanthropists for hiding the scaffold, a shabby and shameful Place de Grève for a society of shopkeepers and burghers who shrink before the death penalty, daring neither to abolish it magnanimously nor to impose it authoritatively." In any event, in 1836 the city built the panoptic prison of La Roquette, near the Bastille, and both death row inmates and their instrument of termination were shifted there. Despite its brief term—only forty-one persons met their end there—the emplacement at Saint-Jacques nevertheless left a significant dent in collective memory as the execution site of the romantic murderer Pierre-François Lacenaire and the would-be regicides Louis Alibaud and Giuseppe Fieschi, not to mention the fictional Le Chourineur, antihero of Eugène Sue's *Mysteries of Paris* (1842–43).

But the association of exurban wasteland with public executions was already cemented in the Parisian mind, as from the thirteenth to the seventeenth centuries the municipal gibbet had been located at Montfaucon, reasonably distant from the city then, now a bit west of the Buttes-Chaumont, roughly on the site of the Bolivar Métro stop. Hanging was the standard method of disposal at the time, and the edifice at Montfaucon, which was

Sheet music for Berthe Sylva's "Rôdeuse de barrière," 1931

The guillotine in an early nineteenth-century woodcut

The gibbet at Montfaucon, a nineteenth-century representation of the fifteenth century

"The border of the *ville lumière*." An *octroi* gate, 1930s

somewhere between two and four stories high, could accommodate as many as fifty gallows birds at once. It was situated on a rocky mount just off a road, assuring that no one in the surrounding region could miss the sight. Although the last executions were held there around 1629, the impression the place left on the Parisian mind was sufficiently indelible that, for example, Serge Gainsbourg could casually allude to it in his song "Laissez-moi tranquille" (1959).

Before the gibbet even existed, and long after it ceased to be, Montfaucon was the site of an immense garbage dump, which persisted after the city's six other dumps were closed down by order of the king in the early seventeenth century. The site incorporated a knackers' yard and a manufacturer of *poudrette*, a manure that combined excrement with charcoal and gypsum—the gypsum quarries were conveniently adjacent. Animal bones were burned and the ash was used in building walls; the hides were picked up by tanners. Soon, chemical plants were established to make use of other by-products, and their runoff flowed in the open a quarter mile or more toward the nearest sewer. Some twenty-five hundred cubic feet of human excrement were carted there every day; at any given time the carcasses of twelve thousand horses and more than twenty-five thousand dogs, cats, goats, and donkeys were left to rot. These along with miscellaneous trash covered the ground in heaps up to five feet high, and of course there were rats, "in such numbers that if the carcasses of quartered horses were left in some corner on a given day, by the following they would be completely stripped; the rats mined the nearby hills and brought down entire houses." The ecosystem could be impressive: fish bait was produced by allowing carcasses to draw maggots; then the maggots drew flies; the flies drew large swarms of swallows; and these in turn drew hunters. In summer, the stink of Montfaucon could sometimes travel as far as the Tuileries. Complaints were lodged by the town councils of Belleville, Pantin, and Romainville, which depended on tourists from the city coming out to enjoy their fresh country air. Although a new dump farther away from the city was mandated in 1817, Montfaucon wasn't finally closed until 1849.

By then the city had moved much closer. In 1841, Louis-Philippe decreed that a new military wall should be built, and engaged Adolphe Thiers (1797–1877) to carry out the work. The fortification was to be a belt some twenty-four and a half miles long, with fifty-two gates, which would be closed at night with iron grilles. Inside the wall was a 500-foot-wide buffer that in 1860 became the *boulevards des maréchaux*. On the outside, the wall projected a *glacis*, an artificial 100-foot-wide slope, and beyond that lay another buffer, an 820-foot-wide ribbon of terrain that was designated a *zone non aedificandi*, "not to be built upon." The wall's circumference included a number of villages that would not be incorporated until 1860, and also "amputated" parts of the villages of Clignancourt, Montmartre, La Chapelle, Saint-Denis, and Saint-Ouen. Its dimensions, which more than doubled the previous size of Paris, established the city limits as they still stand—the present Périphérique highway follows the inner border of "the Zone"—although initially the wall simply imposed itself willy-nilly across blameless farmland and assorted wastes, its circumference determined by calculating the safest range to shield the city proper from artillery fire. The Prussian army proved otherwise in 1871, and demolition of the wall began to be discussed a decade later, although the process wasn't begun until 1919 and took another decade to achieve completion.

"And to think we're Parisians now." Illustration by Honoré Daumier, from *Le Charivari*, 1852

In the meantime the wall and its nimbus took on a life of their own. A lithograph by Daumier shows a peasant couple, standing outside their tiny shack, surrounded by undulating emptiness. In the far distance lies a dome: Panthéon, Val-de-Grâce, or Invalides. They look pleased with themselves. "And to think we're Parisians now," the woman says. Many improbable scenes and landscapes were now folded into the urban sphere: beet fields and vineyards, isolated *folies* and hunting lodges from the eighteenth century, railroad marshaling yards, rural villages that would not have looked out of place in Normandy or Champagne, wayside crucifixes, gypsy camps, scores of *guinguettes* that had thrived outside the tax wall just months earlier, overgrown cemeteries, the huts of rabbit trappers and beekeepers, and numerous stretches of unused land in various conditions of arability and desolation, of uncertain ownership.

Urbanization proceeded at different rates at different points of the compass. At first there were recognizable streets going right up to the wall only in a few places, in Montmartre and the

An old hunting lodge on Boulevard d'Italie, circa 1900

The Outskirts of Paris. Painting by Vincent van Gogh, 1887

Faubourgs parisiens. Painting by Jean-François Raffaëlli, 1880s

Batignolles to the north and around the Point du Jour in the southwest, for example. Soon enough, many of the gates sprouted businesses catering to truckers, primarily wineshops, cafés, and brothels, and hodgepodge neighborhoods of tiny houses made of plaster, wood, brick, tin, clinker (residue from coal combustion), or stacked sardine cans filled with dirt, or any combination thereof. These coexisted with the parts of Belleville and the Batignolles that were being built up conventionally, using material salvaged from Haussmann's demolitions in the center, and with clusters of the horse-drawn trailers used by the Roma and other travelers who migrated according to the seasons, and with wilder stretches inhabited by the sorts of people who preferred it not be known they were inhabited. There were few paved streets, no streetlights, no sewers or, for that matter, plumbing, and water had to be fetched from pumps or streams sometimes a considerable distance away. As construction and land speculation within the wall proceeded apace, the more impoverished or legally compromised or simply contrary of those who lived on its interior fringes began gradually to move out to the Zone, which was not to be built upon but did not remain so for long.

Initially the Zone was a sort of tundra, empty grassland with the occasional lone tree, crossed by trails like deer runs, two-story buildings visible here and there on the far horizon. It was documented more by painters than by photographers. Vincent van Gogh's *The Outskirts of Paris* (1887) shows a vast plain with a windmill and a few barnlike structures in the distance, in the foreground the confluence of two muddy paths, a tumbledown fence, and, incongruously, a cast-iron lamppost. Jean-François Raffaëlli made many paintings of the Zone as desolate farmland, featuring maybe a spavined horse and a few skinny chickens tended by an old woman in black, some unpainted hovels in the middle distance with wash lines strung between them, factory chimneys miles away, the scene perhaps interrupted by a man running past with a loaf of bread under each arm, looking back over his shoulder. Where the Zone was breached by the important roads bound for Italy or Flanders or the sea, there might be newspaper kiosks and perhaps an outdoor urinal plastered with advertising, on a tended surface with no neighboring structures.

The ragpickers were the first to colonize the space. Ragpickers had been an integral part of city life since its unrecorded dawn, but they had never had an easy time of it. Besides the financial precariousness of the trade, there were successive waves of persecution by the authorities. In 1635 the sale of old clothes was prohibited in Paris, forcing ragpickers to work clandestinely or outside the walls. In 1701 heavy fines and corporal punishment were imposed on ragpickers found on the streets at night. In 1828 the city began licensing ragpickers, but in 1832 it attempted to institute municipal trash collection, impinging on their trade. In 1835 a new police prefect allowed ragpickers a permanent market within Les Halles, but a few years later the order was rescinded, and by 1860 they were actively being chased from even their traditional corners. The final blow came in 1884, when Eugène Poubelle, prefect of the Seine, decreed that all houses be supplied with lidded containers for refuse, their contents to be collected by municipal authority; *poubelle* soon became, and remains, the word for "garbage can." Fifty thousand ragpickers demonstrated, but to no avail.

A ragpicker, 1840s

There was a hierarchical caste system among the ragpickers, who might be hereditary members of the professional tribe, or bohemians, or miserable, homeless alcoholics who slept under bridges or in abandoned houses and drank *casse-poitrine* (chest breaker) or *tord-boyaux* (gut twister). The highest-ranked of them, called *placiers*, drove horse carts and were often allowed to skim the trash in houses before it was put out on the street. They generally earned about ten times as much as the ordinary pickers, who collected not only rags and paper but also dead animals. The rags and paper were used for making paper and cardboard; bones went toward the manufacture of charcoal and blacking; broken glass was remelted; animal hides were tanned and the hair bought by wig makers. The *placiers*, however, might find valuable discards, which they would bring directly to market, either at the biannual fairs (the ham fair at Place de la République or the scrap iron fair at the Bastille) or else at the street market on Place d'Aligre or at the ancient Marché des Patriarches on Rue Mouffetard, which according to legend was sanctioned by the church after beggars saved the life of the bishop of Paris around 1350, in return being given the right to sell "untraceable goods and objects."

A flea market, circa 1910

Vendors awaiting the opening of the Marché du Temple, circa 1910

Police Magazine, July 1935

Although these markets endured for another century (and the one on Place d'Aligre in some fashion still exists), around 1860, ragpickers began moving out to the Zone, where they were generally free from police harassment and enjoyed unlimited space to spread their wares. At first the pickers set down their bundles directly off the path through the Plaine de Malassis, where strollers would come by and bargain. Professionals began organizing markets in the 1880s, charging rent to newcomers, who built shacks from available litter, such as old wagons. Saint-Ouen, bordering on the Zone to the north, had been renowned for its delicate white wine, which could not be exported, so that it became a resort of wineshops and *guinguettes*, but after phylloxera (plant lice) destroyed the vines in 1900 the space was entirely given over to what was just then beginning to be called the "flea market." Soon it grew so large it merged with the neighboring market at Clignancourt, while others opened at Les Lilas and Quatre-Chemins (La Villette) in the northeast, Montreuil in the east, Bicêtre in the southeast, and Vanves in the south.

Of these, Montreuil, Vanves, and Saint-Ouen/Clignancourt still exist, the latter grown enormous. Over time the bourgeoisie came in search of antiques; painters such as the young Picasso bought old canvases they could scrape clean and reuse; Apollinaire and later the Surrealists sought peculiar and poetic objects; revivals of bygone styles were initiated through flea market finds. But the inventory of a vendor in the 1890s suggests a more typical display: two fragments of Turkish carpet, some bracelets made of hair, a lot of watches and chains in need of repair, three portraits of Napoléon, a compass, a tobacco grater, a shell box ornamented with a picture of Louis XVI inspecting a pot of lilies, a bust of *L'Intransigeant* editor Henri Rochefort, a chromo based on a painting by Édouard Detaille, and two meerschaum pipes, heavily colored and garnished with "immodest" nymphs.

Meanwhile, the Zone was still, as in Aristide Bruant's song "À Saint-Ouen" (1908), a field "where the harvest was of broken bottles and shards of china." The titular heroine of Edmond and Jules de Goncourt's 1865 novel *Germinie Lacerteux* takes a trip outside the walls, along "little gray trampled paths" through grass "frizzled and yellowed," across the railroad bridge, where she shivers at the "evil ragpickers' encampment and the stonemasons' quarter below Clignancourt," where the houses are built of stolen construction materials, "sweating the horrors they concealed." She feels they hold "all the crimes of the night." But she is able to relax on the mound of the fortifications themselves, since there are children, and a brass ring game, and cafés and wineshops and fry joints, and a shooting gallery, and flags. Sixty years later the tireless flâneur André Warnod went to Montreuil on a Sunday, where

> surrounded by an attentive audience, a blindfolded man predicts the future. Peddlers hawk their junk, probably the same trash travelers try to bribe Africans with—but they, too, are doing a roaring business . . . Behind canvas banners depicting grand tragic hunt scenes, for five sous you can see a live eagle, king of the beasts, poor fallen monarch who has a terribly hard time fitting his beak and his clipped wings into a horrible little cage.

Sheet music for Damia's "La guinguette a fermé ses volets," 1935

He drinks "rude" red wine at the *guinguette* Aux Petits Agneaux, which is painted red like the wine. Wine-red or blood-red buildings keep recurring in accounts and reminiscences of the Zone. In Zola's *L'assommoir* the miserable hotel where we meet Gervaise and Lantier, a two-story hovel next to the Poissonnière gate, is painted "wine-dregs red."

On the private side the Zone had many faces, most of them hidden. It was a community of squatters, after all, who never knew when some political decision might result in their being rousted. And then there were those who preferred to remain anonymous anyway, because of bank robberies or incendiary leaflets or incendiary devices or religious or sexual persuasion or embezzlement or morals charges or skin disease. You had to know your way around. Blaise Cendrars took Fernard Léger to a gypsy camp in 1924:

> I took a path that zigzagged between the tarps, the farmyards, the henhouses, the little gardens, the vacant lots of the *zoniers*, enclosed in walls topped with broken bottles, delimited with barbed-wire fences and old railroad crossing gates, filled with furious dogs with nail-studded

collars, their chains running along a strung wire that allowed them to go crazy from one end of their bare hutch to the other, leaping, barking, drooling with rage, among the empty, dented, crumbling tin cans, the stoved-in barrels, the jagged bits of sheet metal, the bed springs poking up from the slag, broken china and pottery, split soup cans, piles of obsolete household appliances, cannibalized vehicles, disemboweled trash bags, all surrounded by spruces, by scant tufts of lilacs, or else dominated like a Golgotha by the skeleton of a tree, a stunted elder, a tortured acacia, a diseased runt of a linden tree, the stump of its branch capped by a chamber pot, its pollarded top crowned by an old tire.

All sorts of people hunkered down in the Zone, which could resemble the streets of the old Cité spread flat across a gnarled ring of dead ground, and forecast the bidonvilles and favelas and refugee camps of a later era. By the time it was fully incorporated into the Parisian imaginary around 1900, however, the "Zone" evoked in potboilers and the popular press had a radius that extended back into the city itself, annexing big chunks of Belleville and Montmartre and the nebulous neighborhoods in the far south. It became a catchall slum where everything sensational and sleazy and prurient could be relegated. The Zone was frequently cited as the home of the criminals who were called *apaches* at the beginning of the twentieth century, and is nostalgically evoked in Jacques Becker's 1952 film *Casque d'Or*, the romantic apotheosis of fin-de-siècle criminality—although there were *apaches* all over the city, and the actual story behind the movie occurred in Belleville, around the Bastille, near Les Halles, and in the southern suburb of Alfortville. The mature prostitutes photographed by Eugène Atget in the 1920s standing in front of their doorways are often described as denizens of the Zone, although they lived and worked in Fort-Monjol, a flesh market on a street that no longer exists southwest of the Buttes-Chaumont, a considerable distance from the wall. But the Zone, besides the shadowy menace implicit in its very name, was indisputably a convenient place for people to go to ground when they were wanted by the cops, and the fortifications, with their elevation

Gypsy wagons and bombed-out houses in the Zone, 1920s

and unobstructed views, presented an ideal neutral spot for knife fights.

All this is exploited with mythmaking verve in Francis Carco's 1919 novel *L'équipe*, subtitled *Roman des fortifs*. The story, nearly generic now, was less so a century ago: a gang leader is released from prison only to find that his gang has been taken over by a rival; a protracted struggle between the two men ensues. The geography is as stunted as it would have been in the minds of the characters' prototypes: the world is confined to Belleville, the fortifications, the Zone, and a few miles of outlying suburbs. The men on the street are

A murder in the Zone, 1930s

> fugitive personalities whose eyes lit up and went out rapidly. In that sector where the plaster shanties, isolated among vacant lots, gave an oblique appearance to everything, they added to that impression . . . The green shutters—a washed-out green—alternated with little shacks of a sickly yellow, their walls carved up with graffiti, and with the shuttered fronts of unfinished new houses, and when night fell the collection of things incomplete or already dead gave off a feeling of emptiness and weighty unease . . . The flat roofs of banal houses cut a silhouette against the sky that was only occasionally relieved by small chimneys that looked like still-smoking cigarette butts someone had glued there.

Even Carco's unsentimental camera eye could not dislodge the romance of the fortifications. After the wall was demolished in the 1920s its shadow haunted the city for decades. Until the construction of the Périphérique (1958–73), its site, according to Jean-Paul Clébert, was "a filthy ribbon of grass and piles of dirt, but where there remains under the big sky a restful view of loamy hillocks where laughing, grimy kids play all week long and of small, trampled footpaths like those worn down by animals headed to the watering hole." Its fame endured in memoirs and old postcards and in Georges Lacombe's 1928 documentary *La Zone*, in which you can see Toulouse-Lautrec's favorite model, La Goulue, a denizen of the place in her old age, along with a variety of other characters, among them a formidable woman

"Mother of dogs" in the Zone, 1920s

Music on the fortifications, Saint-Ouen, circa 1910

called *mère aux chiens*, "mother of dogs." Its final monument, though, was Fréhel's 1938 song "La chanson des fortifs," the deep-dish sentimentality of which is balanced by the resolute strength of her delivery. All the childhood heroes of the Zone have been translated to other existences: P'tit Louis, the strongman, now owns a garage; Julot is being measured for an endowed chair; and Nini married somebody and acquired a château. The old embankment is now covered by six-story apartment houses with elevators and central heating. "Gone are the fortifications / and the little saloons by the gates. / Goodbye to the scenery of all the songs / the pretty songs of long ago."

Because while the Zone was a netherworld, a gray area, a borderland teeming with the sorts of shadowy activities that thrive on margins, it also at the same time represented a door to nature. Not everyone was comfortable in the heavily regulated parks; even the relative vastness of the Bois de Vincennes might have felt too constricted to people from the wrong part of town. In the Zone you could own the outdoors. You didn't risk being run down by the carriages of the bon ton, weren't subject to constant surveillance by the constabulary. You could drink and dance and smoke and swear while surrounded by garlands of flowers and Japanese lanterns under the trees. People could gather escargots in the trenches of the fortifications and herbs on its mounds, and after the wall came down parts of its site were occupied for decades by a patchwork of tiny garden plots worked

A pleasure boat dock in Nogent-sur-Seine, circa 1910

by slum dwellers who might have to walk considerable distances to get to them. And then beyond the Zone was the *banlieue*.

Before the twentieth century the *banlieue* was primarily farmland punctuated by villages. Its waterways (the Seine, the Marne, the Oise) attracted boaters and day-trippers, familiar to us with their striped jerseys and straw hats in a long continuum that stretches from Manet's rowers at Argenteuil (1874) to Seurat's bathers at Asnières (1883–84) and loungers on the island of La Grande Jatte (1884–86) to Jean Renoir's wedding party in *Boudu Saved from Drowning* (1932) to Cartier-Bresson's picnickers on the banks of the Marne (1936) and Renoir's holidaymakers in *Partie de campagne* (also 1936). There were *guinguettes* everywhere, from the classically minimal shack with a few tables under the trees to more elaborate installations with full restaurant service that might also include seesaws, swings, courts for *boules*, pedal-driven boats for hire, polished dance floors with bandstands, and even fairground rides. In 1848, in the southern suburb of Plessis-Piquet, an enthusiast of Johann David Wyss's *Swiss Family Robinson* (1812) was inspired to build a *guinguette* in the form of an elaborate tree house. Competitors erected their own tree house bistros, and before long the village's popularity as a Sunday destination was such that in 1909 it was officially renamed Plessis-Robinson. Although those establishments are long gone, some that are nearly as old survive today, such as Chez Gégène, on the Marne in Joinville-le-Pont, which dates back to somewhere in the pre-1914 mists and was repeatedly photographed by Robert Doisneau in the 1940s and '50s; it looks much the same as it ever did.

The permanent population of the *banlieue* was all the while steadily rising, with much of the influx coming from the city. Some went out to Pantin or Aubervilliers or Malakoff to buy their *octroi*-free staples and wound up staying. Ex-convicts were often declared *interdit de séjour* (forbidden to enter the capital) and while some became vagabonds, others chose to settle on the fringes. People with just a little bit of money built *bicoques* (shanties) of wood or plaster or concrete blocks, with names such as Malgré Tout, Ça Me Suffit, Mon Bonheur,* that served as sum-

Le Vrai Arbre, the first café in the trees, in Robinson, circa 1910

* "Despite Everything," "Enough for Me," "My Happiness."

The wall and the village of Saint-Ouen, circa 1910

mer retreats and represented the dream of retirement. Now and again some member of the Parisian minor bourgeoisie would round up sufficient cash to indulge a long-standing baronial fantasy and build himself a crenellated castle in the middle of nowhere.* The suburban experience manifested itself embryonically, first in the form of aspirational villas and then, after the First World War, as patchy developments of cheaply built *pavillons* aligned in neat rows, much like the pre-Levittown tract home enterprises in the United States.

In the unregulated *banlieue* these coexisted with muddy fields, gasworks, marshaling yards, stockyards, warehouses, slaughterhouses, military depots, abandoned factories, working factories, acres of rubble, illegal dumps, soccer pitches, convents, orphanages, hospitals where patients stood by the gates to sell their medications, and old-age homes where the inmates waited outside to sell their tobacco allowances. And everywhere there were bars, of every description, some of them corner establishments made of brick, intended to anchor a street of shops that may or may not eventually have been built; some of them plywood shacks with tin roofs although minus the rustic amenities of a *guinguette*, kept afloat by a strictly marginal clientele who inhabited a notional extension of the Zone. And through the postwar years the area saw the emergence of bidonvilles—favelas, that is: whole communities built of scrap and inhabited primarily by immigrants from North Africa, which could vary dramatically in tone. There were reasonably stable hamlets where families predominated and people took pride in their dwellings, of the sort that Didier Daeninckx describes in his novel *Meurtres pour mémoire*, set in 1961:

> She walked toward the water company buildings, where the first inhabitants of the bidonville had made their homes. The company for some obscure reason had let the

* An early model was Alexandre Dumas *père*'s Château de Monte-Cristo in Le Port-Marly, north of Versailles, a lavish Renaissance-style palace with Moorish touches, with an adjacent studio in the form of a miniature Gothic castle, the whole surrounded by English gardens with follies, grottoes, and waterworks. Dumas, flush with success, initiated construction in 1844, celebrated its completion in 1847 with a banquet for six hundred, but then, debt-ridden, was forced to sell in 1848. It still stands.

land go to waste, in the process abandoning four rudimentary structures, big rectangular redbrick boxes. A few families had settled there, and had expanded their dwellings by building upper stories from boards and sheet metal. Over the course of months and years other families had joined them, and today the four structures formed the core and center of an agglomeration of shacks where five thousand people lived.

At the other extreme were encampments, essentially hobo jungles, congeries of single men where violence was perpetually imminent and—unsurprisingly, as their shacks were covered with tarpaper, and as kerosene was the source of both heat and light—fires could erase the whole patch at any time.

Meanwhile, the city of Paris had been attempting to address the problem of housing for the poor since at least the 1840s, and in 1894 the Siegfried Law, which stipulated financing and tax relief for such constructions, gave the impulse a practical footing. Not much was done until after World War I, however, when the housing problem began to reach crisis proportions, and the first proposals fell into two categories: garden cities, an idea borrowed from the British, and HBMs, or *habitations à bon marché*, or "cheap housing." These began to be built in 1928, two hundred thousand low-cost units in addition to eighty thousand medium-range, generally squat six-story orange-brick buildings, the first ones going up on the site of the former wall. The poet Jean Follain noted, with a touch of superciliousness, that "now an entire population aspires to a light-filled apartment. The fairground wrestler, worn down, covered with hieroglyphic tattoos, wants nothing more in this fallen world than walls painted in soft colors." But it didn't take very long for these to decline, or at least for their mass-produced institutional lack of distinction to sap the spirits of their inmates. By 1933 the proletarian writer Eugène Dabit could describe "a circle of buildings, in the middle a courtyard with its flower beds filled with yellowed grass, a few flowerpots on a cement ground. Stairs and hallways all alike. When you were drunk you'd come home to some building, didn't matter which one. Whatever—it was all the same termite mound."

An old-style workers' *cité*, Île-de-France, circa 1910

A bidonville in Saint-Denis, 1963

But the HBMs could not adequately house even the forty thousand inhabitants of the Zone, all of them relocated by 1932. By then there were 2.1 million people living in the *banlieue,* as compared with 2.9 million in Paris itself; by the eve of the war the two populations were equal. After the war an enormous influx from the provinces further aggravated standing problems; there were bidonvilles within the city itself. And the *banlieue* terrified the municipal establishment—it was the "Red Belt," overwhelmingly working-class, reliably Communist at the polls, which editorial Cassandras foresaw seizing Paris in a pincer grasp, making a revolution from the outside in. And the inhabitants of the HBMs were increasingly unhappy. Cendrars surveyed the scene in the text he wrote to accompany Doisneau's photographs of the *banlieue*: "Everything is a sham in those big echoing barracks, from the broken elevators to the cellars where wine sours, turns to vinegar. The only real thing is misery: tuberculosis in proportion to the continual increase of children in cramped quarters, cuckoldry on every floor, worries drowned in drink, and women beaten like rugs."

In 1949 the HBMs became HLMs, *habitations à loyer modéré*, "reduced-rent housing," a telling move from plain speech and toward bureaucratic equivocation. The only possible direction was upward and outward, toward the *grand ensemble*, "the big set"—like a low-budget, reduced-scale version of Le Corbusier's apocalyptic cityscapes. The idea had already been tried out in the 1930s, in the Cité de la Muette in Drancy, which had buildings up to fifteen stories high.* Now, in the early 1950s, partly as a consequence of the agitations of Abbé Pierre, France's most prominent media cleric, who was incessantly leading crusades to bring attention to the plight of the homeless and the ill-housed, the mechanism swung into gear and, one after another, the *grands ensembles* arose: Arceuil, Orsay, Plaisance, Créteil, Massy-Antony, Melun-Sénart, Cergy-Pontoise, Marne-la-Vallée, Sarcelles-la-Grande-Borne, Saint-Quentin-en-Yvelines. And very soon the constructions moved beyond Île-de-France and encircled every major city in the land.

A *grand ensemble* represented by consumer goods, from Jean-Luc Godard's *2 or 3 Things I Know About Her* (1967)

The old *cités* had been rows of attached two-story houses with pitched roofs, grouped into courtyards and culs-de-sac, visually echoing the ancient layout of the walled farm as it can still be seen all over France. The new complexes looked like immense chests of drawers or speaker cabinets, like banks of Univac-style computers, like the Secretariat of the United Nations extended into a vast hedge. There were tower blocks with cross or tripod footprints, and some that were cylindrical, like silos. Their forward-looking architects eschewed the safe and familiar in favor of vanguard designs. Some had enormous walls of windows to which were assigned uniform drapes, while others had little slivers of windows in rows or stacks of two or three, meant more for the visual delectation of outsiders than for the use of the inhabitants. "The landscape being generally thankless, they've gone so far as to eliminate windows, since there is nothing to see," says the narrator of Maurice Pialat's short film *L'amour existe* (1960).

Pialat, who had grown up before the war in one of the little detached *pavillons* in Courbevoie, made his movie as an elegy to the old *banlieue* at a time when it was being mercilessly reconfigured. He acknowledges the grayness and drabness and boredom of the *banlieue* as it was, the German bombs that cratered landscapes already unprepossessing as they were. He cites statistics:

The title frame of Maurice Pialat's *L'amour existe*, 1960

* Ten years later the Cité was converted into an internment camp for Jews, who were sent from there to Auschwitz.

twenty-nine *lycées* in the city as compared with just nine in the *banlieue*, which by then had nearly twice the population. He notes that the new projects segregate not simply by class but by age and family status as well. He suggests that there are more than superficial similarities between the designers and builders of the new *cités* and those of the Todt Organization, the Nazi engineering outfit that gave Germany the Autobahn and the Siegfried Line and gave France the Atlantic Wall. He shows a street sign, flung down and trampled: RUE ORADOUR-SUR-GLANE, it reads. The street had been named after that village in the Limousin where, in June 1944, the Waffen SS massacred 642 men, women, and children—they had targeted another, similarly named village nearby but had gone to the wrong address. Around the fallen sign a group of young men are pummeling and kicking one another, smashing wooden crates on each other's heads, for no particular reason. Love still exists, Pialat's title says, but very little in his footage suggests where it may be found.

5

La Canaille

Censuses have been taken for as long as there has been taxation, and there has been taxation for as long as there have been human settlements, which is to say for as long as agriculture has existed. Still, it has never in any period been a simple matter to establish who "the people" are, or to determine their numbers. "The people," it seems, is a highly subjective category. Think of all those human tribes whose name translates as "the people"—they are legion—which implies that all others belong to some different life-form. Consider that the Roman people in the formulation Senatus Populusque Romanus, or SPQR, might have been considered sovereign by the Republic, but the tally did not include women, servants, or the foreign-born. Elsewhere and at other times, though, "the people" might refer to the vast undifferentiated mass that existed below the level of the nobility and the Church.

That was the case in the French language. Actually, to be more precise, the term usually applied to the roiling multitude before the nineteenth century was *populace*, which my edition of the *Dictionnaire Quillet* (1948) defines as "the inferior people; the dregs of the population." Things began to change after 1789, when the notion arose of the *peuple*, a comparatively neutral term that implied more about quantity than quality. In Victor Hugo's verse drama *Hernani*, the signal work of the revolutionary year 1830, the *peuple* is compared to

Rent strikers, circa 1910

"The bourgeois . . . nothing but a herd of cattle."
Illustration by Gavarni, from *Les petits mordent*, 1853

. . . an ocean, a surge ceaselessly astir,
Into which nothing can be thrown without affecting all,
A wave that can crush a throne and lull a grave,
A mirror in which a king seldom sees himself flattered.
　　(iv, 2)

In other words, the subject had passed from the mob to the crowd. The former is headless and directionless, a chaos, while the latter is a highly reactive organic entity, with its own sometimes unfathomable purposes, that might be temporarily appeased but never quelled. It was around the same time that the term *prolétaire* was repurposed from the Latin to describe that portion of the population that depended for survival on compensation of its labor, as distinct from *capitaliste*, a word first used in French in 1788.

To those who did not consider themselves members of the crowd, it was at best an environmental hazard, at worst a malign force. The people were dirty, treacherous, even murderous; they smelled bad, something that discouraged slumming almost as much as did the threat of crime. But then a view of the crowd from an appropriate distance could dissolve all the lower rungs of class, making the population a single pulsating mass. Thus Balzac, writing in 1834:

> One of the most distressing of spectacles is the appearance of the Parisian population, a people horrible to behold, pale, wan, sunburned. Isn't Paris a vast field incessantly stirred by a storm of motives, in which eddies a harvest of humans which death reaps more often than elsewhere and who are reborn just as clenched as always, whose twisted and contorted faces exude through every pore the desires, the vices, the poisons with which their brains have been swelled— no, not faces but masks: masks of weakness, masks of strength, masks of misery, masks of joy, masks of hypocrisy, all enfeebled, all stamped with the indelible sign of panting greed? What do they want? Gold or pleasure?

But then those were the years, after Napoléon and the brief, tumultuous reigns of Louis XVIII and Charles X, when Paris was becoming a modern city. The bourgeoisie was rising, the aristoc-

The crowd on Sunday morning, at the corner of Rue Saint-Médard and Rue Mouffetard, circa 1910

racy was dimming, the population was swelled by immigrants from all the regions of France, especially the arid south-central. Suddenly, a great many of the faces on the street were unfamiliar, and the narrow alleys and passages and culs-de-sac of the center, constructed for a much smaller population, were bursting with people, who were tucking themselves into every corner, filling the courtyards with workshops, butting ad hoc annexes onto ancient buildings, adding to the pileup of garbage, the cloud of stench, the overflowing gutters; and who, not to mention, were reproducing furiously—by 1830 one birth in three was illegitimate. Anyone who could remember the time before the Restoration was disoriented, even alienated. The city was no longer theirs.

Even so, the rabble had always been the city's fundament. Cendrars evokes the crowd of the Middle Ages, the people drawn by the construction of Notre-Dame:

A swarm of ordinary folk, vagabonds, pilgrims, some wealthy merchant who had taken a vow after eluding highwaymen, along with his servants and his employees who had like him come to work for a while as laborers, those were the people who overran the stonemason's yard, a genuine Zone established in the heart of the city when a cathedral was being built, which generally lasted more than a century, with an influx of the mad, the sick, the

"What's with the racket? What do you want?" "Your charity, please, my lord." Illustration by J. J. Grand-ville, from *Scènes de la vie publique et privée des animaux*, 1842

Rubberneckers—*badauds*—perhaps taking in a dramatic rescue from the Seine down below

illuminated, the devout, of preaching monks, criminals, drunkards, bourgeois, nobles surrounding the yard night and day because it is always entertaining to watch others work . . .

He goes on to note how random members of this mob would be chosen by the stone carvers to pose for one of the myriad statues that crowd the portals and the façade: ". . . all those carved stones are portraits of people who had names (only those of the donors have endured), all those statues were carved on the spot, in real time, without cheating or faking, in the midst of life, with their attitudes, gestures, clothing, and accessories preserved, often with a huge sense of humor or cruel satire . . ." Thus the physical trace of the rabble is retained in the oldest, most august, most sanctified monument of the city.

The names of the crowd are irrevocably lost—to the extent that they had been recorded at all, the documentation was destroyed in the fires during the Bloody Week that ended the Commune in 1871. Their occupations, general appearance, family relations, details of daily living can be guessed at only in the broadest ways. They do possess another monument: the Catacombs, the network of caves (former limestone mines) centered under Place Denfert-Rochereau in the Fourteenth Arrondissement, where beginning in 1780 the contents of the city's graveyards were removed, following an incident in which people were asphyxiated by fumes in their cellars on Rue de la Lingerie, adjacent to one of the common trenches of the Innocents cemetery near Les Halles. The Catacombs contain the remains of somewhere between six and eight million citizens, all of them more or less poor, since the rich got themselves interred in crypts in their family church. Their bones are arranged in architectural formations in certain caves, piled any which way in others. You can examine the skulls and speculate: this one a laundress, that one a sneak thief, this one a monk, that one a rat catcher. They are the people who built the Louvre and the Bastille; who watched Templars and schismatics be burned alive and common thieves and murderers broken on the wheel; who stared at the first elephant, the first rhinoceros, the first giraffe to enter France; who withstood epic floods, disastrous freezes, devastating fires, sudden famines; who died in great numbers from the Plague, small-pox, typhus, syphilis, influenza, whooping cough; who rose up against tax collectors, heretics, foreigners, pretenders, Jews, Protestants, and supporters of Cardinal Mazarin; who ate tainted meat and were trampled during festivals and learned to drink coffee and never once left the city.

The Parisians for a long time were a Nordic people, blond and blue-eyed even after a considerable interval dominated by Romans. Louis Chevalier insisted on a continuity of affinities that stretched across the centuries, basing this perhaps questionable claim on a protracted study of documents high and low going back to the Middle Ages: their wit, he thought, was a permanent trait, along with their subtle irony, their gift for repartee, their need for pleasure, their insistence on being released from all constraints, as well as their deep investment in romance, covering the span from idealistic love to frank carnality. And Victor Hugo introduced the urchin Gavroche as his capsule model of the essential Parisian:

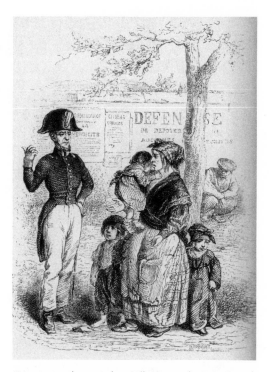

"Necessity obeys no law." Illustration by J. J. Grandville, from *Cent proverbes*, 1845

When it comes to the people of Paris, even the mature adult remains a kid. To depict the child is to depict the city, and that's why we have chosen this sparrow as a subject by which to render the eagle.

It is especially in the faubourgs, let us insist, that the Parisian race is made manifest. They are where you'll find its undiluted blood, its true features. They are where that people works and suffers, and work and suffering are the two faces of humanity. There are enormous numbers of unknown beings; the place is aswarm with the strangest creatures, from the stevedore of La Rapée to the knacker of Montfaucon. *Fex urbis*, cried Cicero; *mob*, added the indignant Burke; rabble, multitude, populace. Those words fall from your lips . . . That abject sand you trample, throw it into the furnace; let it melt and boil: it will become a splendid crystal, and through it Galileo and Newton will discover the stars.

As the nineteenth century drew on, that abject sand became ever less timid about asserting its merit. Already it had mastered

Three-card monte players, circa 1900

the art of seizing and reclaiming insults flung its way. The French language is rich in words for the lower classes that signify dregs, scum, residue, bottom: *la racaille,** la crapule, la vermine, la fripouille, la tourbe.* Perhaps the most frequently employed was *canaille,* which derives from the Latin word for "dog." It was a sign of the times when in 1865 Joseph Darcier and Alexis Bouvier wrote the song "La canaille," which was a resounding hit four years later for Rosa Bordas. Its many verses are rhetorical and uninteresting ("In an old French city / there is a race of iron / . . . / All its sons are born on straw / Their palace is nothing but a shack . . ."), but every time La Bordas, on the stage at a café-concert, engaged the chorus, "C'est la canaille!," the audience would join its second line en masse: "Eh bien, j'en suis!"

This act of self-identification with the riffraff was occurring on the eve of the Franco-Prussian War and just two years before the Commune. You could argue that the socioeconomic structure of the Second Empire precluded vertical mobility and class-jumping aspiration; you could also make the case that those of the *menu peuple* who didn't actually live in misery were more concerned with their homes and families than with social status. If they were lumped they would spit in the eye of the lumpers.

A precedent of sorts had occurred a quarter century earlier, with the publication of Eugène Sue's epochal novel *The Mysteries of Paris.* Sue (1804–1857) was hardly a man of the people—his father was surgeon to the Imperial Guard and he himself was a godson of Empress Eugénie—but, spurred by a bet, he was determined to write the great epic of the people, and disguised himself and hung around the dives of the Cité, collecting material. He started writing right away after his initial immersion, having found two of his main characters brawling in the very first deadfall he checked into. The writing proceeded serially, installments appearing regularly in the *Journal des Débats* from June 1842 to October 1843 and eventually filling ten volumes. The result is a sprawling tableau of lower-class Parisian life, presented melodramatically and as it were operatically, with each of the characters embodying some trait, some station, some princi-

The Mysteries of Paris, directed by Charles Burguet, 1922. The second of six films—and two TV series—based on the novel

---

* During the 2005 riots in the *banlieue,* Nicolas Sarkozy notoriously referred to the rioters as *racaille.*

ple rather than attempting to impersonate individual humans. Le Chourineur is a knife fighter and ostensibly a brute, although not lacking hidden virtues; Fleur-de-Marie, alias La Goualeuse, is a pure flower of the slums, around whom the entire plot revolves; Rigolette is the very image of the *grisette*, the emblematic young Parisian working woman, allegedly charming and lighthearted at all times; the Schoolmaster is a brutal ex-con; La Chouette (the Owl) is a vicious old woman; Ferrand is the notary who enriches himself at the expense of the vulnerable—and so on through the archetypes. The central figure, though, is Rodolphe, something of a superhero. He is secretly grand duke of a Ruritanian principality, but disguises himself as an ordinary workingman in order to solve the problems of one and all, since he is of such flawless essence he feels obliged to parcel out his inherent gifts.

For all the book's shortcomings, the people of Paris saw themselves represented in it. It's true that much of its subject matter might have been familiar to literary consumers from the *Memoirs* (1828) of Eugène-François Vidocq, the convict turned policeman turned detective, or from Victor Hugo's novel *The Last Day of a Condemned Man* (1829). But unlike either of those books, *Mysteries* featured addictive, suspense-filled plot construction, and Sue's direct appeals to the emotions and his partisanship on behalf of the poor, which became more explicit with each passing chapter, broke through class barriers and seized the imagination of the whole city. It had hundreds of thousands of readers; long lines of people appeared every week outside the offices of the *Journal des Débats* to snag the first copies; the illiterate demanded it be read to them. Readers thought that Rodolphe was a real person, and many letters were addressed to him asking for his intercession. According to his friend Alexandre Dumas, Sue to the end of his life received letters, often anonymous, enclosing money for the poor. But somehow the novel also acted as a genuine agent of social change, inspiring investigative journalism that tallied wages paid to factory workers and compared them with the cost of living—something unheard of until then.

The industry of the serial novel, or *roman-feuilleton*, began in 1836 with the publication of *The Duchess of Salisbury,* by Dumas, in *La Presse* and right away became a sensation, the focus of a

Eugène Sue

The bread-crust market. Illustration by José Belon for *Paris anecdote,* by Privat d'Anglemont, 1885 edition

A rally in support of the United Front, Place de la Nation, 1934

three-way rivalry among *La Presse*, *Le Siècle*, and the *Journal des Débats*, the field of combat of such unstoppably prolific novel-extruding machines as Dumas, Balzac, Paul Féval, and Pierre-Alexis de Ponson du Terrail. *The Mysteries of Paris* was the form's first truly major success—Dumas's *Count of Monte Cristo*, to name one of many, was deliberately conceived as an attempt to top it. The serials and the newspapers that printed them were aimed at the petite bourgeoisie, newly literate and possessed of leisure time. There was an understanding that the upper classes might stoop to slumming in those pages as well, but *Mysteries* in addition opened the door to an unexpected new audience: the working class.

Thus was born the concept of the *populaire*, which for all its ups and downs and sundry mutations has never since ceased to be a major component of French culture. It is congruent with the English-language notion of popular culture only up to a point, since the French version is not just a bit older but also much more self-conscious and politicized. It covers a broad terrain: the café-concert, the detective novel, the sports industry, blood-and-thunder plays, six-day bicycle races, comic strips, popular science, true crime magazines, lotteries, sidewalk demonstrations by muscle men and patent medicine vendors, soft porn, torch singers, street purveyors of fried potatoes and roasted chestnuts, neighborhood carnivals, postcards, romance novels, self-help nostrums, *fumetti*, and a great swath of the movies. Historically it has often been subject to attempts by the left to mold it, but in the twentieth century and beyond it has more often inclined toward the right, from the Action Française of the 1930s to the Front National of the present day. The art historian and cultural critic T. J. Clark defined its nub: "Popular culture provided the petit-bourgeois aficionado with two forms of illusory 'class': an identity with those below him, or at least with certain images of their life, and a difference which hinged on his skill—his privileged place—as a consumer of those same images."

When class is a determining factor in society, an ostensibly class-spanning phenomenon puts all the parties into uneasy relationships. The petit bourgeois consumer is squeezed between authenticity on one side and aspiration on the other. The bourgeois always has the option of *s'encanailler* (slumming)—but then she might be encouraging behavior that will later prove a threat.

An illustration by Théophile Steinlen for *Dans la rue*, vol. 1, by Aristide Bruant, 1889

And the lower classes might profit from the situation, but at the cost of being permanently patronized, pursuing their pleasures in a sort of diorama.

The *populaire* can be seen as a mechanism, if unintentional, for keeping the classes in their place. As Clark writes, "It is above all *collectivity* that the popular exists to prevent." The culture of the lower classes is maintained in its private plot, branded for immediate identification—there is little danger of its overstepping its bounds and turning into something more ambiguous, let alone incendiary. The products of the music hall, the penny press, and the vaudeville theater are kept in a different aisle from those of the Comédie Française, the *Revue des Deux Mondes*, and the Opéra; it is made clear that the former are diversions while the latter constitute culture. Not only did this discourage consumers from finding an excess of meaning in the songs and plays of the working class, but it also kept the classes from making common cause. The best-known example of this sort of cultural policing was, and remains, the Académie Française, which in obsessively tending the French language like a heritage garden, preserving the vocabulary and syntax of Racine and Corneille and extirpating creeping foreign influences, has also scrupulously weeded out all traces of argot, which might be employed on a daily basis by a majority of the population but would not find its way into respectable print.

•

"The black man of tomorrow": an Auvergnat, because he is in the coal business. Interesting racial politics from André Gill in *La Petite Lune*, 1878

"These are no brave messengers, who wander through strange lands." The Roma as seen by Jacques Callot, in *Les bohémiens en marche: L'arrière garde*, 1621

The blue-eyed descendants of the Parisii were not the only Parisians, had not been for ages. People had been filtering into the capital from other parts of France in significant numbers since at least the seventeenth century, Normans and Auvergnats and Gascons and Savoyards, who were welcomed because—as is always and everywhere the case with immigrants—they were willing to take on the hard, dirty, and dangerous jobs scorned by the natives. They soon became identified with specific trades, which they monopolized, so that successive generations of newcomers were assured of jobs; the Savoyards, for example, long had a lock on chimney sweeping. Privat d'Anglemont wrote in the 1850s that "the first Auvergnat in Paris must have picked up some change selling scrap iron, likewise the first Norman by selling old clothes. Since that time—time immemorial—all the Auvergnats are scrap metal vendors and all the Normans deal in secondhand clothes."

The Auvergnats, hailing from the Cantal and Puy-de-Dôme departments in the arid Massif Central, have arguably left a mark on the city more indelible than any other group of immigrants. They were first known as water carriers; in the days before indoor plumbing, somebody had to carry buckets up to the seventh floors of houses. In the 1780s Louis-Sébastien Mercier estimated that twenty thousand Auvergnats were so occupied, but by then their sense of enterprise had already granted them many royal letters of patent. The Auvergnats came to dominate the scrap metal trade and the trade in wood; they were tinkers and braziers and knife sharpeners, repairers of china and parasols. Before long they had amassed sufficient capital to begin opening cafés and wineshops and restaurants and hotels, and that is what they are still known for today. The epicenter of Auvergnat settlement had from the beginning been the area around the Bastille. On Rue de Lappe they opened dance halls featuring their indigenous music, based on a bagpipe instrument called the musette. The dances attracted outsiders and changed over the decades; the musette itself disappeared in favor of accordions and clarinets, but the term *bal-musette* remained fixed in the language and in Parisian culture, and the spiritual home of the music remains Rue de Lappe. Somehow, unlike most other groups of immigrants from the Hexagon, the Auvergnats have maintained a distinct identity.*

The experience of groups from outside the country has been somewhat more vexed. The Roma—"the poorest creatures ever seen coming to France within living memory"—arrived, headed by twelve men on horseback, in 1427, with tales of being persecuted by the Saracens for their Christianity. They were denied entry and forced to camp in Saint-Denis. When they were allowed to attend a fair, their women began reading palms, which proved very popular and very embarrassing, both to the public (numerous were the imputations of cuckoldry) and to the church, which sent a friar to excommunicate them all, after which they were shown the road out. They would reappear throughout the centuries—they were a significant presence in the Zone—but their relations with the French authorities were always contentious, and so they have remained to the present day. That is not a matter confined to Paris or to France, of course. The poor Roma suffer the unhappy fate of eternally being cast as the world's stepchildren.

There have been Jews in Paris for so long that there is no record of their arrival. Their first appearance in the historical register comes by way of a mention of forced conversions to Christianity in 581. In that same Merovingian era they may have constituted 20 percent of the population of Île de la Cité; its main street at the time was called Rue de la Juiverie. But numbers and importance did not spare them from being scapegoated every time something went wrong. Philippe-Auguste expelled them en masse in 1182 and called them back in 1198. They began the thirteenth century numbered at around three thousand, but they were down to a third of that figure by 1296. This was surely a result of an incident in 1290, when a certain Jonathas is said to have stabbed a host wafer with his dagger, causing it to bleed. He was burned at the stake, his family converted, and presumably most of his coreligionists decamped, but this did not prevent Philippe the Fair from driving out the remainder in 1306; he called them back almost immediately. Riots were directed against

* The weekly newspaper *L'Auvergnat de Paris* began publication in 1882 and continues to exist, if in somewhat diminished form, in the twenty-first century.

A Jewish bookstore and bookbindery in the Marais, circa 1910

them in 1380 and 1382, and they were again expelled in 1394; the date of their return is uncertain. At the start of the eighteenth century there were only about five hundred Jews in Paris, some of them Spanish Sephardim, some from Avignon (including the families of two major twentieth-century composers, Ravel and Milhaud), but with a solid majority of Ashkenazim from the east, who were starting to arrive in significant numbers. In 1791 the Revolutionary government granted them citizenship, which was formalized by Napoléon in 1808, and then the July Monarchy extended full civil equality in 1831. Their numbers continued to swell, as Jews escaping pogroms in Russia established themselves in the area around the Marché du Temple previously settled by Jewish furriers. (It remains a Jewish neighborhood to the present day.)

Their problems were hardly over. Soon the language began to distinguish between French Jews of long standing, *israélites*, and immigrants, *juifs*. And even the former were not immune to persecution, as demonstrated by the fate of Alfred Dreyfus, as exemplary a member of the assimilated Jewish bourgeoisie as you could have hoped to find. In the late nineteenth century, anti-Semitism was a cleaver that split nearly every subgrouping within the French population; there were, for example, pro-

Semitic and anti-Semitic factions among the anarchists, which by the time of the Dreyfus Affair had roughly equal influence and vehemence, their anti-Semitism ostensibly spurred by the role Jews played in capitalist oppression—not for nothing has anti-Semitism been called "the socialism of fools." Acknowledgments of the Jewish working class are sufficiently rare that the 1908 account by the investigative reporters Maurice and Léon Bonneff stands out as singular:

> Among the workers of Paris there is one group of people, industrious and starving, who have held on to their customs and their language: the Jewish proletariat. Even when laborers have united in solidarity regardless of their origins, Jewish workers, for many reasons, could not assimilate. Most of them exiled, all of them exploited, Jewish workers have endured the burden of religious hatred, stringent economic subjugation, all the miseries of the Old World. The Jewish manual laborer, the Jew far from the shop and the cash register, is generally little known. But the Fourth and Ninth Arrondissements of Paris, the Bastille and Hôtel de Ville neighborhoods, give shelter to a population of Jewish tailors, cap makers, cabinetmakers, smiths, cobblers, sculptors, mechanics, tinsmiths, locksmiths, coppersmiths, and furriers, all speaking the same language: Yiddish.

A propaganda poster denouncing members of the Manouchian resistance network, the twenty-three members of which were all foreigners, many of them Jewish. They were executed early in 1944.

The figurehead of race hatred then was Édouard Drumont, author of *La France juive* (1886) and editor of the poisonously influential newspaper *La Libre Parole* (1892–1924; its motto: "France for the French"). The maverick anarchist writer Georges Darien devoted his 1891 novel *Les Pharisiens* (the title puns on "Pharisees" and "Parisians") to a satirical portrait of Drumont: "He had been *completely* a man of his time, and that was admirable. Like a sponge, his brain had absorbed all its gall and slime, all its bile and spittle, all its manure and filth, and when the day came, all he had to do was to press his dirty fingers onto white paper to let flow an entire generation's covetous passions and unclean desires."

By the late 1890s there was a virtual pandemic of far-right

Le Petit Journal
SUPPLÉMENT ILLUSTRÉ
Huit pages : CINQ centimes

Le dernier ravitaillement du Fort Chabrol
POURSUITE SUR LES TOITS

Supporters throwing supplies down to members of the outlawed Ligue Antisémite holed up in "Fort Chabrol," 1899

organizations that traded in virulent anti-Semitism as a matter of course, such as the Ligue des Patriotes (founded by among others Félix Faure, seventh president of the Republic), the Jeunesses Royalistes, and the Ligue Antisémite. In 1899, in the course of the Dreyfus case, the government feared a right-wing coup and had the heads of those organizations arrested—but Jules Guérin, chief of the Antisemitic League, took refuge with a group of die-hards in a Masonic lodge on Rue de Chabrol, near the Gare de l'Est, where they held out for thirty-eight days. In 1902, Henri Buronfosse, a member of the League of Patriots, blocked the chimney pipe in the house of Émile Zola, causing his death from carbon monoxide poisoning.

In the same era, the hypernationalist Charles Maurras founded Action Française—at once a publication, a philosophy, and a movement that, while it swung back and forth between republicanism and monarchism, and despised Germans even as it kowtowed to them under the Vichy puppet regime, held fast to its xenophobia, particularly with respect to Jews. Maurras, who preached that Jews brought "lice, plague, and typhus while awaiting the revolution," urged that Léon Blum, prime minister during the Popular Front era, be "shot by firing squad, from the back," and that "his throat [be] cut with a kitchen knife." Blum, France's most prominent Jewish politician up to that time, was in fact very nearly lynched on the street in Paris in 1936 by members of the Camelots du Roi, a Maurras-affiliated intimidation squad. And Maurras was hardly an isolated extremist. In 1928 a proposed law brought before the Chamber of Deputies and signed by sixty-five members from both right and left was aimed at destroying the Jewish community:

> The undesirables must be banished. By "undesirables" we mean all foreigners who cannot prove that they follow a profession that contributes to the economic prosperity of the nation. These are for the most part ruffians, croupiers, vendors of secondhand goods, etc.—exotics, who live in France as parasites. Currently they maintain nests of a dangerously unhealthy sort, particularly in the Fourth, Fourteenth, and Eighteenth Arrondissements of Paris, which the City Council has many times singled out for notice.

But of course such crimes and rhetoric were as nothing compared to the *traque* that began in July 1942 with the arrest of 12,884 Jewish men, women, and children, who were taken to the Vel d'Hiv, or Vélodrome d'Hiver, a bicycle racing stadium near the Eiffel Tower, or to a former housing project in Drancy, in the northeastern *banlieue*, before being sent on to Auschwitz. Eventually nearly seventy-six thousand French Jews were arrested and deported, 85 percent of them by French police; only twenty-five hundred returned. In Paris the toll was heaviest in the northeast, from the Marais to Belleville and Ménilmontant. In those neighborhoods, every school building that stood before 1940 bears a plaque by its front entrance commemorating the pupils lost to the Shoah, many of them pulled from their classes by agents of the French Gestapo.

A telephone booth prohibiting use by Jews, during the German occupation

No figure is more illustrative of the perniciousness and license of French racism than Maurice Papon, an ambitious civil servant, at first not especially ideological in his preoccupations, who rose quickly within the Vichy government and got himself appointed to the number two spot in the police department in Bordeaux, with a specific mandate on Jewish affairs. There he was directly responsible for the deportation of 1,560 Jewish men, women, and children. Nevertheless, after the war he simply claimed with no proof that he had been active in the Resistance—he would not be the only Vichy official to successfully pursue this tack—and was quietly absorbed into Charles de Gaulle's Fifth Republic, serving in various high-echelon posts. He spent the better part of the 1950s as an administrator in North Africa, first repressing Moroccan nationalists and then playing a major role in the Algerian War (1954–62), personally taking part in the torture of prisoners. He was named prefect of police for Paris in 1958, a post he would hold for nine years. In that capacity he was directly responsible for a series of massacres.

In October 1961 a nonviolent march of twenty thousand to thirty thousand organized by the Algerian National Liberation Front in protest of curfew laws was kettled on the Pont de Neuilly on its way to the Étoile by a force of more than sixteen hundred from combined police services, who fired into the crowd. There are numerous eyewitness accounts of deaths, but they are unacknowledged in any official document, and numbers remain un-

"Here we drown Algerians": graffito on a quai around the time of the massacre that ended the peaceful demonstration of October 17, 1961. Poster for a 2011 film by Yasmina Adi about the massacre

North Africans applying for their *cartes d'identité*, 1920s

certain. Another, larger demonstration a few days later resulted in sixty-six thousand arrests, the prisoners taken to two sports stadiums. Many were seriously injured (gunshots, fractured skulls, broken bones, lacerations), but medical services arrived five hours late. Once again, there are reports of many deaths as a consequence, but there exists no formal accounting of them. Later that month a large protest march was broken up by police under the pretext that it violated curfew laws; eleven thousand were arrested and, significantly, locked up in the Vel d'Hiv. What was long known on the street (but not made public until an inquiry in 1994) was that as many as two hundred of the pro-testers were murdered by the police, who threw them trussed up into the Seine, where they drowned. The government to this day will admit to only two deaths. Four months later, a protest against the OAS (Organisation de l'Armée Secrète, a death squad op-erated by French police and military personnel in Algeria) was violently attacked by police, resulting in the deaths of nine trade union members at the Charonne Métro station. That event proved impossible to minimize; a plaque marks its site.

Papon was finally forced to resign in 1967 as a consequence of the furor after the 1965 kidnapping in Paris and subsequent dis-appearance of the Moroccan activist Mehdi Ben Barka, a matter that remains impenetrably murky even now. But Papon was eased into a series of comfortable jobs, including as head of Sud Aviation, the company that built the Concorde supersonic jet. He was finally convicted in 1998 of dispatching eight "death trains" during his tenure in Bordeaux and sentenced to ten years in prison—the usual sentence would have been life—but was released after less than three years on the grounds of ill health. He died in his own bed at the age of ninety-six.

•

Algerians began immigrating to France in 1915, as a direct consequence of Algerian conscription into the French army during the war. By then, Algeria had been the property of the French for eighty-five years; for sixty-seven of those years it had been administered as three *départements*. In between those two dates, fifty thousand French citizens had emigrated there and had benefited from wholesale confiscations of tribal land. By the late nineteenth century, with the influx from France continually on the rise, any halfway significant town reasonably close to the Mediterranean looked indistinguishable from a provincial burg in France, with the Algerians themselves relegated to the margins and used as servants and cheap labor. In Paris they found work in industry (mines, gasworks, assorted manufacturing) and gravitated to the northernmost parts of the northern arrondissements and their adjacent suburbs. The first bidonvilles in the *banlieue* date back to the 1930s. The Algerians were especially vulnerable to tuberculosis, the cause of fully half of their deaths. They were harassed in innumerable ways large and small—for example, "Arab" cafés were required to close at 7:00 p.m. In the mid-1950s a Dutch journalist covering Paris-by-night was given an escorted tour by a police commandant, who told him that the city contained

> 200,000 Algerians . . . who are on a war footing with the French . . . Every North African who walks the streets after midnight is suspect. The chief proposed to us that he should arrest one of them, so that the photographer could make a picture of it. Just one or two at random, because they always had something on their records. And if, by any chance, they hadn't done anything, then they were certainly going to do it soon.

The corner of Rue de la Goutte-d'Or and Rue de Chartres, circa 1910

A Sudanese man being exhibited in a "native village" at the 1906 Colonial Exposition in Marseille

Although Algerians were singled out because of their country's status as a French possession, and later because of its very long and brutal war for independence, accounts official and otherwise usually fail to distinguish among North Africans (Algerians, Moroccans, Tunisians), who are in any case ethnically intermingled. Formerly known collectively as Kabyles, today they are more commonly referred to in French as Maghrébites. While they have made their own the neighborhoods of Barbès and Goutte-d'Or, east of Montmartre—looking down at Boulevard de Rochechouart from the *métro aérien* at the appropriate times reveals a vast field of backs bent in prayer—and many have assimilated and have moved into the top professional tiers, an enormous number are stuffed into housing projects in the *banlieue* and relegated to the worst jobs.

For many years, immigrants from sub-Saharan Africa fared a bit better than those from the north—their numbers were smaller, and they were viewed by even the most racist of the French as a novelty rather than a threat. There was more than a bit of wishful thinking in the air as a result. Marc Kojo Tavalou, who was born in Dahomey (now Benin) in 1887, volunteered for the French army in 1914, was naturalized the following year and a bit later admitted to the bar, helped found the Ligue Universelle de Défense de la Race Noire in 1924. That same year, he addressed Marcus Garvey's Universal Negro Improvement Association at a meeting in the United States, urging that "the great black family make Paris its spiritual Palestine," and later wrote that "France is the only country that not only lacks racial prejudice but labors toward its eradication." Meanwhile, at that very same time, visitors to the Paris zoo (Jardin d'Acclimatation) could take in an "African village" in which a troupe of costumed natives engaged in typical activities, such as dances, for their benefit. The theme of the window display at the Galeries Lafayette for Christmas 1930 was a beauty contest in an African village, which provoked the laughter of passersby.

That laughter was perhaps better than violence, and foreigners could get the superficial impression that Paris was more evolved in racial matters than, say, the United States, at a time when the annual toll of lynchings there was in the dozens if not scores. Sherwood Anderson, visiting in 1921, noted black and white students in Left Bank cafés engaging in intellectual discussions, while American racists looked on aghast: "There is deep anger," he wrote, then quoted something he overheard: "'I saw a nigger with a white girl and the white girl's mother, walking openly in the street. My fingers itched to have hold of a gun and shoot—all of them.'" But American racism could actually be enacted in the streets of post–World War I Paris, as described by Louis Aragon in his novel *Aurélien* (1944): "There was a commotion, shouts . . . On the terrace a drunken sailor was hoisting a marble-topped table. Women were screaming. We saw a tall, lean negro in a gray flannel suit, protecting himself from the table with his arms as he was struck . . . He had been hit in the face, and blood was flowing as the table continued to rise up and come down."

There was Parisian resistance to this, at least from one sector of the population: "'They're disgusting! This is France, not Chicago!' So shouted the pimps and prostitutes who always took the side of the blacks. Pressing his fat, bejeweled hand on a woman's shoulder, a tall guy went on: 'They piss me off, those Sammies! Are the Senegalese niggers or not? Who cares? They fought for us, the Senegalese!'"

The American racism was not confined to war veterans: "One of the gentlemen says that last night he was in a champagne bar where some Americans—not sailors but very stylish people—had them throw out a black customer." Aragon further notes that even the most violent incidents seldom made the newspapers, for fear of antagonizing the U.S. embassy. Aragon was, of course, a hard-shell Stalinist, and his book appeared on the stands not long after the Liberation, while the Americans were being lionized in Paris, so you would think a grain of salt might be in order. Given the state of race relations in the United States at that time, though—race riots in 1919 in Chicago, Omaha, Knoxville, and Longview, Texas; the Ocoee, Florida, massacre of 1920; and the devastating Tulsa riots of 1921—his account does not sound unlikely. It was perhaps this context that helped inform the famous if conditional Parisian hospitality toward African Americans, beginning in the 1920s.

Somehow, despite everything, Paris by the twentieth century had developed a worldwide reputation as a cosmopolitan magnet

Josephine Baker, probably in the early 1930s

Assorted Parisians gathered in Ménilmontant, circa 1910

and a refuge. A census in 1889 enumerated citizens of forty-nine different countries living in the city. There were large numbers of Belgians, Italians, Swiss, and Russians, but also, for example, 524 Brazilians, 861 Turks, 63 Haitians, even a lonely pair of Abyssinians. Forty years later greater Paris held 33,000 people from the French possessions in Africa alone, and Île-de-France was 9.2 percent foreign-born.* The crowd on the street was by then mixed as a matter of course, as Carco noticed in his 1925 novel *Perversité*:

> He turned the corner onto Rue du Commerce. In a bar all lit up and filled with mirrors, people were listening to a phonograph: regular folks, soldiers and housemaids, Japanese and Moroccan workmen in European dress . . . There were crowds everywhere, and whenever the streetcars that scraped the sidewalks passed by with the sudden rumble of their wheels and the ringing of their bell, every sort of men and women, some with babes in arms, jumped back quickly . . . The men around him mostly shepherded women and young bareheaded girls, they themselves showing ravaged faces under their caps. There were many foreigners in the throng: swarthy Arabs, Chinese, Italians with little black mustaches, filthy Spaniards, Russians with red lashless eyelids, Germans, fat Belgians . . .

All those people had become or were in the process of becoming Parisians. They were perhaps engaged in sharpening their repartee, straining against their existential confines, falling prey to romance.

---

* In the past decade that last figure has increased to 16.9 percent. (New York City, by contrast, is 36 percent foreign-born, about the same percentage as in 1900.)

6

Archipelago

The lives of the poor were defined and delimited by the institutions that marked, like an enormous clock, every stage in their lives. Those were the landmarks of the people. In the early nineteenth century, when country cousins came to visit, they would be shown Les Halles, Place de Grève (the symbolic locus of government, primarily because of its function as the site of public executions), hospitals, cemeteries, and the Morgue. Balzac, who did not manage to devote a novel to the lives of the poor in his immense *Human Comedy*, did intend one, although he left only a five-page fragment; it was to be called *The Hospital and the People*. People's lives turned around the hospital, not only because the poor were more vulnerable to disease and injury (poor diets, thin clothes, inadequate shelter, hazardous occupations, street crime), but because those who were better off were *attended*: by courtiers, servants, employees, functionaries. Their doctor was most likely a social acquaintance; he lived nearby and would come over at once when summoned by a servant. The poor, on the other hand, had no choice but to attend themselves.

A century ago the novelist Lucien Descaves took an inventory of the eastern end of the Fourteenth Arrondissement, where he found

The Mont-de-Piété, the state-run pawnshop, on Rue Servan, circa 1900

> a long series of walls behind which misery and suffering are relegated, as in contiguous lazarettos. The whole

neighborhood, in fact, is covered with them. Every misfortune has its block, where it is immured and, as it were, sampled. It is an archipelago of miseries. It seizes people when they are born and does not let go until they die, replete with the illusion that they have lived. Their destinies are inscribed within a triangle which ineluctably draws them back. At its top is the charity refuge for children; at its base is Cochin Hospital, the Santé prison, Sainte-Anne asylum; on one of its sides is the Ricord gate [of Cochin] and the lying-in hospital; on the other, the former place of execution . . . There's not far to go and no chance of straying; all those buildings intercommunicate.

For as many as a thousand years the principal hospital in Paris was the Hôtel-Dieu, which tradition supposes was founded in 651, although hard evidence for its existence begins only in 829. Long before the construction of Notre-Dame it was the signal institution on Île de la Cité, where it remains (although it was moved to the north side of the island under Haussmann). Periodically over the centuries smaller hospitals founded by some religious order or other would crop up, prove inadequate, and close within a few decades. Conditions everywhere were appalling; overcrowding was inevitable; medicine was primitive; hospitals often seemed to exist less to alleviate the sufferings of the afflicted than to minimize contagion—they were warehouses of misery. And they could not, of course, cope at all with the epidemics that would wash like waves over the population at unpredictable intervals, especially in the premodern world.

The Plague, which first attacked in 1348, kept striking until the middle of the seventeenth century. Leprosy had more or less disappeared by the end of the Middle Ages, but then syphilis arrived from the New World and sowed destruction in the fifteenth and sixteenth centuries. Smallpox and influenza recurred until well into the twentieth. Measles and whooping cough, now thought of as easily preventable childhood diseases, took a significant toll in the nineteenth century, as did diphtheria and typhoid fever until sanitary conditions improved. Tuberculosis has not yet stopped in our own age, and now there is AIDS.

The nineteenth century was marked above all by the five out-

The Morgue. Engraving by Charles Meryon, 1854

breaks of cholera, in 1832, 1849, 1865, 1873, and 1884; a sixth in 1892 was contained before it could cause much damage, after which the reign of the disease was finally over. The first one, which claimed 18,402 lives over the course of two months, was especially terrifying. The first reported victim was a porter on Rue des Lombards, and the outbreak spread quickly through the parishes of Saint-Merri and Sainte-Avoye, followed by the Cité and beyond. It was widely noted that the victims were all from the lower classes, although the conclusions we might draw from this (concerning sanitation, for example) were not available to the inhabitants of that time. The press reported that the disease was not believed to be contagious. It was also thought that death was instantaneous. In his *Mémoires d'outre-tombe*, Chateaubriand describes a worker raising his glass to cholera, then dropping stone dead when he set it down. The most common explanations hovered around imputations of witchcraft. The panic was certainly immediate. "Not only did the murder rate double, but the mob gave itself over to massacres: unfortunate passersby, deemed solely on the basis of their ugliness to be guilty of spreading the disease by poisoning fountains and food stocks, were murdered on street corners or squares or tossed into the Seine." The epidemic inevitably exacerbated class tensions. A worker was quoted as alleging that mass rubouts of potential insurgents were occurring in the prisons, on the pretext that these people were responsible for the epidemic. It was of course no coincidence that the streets where the disease first broke out in March were the very same ones where revolt (the brief uprising employed by Hugo as backdrop for the climax of *Les misérables*) broke out in June.

Cholera is caused by a bacterium and usually transmitted by water from a contaminated source. Everyone who drinks from that source is susceptible, although people who are already malnourished will be more susceptible still. Those facts were not known then; the cholera bacterium was not isolated until 1854, and its effects weren't widely recognized until the 1880s. There seemed to be a sense that infected water was involved—those poisoned fountains—but nobody would have had any idea that the principal cause of death is dehydration. The chief symptom is profuse if painless watery diarrhea, which might have passed unnoticed amid the general unsanitary conditions of the day. Other

"Here comes cholera!" Illustration by Adolphe Willette, from *Le Chat Noir*, 1887

A *tapis-franc*. Illustration by José Belon for *Paris anecdote*, by Privat d'Anglemont, 1885 edition

symptoms (muscle cramps, vomiting, chapped skin) might not have seemed especially unusual or alarming, either. People just died, in large numbers, at least 60 percent of those infected. Members of the other classes simply looked on helplessly, if they cared at all.

Maybe they aestheticized the disaster. The English literary scholar Enid Starkie, biographer of Baudelaire and Rimbaud, sketches an arresting scene:

> . . . suddenly, in the middle of the Carnival, just as if it had flown into the city hidden under the wings of spring, the plague swept across the Channel and lit on care-free Paris. A harlequin felt an icy hand suddenly clutch at his legs, creep up his body, paralysing his limbs. He tore off his mask in agony and the onlookers saw that his face had already turned purple. Next the whole company of pierrots were struck down by the cholera as they danced. They were carried from the ballroom to the *Hôtel-Dieu*, thence immediately to the morgue, and they were buried in their fancy dress, with the powder and paint not washed from their faces.

Never mind that those don't sound like the symptoms of cholera. Starkie seems to have based her account on the *Journal intime* of Antoine Fontaney, a minor poet who himself died of tuberculosis at thirty-four a few years later (and whose journal wasn't published until 1925). Her point is that the cholera outbreak nourished a cult of morbidity already festering among the young Romantics. Fontaney describes visits to cemeteries to take in the mass burials, a visit with Prosper Mérimée to the Hôtel-Dieu to gaze upon the cadavers, a soirée at Victor Hugo's at which Franz Liszt played Beethoven's Funeral March, a fantasy in which the resurrected dead strode through Paris in their shrouds to the sound of the music. "And Darkness and Decay and the Red Death held illimitable dominion over all" (although Poe wrote those words only ten years later). Those Romantics were gripped by mingled dread and awe, and distanced those emotions by converting them into an exquisitely putrescent aesthetic frisson—the sublime, the heights as measured from the abyss. Was the spectacle an incarnate metaphor that stood in for the scourges of their own class, but safely distant? Would they have been able to dramatize thus if they or their intimates had been at risk? Or maybe we insufficiently credit their lack of irony.

Those Romantics were bohemians, which is to say that they were trying to evade the strictures of class, whichever one they came from. Some of them lived in hovels, and some of them lived in the ruins of the ancien régime—camped out in abandoned *hôtels particuliers* with one or two exquisite pieces of furniture and hardly any other possessions, for example. The poor did not have those sorts of options. They lived in miserable furnished rooms for which they were charged as much as decent ones cost in other parts of town. Or else they lived in flophouses—ICI ON LOGE À LA NUIT—where thirty sous would get you a meagerly furnished private room with sheets on the bed, 10 sous a cot in a dormitory, and two sous a spot on the floor, the only further amenity being the ropes strung in a grid to separate the flops from one another. Later on in the century, when space was at a higher premium, the ropes became supports for the sleepers' arms and heads—they slept sitting—and the tension was loosened at first light, waking the clientele by sending them sprawling. If the tenants missed a payment, their goods were seized and sold by the proprietor. Aside from the filth, the noise, the fights, the bugs, what also made it hard to get a decent night's sleep was the near-constant presence of the police, who were always shining lanterns into faces in search of some fugitive or other.

People also lived in their workplaces. Ragpickers, for example, were packed by the dozen into the same rooms, airless and lightless, that were employed for washing rags. Unsurprisingly their death rate from cholera was three times the city average. But they also lived in somewhat more reasonable circumstances if they were lucky, such as Cité Doré, which was effectively a self-governing community, where sheds were laid out in avenues and streets and squares like a miniature of the city, where health was a priority and drunks and violence were dealt with peremptorily. There a week's rent was usually equivalent to a day's wage, and a missed payment was met not with eviction but with the removal of the shed door, in winter as in summer, until the matter was

"Lodging for the night," 1840s

Scenes from the homeless shelter Asile Fradin, 1893

Hôtel du Compas-d'Or, Rue Montorgeuil. Photograph by H. Stresser, circa 1900

A *cour des miracles* on Rue du Caire. Engraving by Célestin Nanteuil, 1840s

rectified. According to Privat d'Anglemont, Cité Doré was "far away, at the end of an inconceivable faubourg, farther than Japan, more unknown than the interior of Africa, in a neighborhood no one has ever passed through"—actually it lay between the Jardin des Plantes and the Gare d'Orléans (now the Gare d'Austerlitz)—and he describes it as "incredible, incomparable, strange, awful, charming, distressing, admirable."

In the mid-nineteenth century there were other *cités*, tucked into little-trafficked parts of the outer arrondissements, in which ragpickers, everywhere the lowest of the low, banded together and kept one another from sliding into the misery, disease, alcoholism, and violence that marked most lives in slums such as the Montagne Sainte-Geneviève, to which most of them were consigned. A few *cités* were cooperative enterprises, others were more authoritarian. Cité Foucault, one of the latter, was also known as Cité de la Femme en Culotte: of the "woman in trousers." Sophie Foucault, cousin of one of Napoléon's field marshals and daughter of a businessman who lost everything, was well educated but suddenly confronted with the need to make a living. She elected to become a compositor in a print shop, a difficult job both physically and intellectually, since it involved correcting manuscripts on the fly while setting them in print. Observing that women were paid half as much as men, she decided to pass as a man despite the fact that she was small and delicate. By the time her gender was exposed she had saved enough money to buy a tract of land off Boulevard de Clichy, where she erected her *cité*. She ran the place with a firm hand and was beloved of all, it was said, continuing in male drag for the rest of her life—its end date is unrecorded, as is the ultimate fate of the *cité*, which seems to have been situated in or near the Petite-Pologne slum, razed by Haussmann.

The autonomous *cité* had its antecedent in the *cour des miracles*, a peculiar institution dating back at least to the Middle Ages and perhaps earlier. Hugo describes it in *Notre-Dame de Paris* as

a sewer from which flowed out every morning and to which flowed back every night that stream of vice, beggary, and vagrancy that always floods the streets of the capital; a monstrous beehive to which all the hornets of the social order returned in the evening with their plunder . . . an immense changing room for all the players in that eternal comedy which theft, prostitution, and murder enact on the streets of Paris.

A *cour des miracles* was a cluster of houses that by some mix of tradition, common accord, and benign neglect was deemed off-limits to the law and, as lore has it, where a sort of permanent feast of misrule persisted. The name derives from the fact that miracles were a daily occurrence there—the blind could see, the hunchbacked stood straight, the clubfooted ran and danced, leprous skin became clear and unblemished—once their disguises had been put away for the night. The inhabitants were generally known as *gueux* or *argotiers*, the latter with reference to the fact that they spoke a secret language known only to them, at least as of the fifteenth century, when François Villon made use of it in his poems; its earliest vocabulary derives from the language of the Roma. The intricate social structure is illustrated by the abundance of names the *gueux* had for their highly specific professions: *rifodés* posed as families (they were usually unrelated) and begged in the streets, holding out a certificate that claimed their house had been destroyed by "fire from the sky"; *hubains* presented a document stating that Saint Hubert had cured them of rabies contracted by a dog bite; *coquillards* displayed seashells as proof that they had lately returned from a pilgrimage to Santiago de Compostela in Spain; *sabouleux* were fake epileptics; *piètres* were fake amputees; *francs-mitoux* were fake lepers; *capons* were gambling shills; and so on. They were ruled by an elected chief called the King of Thunes, or Grand-Coësre, who carried a cat-o'-nine-tails and whose banner was a dead dog impaled on a pitchfork. Their relationship with the church was hand in glove: fake lepers would claim to have been cured by a certain statue or relic; donations from the devout would pour into the abbey; the monks would share the proceeds with the *gueux*.

Nineteenth-century chroniclers couldn't agree on how the *cours des miracles* had been established in the first place: was it by right of asylum, or through an understanding with the corporation of the *argotiers* the way the city maintained compacts with

Gueux having relieved themselves of the constraints that made them appear crippled, blind, or with amputations. Illustration from the seventeenth century

The former office of Jacques Hébert's revolutionary newspaper *Le Père Duchesne*, once part of the *cour des miracles*. Photograph circa 1900

The dog barber: "The poor dear animal—such patience!" Illustration by Honoré Daumier, from *Le Charivari*, 1842

other guilds, or was it simply a matter of a long-standing blind eye? In any case, there were as many as a dozen of them between the thirteenth and eighteenth centuries, all then located on the far fringes of the city and not easily accessible. The only one that lasted up to the revolution was in the Sentier, off what is now Rue du Caire—very much in the center by then, although it had once abutted the wall built by Charles V and remained protected by a labyrinthine approach through alleys and culs-de-sac and down a long, rough, crooked incline. The seventeenth-century historian Henri Sauval described

> a mud house, half-buried and falling over from age and rot, not four square fathoms [i.e., 576 square feet] in size, which nevertheless sheltered more than fifty households loaded down with an infinite number of children legitimate, illegitimate, or stolen. I'm told that this house and the others contain overall some five hundred large families piled atop one another. As large as the courtyard is now, it was once much larger, and was surrounded on all sides by low, sunken, dark, shapeless dwellings made of dirt and mud and filled with the evil poor.

During the revolution it was taken over by ironmongers' workshops and the office of *Le Père Duchesne*, Jacques Hébert's scabrous newspaper. The era of the *cour des miracles* was officially over, although there were survivals of a sort. Privat d'Anglemont describes the cloister of Saint-Jean-de-Latran, across from the Collège de France. The church itself, destroyed during the revolution, had long offered asylum to the bankrupt and debt-ridden, to forgers and libelers and perjurers and refractory apprentices. As late as the 1840s the right of asylum was apparently still in effect in the ruins, with its four wings laid out in the sign of the cross (the Father, the Son, the Holy Ghost, and the Amen), its gardens, and its "innumerable quantity of houses—no, we're wrong, it is a single house with many staircases, behind which lurk the sort of ignoble, sordid, stinking cesspools that are decorated with the term 'courtyard.'" It gave shelter to a population that owed fealty "much more to the Kingdom of Bohemia and the Egyptian Empire than to the Republic." That is to say, its inhabitants included buskers, street singers, sword swallowers, egg balancers, acrobats, tooth pullers, and fire eaters.

More than likely its other tenants included practitioners of the short con, but the ones Privat lists are all trying for an honest living, however improvised. There were rag washers, doll dressers, makers of matches, of toy boxes, of toy parachutes, people who cut up rabbit fur to make felt, women who put wicks in lanterns, who unglued the silk of men's hats, who made funeral wreaths from hoof scrapings, people who abridged famous plays for use in puppet theaters. The jobs that people invented for themselves were one of Privat's preoccupations, and he collected hundreds of examples from all over the city. Madame Thibaudeau swept jewelers' shops for no pay so that she could recuperate gold dust. Madame Vanard, widow of a perfumer, was a *zesteuse*: she picked up lemon rinds from the stalls of *limonadiers* and sold the zest to makers of Curaçao, syrups, and essences. Old Monsieur Beaufils bought nightingales, canaries, and finches and, after educating them in song for six to eight weeks, resold them for four times what he paid. The Meurt-de-Soif family—the name, apparently real, means "dying of thirst"—bought old suits, turned them inside out, restitched them, and resold them.

Jacques Simon was awarded two goats by the government as a premium when his wife gave birth to triplets after previously

"Shut up when I'm singing, you stupid blackbird!" Illustration by J. J. Grandville, from *Les métamorphoses du jour*, 1829

The last woman employed as a public letter-writer, on the steps of the *mairie* of the Eighteenth Arrondissement, Montmartre, circa 1910

producing twins. The mother and babies then died, but the goats multiplied, and Simon became a *berger en chambre* (an indoor shepherd), with a flock of fifty-two in a sixth-floor walk-up on Rue de l'Écosse. He sold milk from goats that were fed individual herb-based diets aimed at specific maladies the milk was intended to cure. Mademoiselle Rose, who inherited the job from her mother, was an ant farmer; she sold the eggs to pharmacists and to the Jardin des Plantes for pheasant chow. Monsieur Salier sold maggots. Mathieu Leblanc sold bespoke verses for all occasions. Monsieur Jaeglé wrote little pocket guides to the law for the use of various professions (porters, laborers, concierges, etc.). Monsieur Auguste collected stray legal papers and altered them to suit for people seeking admission to the courts of justice, which required something stamped and initialed. Mère Moskow rented out clothes; a shirt cost twenty centimes a week.

There were men with noble titles rendered meaningless by the revolution but that nevertheless held snob appeal; some of these men made a living acknowledging others' bastard children—but Privat mentions one who unexpectedly inherited a fortune and promptly lost it all to his elected heirs. A *détripé* was a professional witness, who would collect information at the scene of a crime and become the event's leading expert, so that the court would have no choice but to hire him. A *réveilleuse*—always a woman, apparently—was in charge of waking others whose jobs demanded an early rise, especially at Les Halles. An *ange gardien* was engaged by upscale wineshops and cabarets to walk drunks home. A *riboui* remade shoes, extending their lives by only about a week (the product was dubbed *dix-huit*, "eighteen," a pun on *deux fois neuf*, which can mean "twice new" or "twice nine").

Les Halles employed many hundreds, from the famous *forts* (strongmen, who wore distinctive sombreros and hoisted enormous baskets of produce) to people with very specific occupations: egg candlers, builders of vegetable pyramids, fatteners of pigeons, fish stall display artists, breakers of mutton heads to extract the brains and the tongue (whose workplace was called a *massacre*), people who flattened ducks' breastbones with a rod to make them look plumper. There were many whose jobs involved some sort of counterfeiting: people who collected ham bones and jammed them into sundry cuts of meat, people who sprayed mouthfuls of fish oil on the surface of a bouillon to make it look

"We passed the shop of a blacksmith who had become a cobbler." Illustration by J. J. Grandville, from *Scènes de la vie publique et privée des animaux*, 1842

fattier, people who painted turkey feet with varnish to disguise the progressive lightening in color that marks the days elapsed since death, and the confectioners of cocks' combs (which were used in ragouts or as trimming) from beef, mutton, or veal palates. One of these told Privat that all combs are irregular: "Look at mine, by contrast. If the roosters could see them they'd all die of envy. See how mine are notched, carved, proportioned—they are perfect!"

When it came to food, not much went to waste. Bones were cycled four times over: from butchers to restaurants to vendors of cheap soup to *gargotiers*, who peddled hot water colored brown with carrots, burned onions, and caramel, and improved with a misting of fish oil. A *boulanger en vieux* (which might be translated as "secondhand baker") collected stale bread, which could be sold as crumbs or for feeding animals; one of them allegedly figured out a way to restore the crumbs to flour, from which he made gingerbread for sale in the streets. Restaurant dishwashers could make a decent living selling not only bones and vegetable peels for various uses but also the remains on diners' plates. These were collected by entrepreneurs called *bijoutiers* (jewelers), who used them to concoct a slumgullion, called *arlequin* (motley) or *hasard de la fourchette* (luck of the fork), that remained standard fare in the cheapest hash houses until around the middle of the twentieth century. There were more purely sinister ways of extending the food supply, of course, such as the adulteration of bread, which might involve alum, boron, copper sulfate (a.k.a. blue vitriol), carbonate of magnesium, carbonate of ammonia, carbonate of potassium, chalk, plaster, clay, or alabaster. In the 1870s it was estimated that forty thousand Parisians did not eat every day, "but even when they do not dine they all take their coffee, which gives them strength."

Recycling was fundamental to the economy, and there had always been people who carved out their own particular niches, such as the billboard stripper observed by Restif de La Bretonne before the revolution, who waited until the date of a performance had passed to collect all the playbills posted to the walls, selling individual bills by weight to the grocer and those that were stuck together to the cardboard maker, and used as fuel the ones too filthy for resale. Place Maubert, from the late nineteenth century until the 1960s the domain of the clochard, was the center of the

Porters, known as *forts* (strongmen), at Les Halles, circa 1900

"He's hungry, he claims—the sloth. I'm hungry, too, but I take the trouble to go dine." Illustration by Gavarni from *Baliverneries parisiennes*, 1846–47

A soup vendor in Les Halles, circa 1910

A news hawker. Illustration by J. J. Grandville, from *Les Français peints par eux-mêmes*, 1840–42

trade in secondhand tobacco, of which there were two grades: coarse, gleaned from cigar ends and pipe scrapings, and fine, twice as expensive, collected from cigarette butts. While the very poor might sometimes hunt and eat cats, the moderately poor were known to keep cats as pets. As soon as one died, though, its keepers skinned it, salted down its hide, and sold it to a maker of cat's-fur mittens, which as late as the 1930s were sold in pharmacies and bought by Parisians whose rooms had no heat, and who rubbed themselves with the mittens in winter to stay warm.

Parisians long maintained a folkloric appreciation of their street trades, which were celebrated in such popular art media as broadsides, chinaware, and eventually postcards. The sidewalks and center strip of the Boulevard du Crime featured, in addition to its wrestlers, acrobats, and magicians, a profusion of vendors: of water, eggs, greens, oysters, handkerchiefs, underwear, English pears, herbal teas, matches, rags, roasted chestnuts, sausages, fried potatoes, apples, fowl both living and cooked, and coconut water in the summer and, in the winter, oranges and *mottes*, which were bricks of compressed coal dust that burned without flames—just smoke, which made them the fuel of the poor. Along the banks of the Seine there were dog barbers, sailors' barbers, mattress carders, fish bait vendors, washerwomen, stevedores, and sand carriers and dray loaders and barrel rollers for hire. On Maubert there were sock darners, birdseed vendors, public writers, confectors of sugar pipes and little windmills with feathers as blades, gluers of paper bags and cones for grocers, and people who made the rounds trying to sell dubious objects they'd stolen or recovered from the trash. In courtyards and *portes-cochères* people sold newspapers, *frites*, and coffee. Everywhere there were buskers, acrobats, contortionists, street dentists, street jewelers, weight lifters, hurdy-gurdy players, snake handlers, flower girls, old-clothes dealers, bill posters, lamplighters, glaziers, china menders, shoe repairers, knife grinders, silver polishers, window washers, carters and porters for hire, chimney sweeps, and vendors of ink, fish, potatoes, herbs, baskets, umbrellas, shoelaces, pencils, whips, rabbit pelts, licorice water, and lemon juice.

Aside from those with marketable skills, many of these people were generally classed as *camelots*. The term means "hawker" or "peddler," but in the eyes of a late nineteenth-century police commissioner, a *camelot* was "by turns a pickpocket, a pimp, a three-card monte operator, an obscure informer for the Sûreté . . . His getup is grotesquely affected: a wide-brimmed soft hat or a barely perceptible hat or else a silk cap with an enormously high crown; brightly colored neckerchief; tight light-colored trousers; velvet or floral-patterned waistcoat with prominent watch chain." Certainly that avenue of enterprise attracted people who couldn't afford leisure, lacked the connections to obtain sinecures or the inclination to join the artistic bohemia, but who demanded a certain budget of freedom in the use of their time. They corresponded to the original use of the term *bohemian* before it acquired artistic associations in the early nineteenth century, which referred to people who stood outside the social system and treated as porous the line between the law and the lawless. Chevalier quotes a 1913 *Guide des plaisirs* that takes the trouble to analyze the sorts of men who enjoy the favors of prostitutes without having to pay:

A boulevard peddler, circa 1910

> Generally that sort is not capable of regular attendance at a job in an office or a workshop, and anyway he does not like bosses, so he tends to become a *camelot* or an itinerant of some sort . . . because he always chooses a task that will give him freedom and the open air—things of which he's often been deprived and which he fears losing even for a day. Some only go to the racetrack, whether as mere players or as bookmakers; others are dancers, acrobats, equerries, coachmen, automobile drivers, waiters, wrestlers, boxers, etc.

So perhaps they were jailbirds, and maybe they were independent-minded, and certainly they were unconcerned with social proprieties. They had no particular desire to establish themselves as family men or ornaments of their community. But it's also more than likely that they were just following a path laid out for them by society since childhood. In them you can detect the features of Gavroche, all grown up:

"If I could read, I'd never want to read old junk like that." Illustration by Gavarni, from *D'après nature*, 1857–58

> He doesn't eat every day, but he goes to the show every night, if he feels like it. He doesn't have a shirt on his

back, or shoes on his feet, or a roof over his head; he's like the flies of the air, who don't have any of those things, either. He is seven to thirteen years old, lives in packs, pounds the pavements, sleeps in the open, wears old pants of his father's that fall past his heels, an old hat from some other father that comes down over his ears, a single suspender with yellow edges; he runs, snoops, sneaks, wastes time, breaks in pipes, swears like a sailor, haunts the dives, knows thieves, banters with the whores, talks slang, sings dirty songs, and hasn't a mean bone in his body . . . He has his own jobs: hailing cabs, lowering the steps of carriages, collecting tolls for helping people across the street in heavy weather . . .

Other children, especially the ones who had families, were conscripted into the hard-labor ranks from an early age, in factories and ateliers and on the docks. Georges Cain relishes the poetry of a notice tacked up in a courtyard: "Little hands wanted for flowers and feathers." He avoids considering the possible consequences for those hands, such as a lifetime of degenerative arthritis. The makers of silk flowers at the beginning of the twentieth century (all of them women) were paid by the gross. The artisan who fashioned 144 chrysanthemums, highly detailed, each petal individually notched, received two francs and twenty-five centimes for fifteen hours' labor. A very experienced worker could turn out twelve dozen forget-me-nots in two days and net two francs seventy centimes.

At least until the middle of the nineteenth century, a great deal of labor was not apportioned by gender. In farms and factories alike, everybody did everything, and it was liberal reformers who were indignant at the sight of women hauling and heaving. In Paris this equality of labor (which might or might not have extended to equality of pay, depending on the trade) was to some degree maintained at Les Halles, where women engaged in all but the heaviest physical work pretty much until the end of that market. There were occupations that had always been dominated by women—burnishing, for example, or the flower market trades, or a great deal of couture. But the laundresses were a case apart. They had loomed large in the Parisian imaginary at

A vendor of funeral wreaths, Marché du Temple, circa 1910

least as far back as the early eighteenth century, and they remained so well into the twentieth. "In the eyes of Parisians they were one of the most important orders: the most solid, the most active, the loudest and in many respects among the most formidable. They were powerful in many ways: in their numbers, in their organization, and in the ways they had of standing up for themselves." Washerwomen were certainly numerous (ninety-four thousand of them, according to an 1880 count*) and they were certainly visible. Anyone walking along the Seine or the Canal Saint-Martin could see the *bateaux-lavoirs* docked on its banks, where long rows of women on their knees scrubbed with ashes or soap and rinsed the laundry by immersion. And they were everywhere on the streets, delivering their loads, so that they took on a certain romantic aura and became ubiquitous in nineteenth-century art, in works by Daumier, Degas, Toulouse-Lautrec, Bonnard, and many genre painters. Zola's *L'assommoir* (1876–77) portrays Gervaise, who begins as a laundress and then briefly achieves bourgeois respectability, with a boutique of her own, until her profits are literally drunk up by men; at the end she is once again a laundress, but now unable to iron because of the tremors in her hands.

Steam rose from the corners and spread a bluish veil across the room. Heavy droplets hung in the air, exuding a soapy, clammy, insipid odor; sometimes stronger whiffs of bleach predominated. At washboards on both sides of the center aisle were rows of women, their arms bare to the shoulders, their necks bare, their skirts drawn up, showing colored socks and big lace-up shoes. They beat the washing furiously, laughed, tilted backward to yell a word through the din, leaned over their tubs, rough, ungainly, brutal, as soaked as if they'd been in a downpour, their skin reddened and steaming. Around and under them ran a great stream: buckets of water transported and dumped, cold-water faucets left wide open to piss from on high, splashes from the wash stations, drips from rinsed clothing, the puddles they trudged through, leaking out in

* There were also ten thousand men in the trade.

Washerwomen on the banks of the Canal Saint-Martin, circa 1910

Aujourd'hui faut à ces d'moiselle
Des machins avec des dentelles
Et des vrais bijoux en vrai or,
A la Goutt'-d'Or.

"Today women want / Stuff with lace on it / And real jewels in real gold, / In the Goutte-d'Or." Illustration by Théophile Steinlen, for Aristide Bruant's *Dans la rue*, vol. 2, 1889

little streamlets on the slanted flagstones. And amid all the shouts, the rhythmic thumps, the murmuring sound of rain and that thunderstorm rumble stifled by the wet ceiling, the steam engine, over to the right, all white with fine dew, panted and snored unrelentingly, the dancing agitation of its flywheel seeming to guide the whole enormous racket.

The laundry, an "enormous shed," was probably the size of one of the larger ateliers in the city, where manufacture remained small-scale until late in the nineteenth century. Many of the workshops had their origins in the aftermath of the revolution, when they opened in "huts encrusted on the sides of former mansions" and in courtyards bought at auction by artisans who had been sansculottes. An 1866 census noted that while one out of ten employed Parisians was in "commerce," three out of five were in "industry." They were printers, tailors, hosiers, glaziers, tinsmiths, gunsmiths, brewers, bakers, butchers, carpenters, joiners, metalworkers, tanners, glovers, saddlers, bookbinders, shoemakers—much the same list as a century or two earlier. Most ateliers were headed by an *ouvrier-patron* (the boss worked alongside his employees), and neighborhoods brought trades together in chains of supply and demand, what today would be called synergy.

Until the late nineteenth century the single most industrialized part of the city lay along the course of the Bièvre—the name comes from the Old French word for "beaver"—a river that ran northeast from its source in a pond near Versailles, entered the city just west of the Porte d'Italie, and flowed into the Seine near the present Rue des Grands-Degrés, opposite Notre-Dame (later shifted over to near the Pont d'Austerlitz). Twelfth-century monks were the first to divert its course, and dug a canal to power a grain mill. It was fully canalized by 1844; it began to be covered over around 1874, the task completed mostly after the Great Flood of 1910, the narrow Bièvre being disproportionately prone to flooding. Visitors to the area today often have no idea that a river runs under their feet. It was for a long time a sewer, collecting the outflow of abattoirs and hospitals as well as households, and its water was used by the tapestry manufacturers of the Gobelins along with tanners, dyers, and curriers of

The Bièvre, between Rue Mouffetard and Rue Pascal, around 1860 leather. Those uses destroyed the Bièvre, turning it into a festering source of epidemics, creating immense mires of brackish mud on its edges, and polluting it irredeemably. "Colored in every hue, yellow, green, red, ferrying noisome offal right alongside us, slimy, virtually immobile, nauseating, with a texture like clotted blood, with no reflections on its surface on a cloudy day, with heavy clumps of greenish foam slowly sliding by," observed Georges Cain in 1908. For more than a century it was a place of horror. In a passage set around 1824, Balzac has seven-year-old Hélène d'Aiglemont, jealous of her mother's love, push in her little half-brother, Charles:

An alley by the Bièvre, circa 1900

> No eyes . . . could locate the exact place where the child had been swallowed up. The black water bubbled over an immense expanse. The bed of the Bièvre was covered by ten feet of mud at that spot. The child had to die; it was impossible to save him. At that hour on a Sunday, everyone was at rest. The Bièvre has neither boats nor fishermen. I could find no pole with which to sound the depths, and could see nobody at all in the distance.

Marville's photographs of the 1860s show a turbid canal barely wider than a sidewalk, its banks covered almost to their edges with sheds projecting from high factory walls and heaped with sacks, barrels, sawhorses, and everywhere men wearing long aprons pressing hides. Postcards of the Île des Singes made fifty years later show the same scenes, but much more broken-down and sordid, everything piled with trash and tumbling into ruin.* Joris-Karl Huysmans, writing in the late 1880s, saw

> in the air, thousands of dried rabbit pelts knocking against one another, spotted with blood and furrowed with blue veins . . . and through the windows you can see . . . workers skimming the horrible stew in the vats, or raking hides over a trench . . . The alley is completely white: the roofs, the pavements, and the walls are all rimed. Endless

Tanneries on the Île des Singes, circa 1910

* The island lay between two arms of the river, one covered, the other open. *Singes* are literally "monkeys," but here the term means "bosses."

The gates of a tobacco factory, Rue des Meuniers, circa 1910

End of the workday at Delaunay-Belleville, in Saint-Denis, circa 1910

End of the workday on Rue de la Haie-Coq, in Auber-villiers, circa 1910

snow falls in the middle of summer, a snow made of the ambient scrapings of hides.

What wasn't thus whitened was stained red by tanners' bark, the overpowering acrid stench of which filled the whole area.

By the late nineteenth century, the industrial zones of the city had expanded, especially toward the northeast. La Villette contained not only most of the major slaughterhouses (except for the ones in the south, at Vaugirard and the horse butchery at Porte Brancion), but also soapworks, saltworks, glassworks, breweries, distilleries, chemical plants, and factories producing candles, perfume, matches, enamel, bone black, pianos, and freight cars. La Chapelle, with its gasworks and vast railyards, was not far behind. There were major industries along the Seine at both its eastern and western extremities within the city—Quai de Javel, in the Fifteenth, was named after the bleach industry, for example, and the Citroën plant long dominated the land behind it. Smaller factories were crammed into any available space in all outlying arrondissements except the Sixteenth and the southern reaches of the Seventeenth. And all those industries had their even larger analogues in the northern, eastern, and southern *banlieue*.

That was a story repeated throughout the Western world as the consumer market expanded and transport became cheaper and more reliable. It was a gold rush for industrialists, who were not generally concerned overmuch with the safety or well-being of their employees, and it was further spurred by streamlining processes imported from the United States, such as the time management of Taylorism and the assembly-line techniques of Henry Ford. In America the price in human suffering was chronicled extensively by Lincoln Steffens, Ida Tarbell, and Upton Sinclair, crusading journalists who earned the derisive label "muckrakers." France had its own investigators, Maurice and Léon Bonneff, who were born two years apart in the early 1880s to a poor family of embroiderers in the Franche-Comté. They left school to go to work at the usual age of twelve or thirteen, and then in 1900 made their way to Paris, where a chance encounter with the old Communard historian Gustave Lefrançais and his secretary, the writer Lucien Descaves, encouraged their literary ambitions. Individually they tried their hand at writing plays, but within a few years found their true vocation as investigative journalists, writing for Jean Jaurès's *L'Humanité* and jointly producing several major works: *Jobs That Kill* (1906), *The Tragic Lives of Workers* (1908), *The Working Class* (1910), and *Merchants of Madness* (1913). These failed to have the impact they should have, in part because they were refused by the major publishing houses and wound up being issued by small leftist presses, also because the brothers both died young. On their own they also wrote a novel apiece. Léon's *Aubervilliers*, a diorama portrait of that city in the northern *banlieue*—"stinking from the exhalations of the fertilizer plants, renewed by the breath of the gardens and the fields . . . the city where dead animals are cooked and harvests are abundant . . . the cauldron of hell and the bounty of spring"—shows the influence of Sinclair's *The Jungle*. It was partially serialized only after the war and not published in book form until 1949 (it alone of their works is in print today).

The Bonneffs' purview was at once broad and intensely focused; no detail was too small for them. They noticed, for example, that if the ragpickers' path was stony, the sedentary job of the women who sorted the rags was at least as dangerous:

> They work over rectangular grates around three feet long, perforated with little close-set square openings. The dust emitted by the rags falls through the openings of the grate, but it also spreads through the workroom. The ateliers of the major rag recyclers are generally spacious and the sorting rooms sufficiently large, with windows that allow for aeration. But the danger is no less for the employees, who inevitably inhale the noxious particles emitted by the rags . . . Ailments of the throat and lungs are common among the workers, and tuberculosis has claimed numerous victims among their ranks. In this business there are few elderly employees.

Two decades before George Orwell got a job belowstairs in the Hôtel Lotti and subsequently chronicled his experiences in *Down and Out in Paris and London* (1933), the Bonneffs were alert to the fate of dishwashers in fancy restaurants:

"Get a move on, you lazy animal!" Illustration by J. J. Grandville, from *Les métamorphoses du jour*, 1829

Restaurant kitchens are like the ovens of a bakery: because customers don't visit them, the owners make the rooms narrow, low-ceilinged, airless, and ill-lit. They are generally basements where the gaslights are kept on around the clock. Ventilators, stingily perforated, allow only a feeble current of air. The heat emitted by the ovens—red-hot during business hours—the odors of oil, fat, grilling meat, smoking coals make breathing difficult. From 11:00 to 1:30 and again from 6:00 to 9:00—and often later—the constant temperature is 130°F . . . The dishwasher stands on a plank in front of the brazier that heats the water. The heat is such that his apron catches fire; he has to change it every two hours. And all day long, except for two hours' rest in the afternoon, he stirs up evil-smelling water, hot and dense water the sight of which alone is nauseating.

The Bonneffs chronicled trade after trade, not only in Paris but all over France: bakers, shop assistants, railroad workers, postal employees, construction workers. They cataloged the ailments specific to jobs, such as lead poisoning (painters, weavers, lacemakers, electricians), arsenic poisoning (florists, tanners, taxidermists), mercury poisoning (hatters), and respiratory illnesses of all kinds, from tuberculosis to black lung. They pursued their investigations by getting themselves hired, at job after job, with the help of confederates. By simply recording observed facts, in clear and chastened language with a total absence of rhetoric, they effectively damned hundreds of industries. You think as you read that the sheer accumulation of outrages could not have failed to affect readers and lead to social changes. But the Bonneff brothers weren't as fortunate as their American analogues, in part because of the political climate, in part due to unfortunate timing. Jean Jaurès was assassinated on July 31, 1914; Germany declared war on Russia the following day; Maurice Bonneff died in combat on September 24; Léon succumbed to wounds suffered on the front line on December 24. Today they are mostly forgotten, their only memorials three streets named after them in Bezons, Limoges, and Champigny-sur-Marne, once "red" cities.

7

Le Business

Prostitution, a phenomenon as old as commerce and travel, has been so long associated with Paris in popular culture that you could almost get the impression it was invented there. The traffic in women was of course a harsh and often deadly commerce for those who were its merchandise. It was also for a very long time viewed (and not solely by men) as an essential part of the city's fabric, of its ambiance, a signpost announcing that it was a place apart, exempt from the imperatives of labor, family, and fatherland that ruled the surrounding nation. For Maupassant's Georges Duroy, Bel-Ami in the novel of that name, the culture of prostitution is fundamental to the pleasures of *flânerie*:

> His pocket empty and his blood boiling, he lit up upon contact with the streetwalkers who murmured, on the corners: "Come with me, pretty boy." But he didn't dare follow them, unable to pay, and also he awaited something else, other kisses, less vulgar ones.
>
> He nevertheless loved the places where prostitutes swarmed, their dance halls, their cafés, their streets. He loved to jostle them, to talk to them in familiar terms, to whiff their violent perfumes, to feel close to them. They were women, after all, women devoted to love. And he didn't treat them with that contempt innate in family men.

On the turf, 1930s

At the entrance to a gambling den in the Palais-Royal, 1815

Forty years later, Francis Carco sang the same song: "It wasn't so much the whores that I loved so much as the black streets, the shops, the cold, the thin rain on the roofs, the chance encounters, and, in those rooms, an atmosphere of harrowing abandon that clutched my heart." Paris may have been the capital of the nineteenth century; it remains the capital of contradictions.

Prostitution in Paris dates back at least to the Gallo-Roman era, although we don't hear much about it until the Middle Ages, and then mostly in connection with attempts to suppress it, such as by immuring whores in convents. The sainted Louis IX tried in vain to expel them from the capital in 1254; Parliament attempted with no greater success to close the brothels in 1272; a law of 1360 forbade prostitutes from wearing the same clothes as women not in the profession. Around the same time it was noted that thirty streets, in a city much smaller than today's, were given over in whole or in part to the ambulatory trade. In the following centuries prostitution underwent vicissitudes of toleration and repression—the latter in particular by the Protestants and by the woman-hating Henri III (1574–1589)—until, in the late seventeenth and eighteenth centuries, it emerged as a highly fashionable pursuit, with bordellos ever more richly appointed and exclusive. It was then, for example, that certain houses began publishing illustrated catalogues, so that finicky prospective johns could make their selection without mussing themselves.

It was then, too, that the sport of estimating numbers began in earnest. A police report in 1762 guessed there were between six hundred and seven hundred prostitutes in the capital. Restif de La Bretonne in the 1780s thought there were twenty thousand. In 1802 the minister of police suggested thirty thousand, whereas in 1810 the police prefect estimated eighteen thousand, although half of those were kept women. Around the same time, it was believed there were between six hundred and nine hundred working women in the Palais-Royal alone. In 1812 around nine hundred prostitutes were formally registered with the police; twenty years later the number had jumped to thirty-five hundred—but only women working in brothels were then required to register. "In the 1850s it was estimated that London had about 24,000 prostitutes but Paris, with almost half the population, was said to have 34,000." A couple of decades later

Maxime du Camp claimed there were one hundred twenty thousand working women in the city, although du Camp was an end-of-society hysteric whose statements should generally be handled at arm's length. Meanwhile, from the late 1850s to the late 1870s, between six thousand and fifteen thousand prostitutes passed every year through the Dépôt, the medical dispensary to which working women were dispatched for inspection by the sanitary police. Those numbers are actual, not speculative.

The women who walked the streets, whose status was tolerated rather than strictly speaking legal, were only a percentage of the population. They fell into two broad categories: *respectueuses*, who worked for a pimp, and *insoumises* ("rebels"), who didn't— the latter often tended to be very young, although some were so young they were pimped by their mothers. Many women worked legally in houses, of which there were hundreds at any given time. And then there were the more ambiguous sorts: the actresses and dancers and models, the kept women, the courtesans, the *grandes cocottes*, the demimondaines, the *horizontales*, the *amazones*, the *lionnes*, the "marble girls," the "man-eaters." Around the parish of Notre-Dame de Lorette, just south of Montmartre, were the *lorettes*, an elastic designation for courtesans and kept women whose relative fortunes could be determined by their address: the ones who did well lived as close as possible to Rue de Provence to the south, whereas the less successful were scattered northwest toward the Batignolles. Delacroix in his journals recalled that when he was a hot-blooded new arrival, around 1822, "the first thing that assaulted the eyes of my virtue was a magnificent specimen of a *lorette*, all dressed in satin and black velvet, who in descending from her cabriolet, and with the insouciance of a goddess, allowed me to view her leg up to the navel."

Alexandre Parent-Duchâtelet, first holder of the chair of medical hygiene at the University of Paris, who wrote *De la prostitution dans la ville de Paris* (1836), the first systematic study of the phenomenon, noticed a great many things, such as the class division in the profession as epitomized by the women's noms de guerre. In the high-toned houses, they tended to sport such floral-scented labels as Aspasia, Sidonia, Azelina, Calliope, Lodoiska, Olympia; at the other end of the spectrum, among the women who worked the pavements around Les Halles or

An illustration by Théophile Steinlen for Aristide Bruant's *Dans la rue*, vol. 2, 1889

"Of course the upper half is more beautiful than the lower half, but it's also more expensive." Illustration by Gavarni, from *Les lorettes*, 1841–43

Sheet music for "Sur le trottoir" (On the pavement),
by Fréhel, 1929

the Quartier de Bréda, you might find Belle-cuisse (Nice Thigh), Faux-cul (Fake Ass), La Ruelle (the Alley), Le Boeuf, Crucifix. It should be noted that the two groups were not mutually exclusive. Members of the first could all too easily wind up in the second as they aged or after they suffered illness or injury.

From time immemorial there had been whores around Les Halles, along Rue Saint-Denis and its dependencies, near Place de Grève, and in the Cité, especially on the long-gone Rue Glatigny, known as Val d'Amour. What these places had in common was that they were common ground—markets, squares, arteries where the classes were most likely to mix, this as distinct from purely working-class neighborhoods, such as the Faubourg Saint-Antoine, where street prostitution was rare and whorehouses were relatively few. With the opening of the new neighborhoods beyond the boulevards in the early nineteenth century, the landscape expanded. Notre-Dame-de-Lorette may have been noted for its better class of *entraineuses*, duly ensconced in plush apartments and seen primarily on their way to the theater, but it overlapped considerably with the Quartier de Bréda (centered on Rue de Bréda, since renamed Rue Henry-Monnier), which became the byword for *basse prostitution*, hard-up women living in poverty and working for small change, the two extremes coexisting so thoroughly that only class-ridden habits of mind can explain why the areas were thought of as distinct. Zola observed the phenomenon: "On the sidewalks of Rue Notre-Dame de Lorette, two rows of women brushed the shop fronts, their skirts trussed up, their noses down, all business, hurrying toward the boulevards without glancing at the window displays. It was the famished descent of the Quartier de Bréda in the first glow of the gas lamps."

Soon enough, as the city expanded yet again and another set of boulevards was opened, the Quartier de Bréda was absorbed by the larger and more robust nexus centered on Place Pigalle, which opened onto Boulevard de Clichy just one block north. (Even today, Pigalle presents the most visible face of the Parisian sex trade.) Not long after that, the lowest rung moved to the exterior boulevards, now the *boulevards des maréchaux*, which were convenient to the Zone, the slaughterhouses and gasworks and factories, and were generally beneath the notice of the vice squad. Zola again, decades later, sets the scene:

For almost twenty minutes they had been there, in the murk of the outer boulevard where prowled the lowest prostitution, the obscene vices of the poor neighborhoods. Drunks had jostled them, and the shadows of whores had grazed them as they came and went, chattering, under the curses and blows of their pimps. Sordid couples sought the darkness of the trees, stopped along benches, tucked themselves into recesses of indescribable filth. It was like that in the whole neighborhood, with dives all around and vile flophouses with their miserable assignation rooms, with no glass in the windows and no sheets on the bed.

Whore, pimp, and john. Illustration by Subin de Beauvais, circa 1900

Then, until the First World War, there was the final stage: Fort-Monjol, for streetwalkers who had outlived the actuarial estimates. Some kept working well into old age in this warren of streets where the women sat on chairs in front of their doors; one of them worked out of a gypsy wagon. You can see them in Atget's photographs. They don't look miserable, but nevertheless "every skin disease of humanity seemed to have met up there: mealy psoriasis, purulent acne, flabby boils, inveterate staphylococcus and streptococcus, tumors, scabies—all flourished in the saltpeter of those stinking walls alive with vermin." The deadliest taunt among whores was "You'll end up at Monjol."

The arc of prostitution was a short rise and a long fall. Girls would come from the faubourgs or the *banlieue* or the provinces when they were fourteen or fifteen, or younger, and they might reach their apex there and then—but afterward they would have to keep working anyway, for as long as their bodies could endure it. They would shuttle among the various arenas—from sidewalk to stage, from Saint-Denis to the outer boulevards, from specialty house to Fort-Monjol, from furnished room to South America—and sometimes they managed not to be killed in any of them. Often the arc was sawtoothed, as shown by the career of Zola's Nana. She is first glimpsed in *L'assommoir*, the daughter of Gervaise, a pretty girl restlessly beginning adolescence as her mother is plunging into the depths. She goes out on pretend errands that last longer and longer until one day she doesn't come home. A neighbor soon sees her in a handsome carriage, dressed to the nines.

Rue Asselin and the Hôtel du Fort-Monjol, circa 1910

Zola's *Nana* in its first American paperback edition, 1941

At the start of the novel bearing her name, she is fifteen and onstage, drawing an eager male public but not because of any acting skills. She entertains admirers in her new apartment on Boulevard Haussmann ("which the proprietor rented to single ladies to give the plaster a chance to dry"), admirers who run the gamut from nobles to merchants to impetuous but penniless youths. But she gets bored and needs money, so before long she is once again, with her friend and lover Satin, walking the streets:

A hundred meters from Café Riche, as they arrived on their beat, they let down their skirts, which they had been holding up carefully in one hand, and from then on, mindless of the dust, sweeping the sidewalk and rolling their hips, they walked slowly, slowing down even more when they crossed the field of light of a big café . . . In the darkness their whitened faces, spotted with lipstick and eyeshadow, took on the disquieting charm of some bogus Oriental bazaar set down in the street. Until eleven o'clock they remained in high spirits even as they were jostled by the crowd, only occasionally tossing a "stupid shit" at the backs of oafs who had stepped on their train . . . But as the night wore on, if they hadn't made one or two trips to Rue de la Rochefoucauld, they became evil bitches, their hunt turning desperate.

After managing to evade a police raid that sweeps up Satin, Nana finds her way back to the stage, where she bombs. Somehow, though, she soon manages to become a fashion plate, a cynosure at the races, the lover of great men—but then a scandal sends her off to parts unknown, perhaps Russia, from which she returns mortally ill. Zola, in his twin roles as novelist and reporter, makes Nana a rounded and singular character who is at the same time representative of a phenomenon. He had some dubious genetic theories, hardly uncommon at the time, about how such a figure represented the wrath of the people against the aristocracy, and he baldly issues his thesis from the mouth of another character: "as tall and beautiful as a plant growing in a manure pile, she avenged the wretches and the forsaken whose product she was . . . She unwittingly became a force of nature, a ferment of destruction, corrupting and convulsing Paris between her snowy thighs." Nevertheless her path is credible in its outline, and you do not have to be a nineteenth-century moralist to see how such a story could not fail to come to a bad end. The legendary putative happy ending—the whore who marries into cosseted respectability—is alluded to and given a name (Irma d'Anglars, "a party girl such as they don't make anymore," who is now ninety and "thick with the priests"), but it is presented as something woozily distant and just barely verifiable.

It goes without saying that prostitution, in the nineteenth and early twentieth centuries especially, kept the flame at a constant simmer beneath the cauldron of class; it was a destabilizing agent in the very bosom of the city. "I have made a pact with prostitution to sow discord among families," wrote the Comte de Lautréamont in the person of his monster, Maldoror. "I've often wondered whether . . . in producing these beautiful women whose mission seems to be to ruin and cretinize the haute bourgeoisie and the last remnants of the nobility, they were not continuing quite peacefully the work of the most violent clubs of 1793," mused Maxime du Camp, chin in hand. Prostitution, carelessly or ruthlessly, blurred every kind of line. "We find in the same bed, each given his day and accepting it without jealousy, the son of a good family, the draper's assistant, and the tenth-rate actor," complained another pamphleteer. Not only was it not possible for the bourgeois majority to frequent only the *grandes horizontales*, let alone make one of them his exclusive property, as Leopold II of Belgium managed for a while with Cléo de Mérode, but cross-class affiliations were built into the system. Doctors and bankers liked their rough trade. There were indeed women called *femmes à lipettes*, who catered to the working class by choice, but the most sordid circumstances primarily drew the bourgeois, who sought out obese women, disfigured women, amputees. For that matter, there were those who liked their women big, strong, and battle-ready, such as the whore in Montmartre in 1910 who, feeling disrespected, successively knocked cold a waiter, a café owner, and a policeman, and required a whole platoon of cops to take her down. "But certain connoisseurs appreciate that. Those women are brutal and vulgar, but they are 'genuine.' Among so many who are scrawny,

"Charitable sir, may God keep your sons away from our daughters." Illustration by Gavarni, from *Les lorettes vieillies*, 1851–53

Marthe Miette, a *lorette*, circa 1860

rickety, anemic, tubercular, they stand out for their robust good health, whether farm girls or factory girls."

There was little opprobrium attached to the practice of frequenting prostitutes, except among the strictest Catholics, who were not so much in fashion in the mid-nineteenth century. Whores had access to all but a few of the leading male citizens, and while blackmail would not have been terribly feasible then, they could give the men syphilis. But while attention has primarily focused on the ruin that syphilis brought to the bourgeois intelligentsia—the lives and deaths of, for example, Baudelaire, Flaubert, Maupassant, Manet, Gauguin, Van Gogh; the physical and mental deterioration chronicled by Alphonse Daudet in his almost unendurable journals—it should be borne in mind that the toll was much greater among the prostitutes, who generally did not have recourse even to the ineffective medicine that was available before Paul Ehrlich discovered Compound 606 (later called arsphenamine) in 1909. Unrecorded are the sufferings they endured in the Dépôt, the women's prisons of Saint-Lazare and Les Madelonnettes, and the insane asylum La Salpêtrière.

The most routine and quotidian torment prostitutes endured came from their pimps. Beginning at twilight or the end of the working day, whichever came first, they

The exercise yard at Saint-Lazare, circa 1900

> hang out on a corner, in a recess, in a dark wineshop, in the hallway of a cheap hotel, their hands in their pockets, their trousers molding their equivocal forms, a silk cap atop their pomaded hair, spit curls on their temples, a cigarette dangling from their lips. With their neck muscles strained and all the features of their greasy, pale faces fixed in a brutal and anxious state of expectation, they survey their employees accosting men on the street . . . When night falls, the same scenes are played out more violently in the glow of the gaslights . . . They follow their women on the prowl, empty their pockets, and beat them unmercifully if the take is low.

A man became a pimp because, as a career, it easily outshone factory labor or peddling. The man had muscle, perhaps had a solid grounding in petty crime, or perhaps he seduced a girl whose prospects were no better than his and they more or less jointly decided on their path. Pimping, in addition to the possibility it accorded the poor boy to become an employer (a capitalist) without having to scare up a monetary stake, was also a trade imbued with its own elegance. Witness the pimp of the 1840s striding along the Boulevard du Crime: polished pointy-toed boots, jacket with nipped waist, cream or dove-gray hat tipped over one ear, brocaded waistcoat, pomaded sideburns, small gold ring in one ear, heavy watch chain, multiple rings, medallions made from the braided hair of his women. Mutatis mutandis, many of these elements were preserved over the decades and centuries, even as, for example, the hat became a cap and then a fedora. Then, too, the nineteenth-century pimps, for all their sins, were denizens of an organized underworld culture with its own laws of hierarchy and territory and mutual aid, in which disputes were adjudicated by a panel of senior members and perhaps settled by a duel, and in which job protection and benefits were markedly superior to those of any legitimate enterprise. After the war, however, all was chaos.

A reporter in the 1930s attended a lecture given in a Montmartre café by a veteran pimp known as Henri le Marseillais to a group of aspiring young macks. The killers and thieves who composed the criminal underworld had their standards, he asserted: loyalty, courage, propriety. But now they were under assault by riffraff. Just about everybody wanted to live off women, no matter how ill suited they were to the task: traitors, informers, hijackers of other men's stables, frauds, slanderers, weaklings, false friends, plunderers of every sort, drudges tired of their jobs, cheaters blacklisted by the gambling houses, embezzlers just out of jail, bums who'd left their bridges, washed-up ex-athletes, pantywaists, failed artists, sandwich men. The mores of the past had been lost. The last of the *vrai de vrai** had traveled, gone to America, been corrupted. They allowed their women to drink and, worst of all, to take cocaine, for a dose of which they'd deliver their man's head to the authorities, already separated from

A pimp, 1890s

---

* "Real ones of real ones," as A. J. Liebling rendered it in his 1947 piece "French Without Scars": a traditional label attesting to the authenticity of senior underworld figures; compare to "OG": original gangster.

A pimp settling his accounts, 1884

its shoulders for their convenience. And the new breed of pimps tolerated competition! When some tinhorn gave the spiel to one of their women, they registered their indignation with all the ferocity of a notary mailing out a cease-and-desist.

But even before the war, would-be pimps came in all flavors. Chevalier relates a *fait-divers* of January 1912, when a Montmartre prostitute, very elegant and sought after, who worked solo out of her apartment, happened to encounter a Corsican on Boulevard de Clichy at three o'clock in the morning and agreed to accompany him back to his hotel. The Corsican got straight to the point: she was to work for him. She demurred, pointing out that, for one thing, she had the clap and in fact was scheduled for a hospital visit the following day. Enraged twice over, he strangled her, smothered her with a pillow, and stuffed her corpse under the bed. Undeterred, he promptly returned to the boulevard and soon found another woman to bring up to the room. Once there, they heard footsteps on the stairs—a police raid! The woman ducked under the bed. Her screams woke the whole neighborhood.

Small wonder women were increasingly inclined to work on their own. A 1930 study alleged that "a majority" of streetwalkers were "clandestines," and that a great many worked out of semilegitimate settings: *hôtels de passe*, dance halls, teahouses, cafés, shops, movie theaters. Both of these assertions appear a trifle optimistic. An American writer thirty years later noted the presence of freelance whores, known as *amazones*, who worked out of their own cars, as well as a certain number of bohemian *insoumises* in the cellar nightclubs around Saint-Germain-des-Prés, but the same old pimp-controlled street trade still prevailed. Prices ranged from one dollar American on Rue de Budapest, hard by the Saint-Lazare train station, through a midrange six to eight dollars in the bars on side streets near the Opéra, all the way to a possible fifty dollars in the Sixteenth, the Bois de Boulogne and de Vincennes, and along the Champs-Élysées. Before the Sarkozy Law passed in 2003, the sites of street prostitution mostly adhered to the traditional locations, some of them centuries old: Rue Saint-Denis and its tributaries; Place de Clichy, not far from Pigalle; Place de la Madeleine, near the financial center; Avenue Foch, in the heart of the haute bourgeoisie; the exterior boulevards in the Sixteenth and Seventeenth; and the Cours de Vincennes on its way to the Bois. The locations outside the center of the city appeared more upscale, but also tended to involve automobiles (the clients'), which exposed the women to more immediate danger from psychopaths. If pimps were in the picture, their protection was unavailing.

The other option that had always been available to women was to work in a brothel, a *maison close*. Until 1946 these were legal, and though there were repressive periods when they were regularly raided and shaken down by the constabulary, most of the time they enjoyed official patronage and safety from graft, reformers, and trouble. The employees were spared from having to report to the Dépôt by a house physician who made regular inspections and treatments on site. Brothels ranged from minuscule establishments with just a couple of employees to major lupanars containing ballrooms and restaurants, and from the sordid to the respectable, even familial. Brothels often served multiple social functions in addition to their principal industry. Maupassant's "La Maison Tellier" (1881) describes a house's role as anchor in a small city—when it closes for a weekend the whole town is thrown into turmoil—but even in Paris there were clients who came just to socialize, to drink with the madam, to make business connections in much the same way that the houses of fraternal orders functioned in the United States. For the women, a brothel could be home and jail at one and the same time, as expressed in the *réaliste* singer Damia's song "En maison" (1934). She enters the house at eighteen, under an assumed

Parisian prostitution in the American imagination: Francis Carco's *Rue Pigalle* (1927), given the drugstore treatment, 1954

The workforce, with monsieur and madame and their dog, 1930s

Sheet music for "En maison," by Damia, 1934

The parlor of a brothel, 1930s

name, and although the work is taxing, she likes the music. She travels (Bordeaux, Marseille, Toulon), but always by going from house to house, so she doesn't see very much of the landscape, and the men are the same everywhere. One of them offers to marry her, however strange an idea that might be, and she takes him up on it. So then she has a parlor, jewels, people kissing her hand—but finally it's not so different from being in a brothel, only minus the music. So one day she returns to the life she used to lead, in a *maison close*.

The glamour period of the brothel begins toward the end of the nineteenth century. La Fleur Blanche, centrally located on Rue des Moulins, opened as a house of prostitution during the Second Empire, but it became famous in the wider world in the 1890s chiefly as a result of paintings by Toulouse-Lautrec, who kept a room there and sympathetically documented the most humdrum aspects of its life: the medical inspection, the laundry-man, the communal meals, the owners and their dog, and the hours of boredom endured by the employees, who lounged end-lessly on sofas in their underwear. (It was another house, on Rue d'Amboise, where he painted individual vignetted portraits of sixteen of the women.) Le Chabanais was opened in 1878 on the street of that name, near the Palais-Royal, by a certain Madame Kelly (née Alexandrine Jouannet). It may not have been the first luxury brothel, but it quickly became the most famous. It was a destination bagnio for the crowned heads of Europe, who leg-endarily indicated visits in their schedules as "appointment with the president of the Senate." The star boarder was the future Edward VII of Britain, known as Bertie, who had a truly re-markable stirrup chair built to his specifications and kept on the premises for erotic configurations that can only be surmised. Its theme rooms were celebrated: Pompeii, medieval torture cham-ber, Moorish, Louis XV, and Japanese. (The last was awarded a prize at the Exposition of 1900.) For all the high-tone trappings, the establishment's male support staff included characters with such names as Georges le Cuirassier, Ernest le Sourd (the Deaf), and Nez Pointu (Pointed Nose).

As you might suspect, not all houses partook of this glam-our. There were, for example, the so-called *maisons d'abattage* (slaughterhouses), which were cut-rate brothels that operated like factories. Of the twelve such houses counted in 1939 by the authors of the special issue on prostitution of *Le Crapouillot*, most were on the outer boulevards, but Le Moulin Galant, on Rue de Fourcy, lay between the church of Saint Paul and the Hôtel de Sens, in the Fourth. It employed sixty women who worked, often continuously in eight-hour shifts, for a set rate of five francs fifty—the fifty sous was for the use of a towel—unless patrons were sluggish in moving beyond the parlor, in which case there might be spontaneous price reductions and even auctions. The couple who ran the house, having given it a fresh paint job and exacting standards of cleanliness, by their lights, were eventually done out of it by a consortium of Parisian and Corsican gangsters, a crew with such monikers as Charlot Paletot de Cuir (Leather Coat) and Armand le Fou (Crazy Armand). Efforts by the former owners to press a lawsuit were ignored by the courts.

There was never any shortage of women available to staff the houses, rather the contrary, and traffickers of all sorts had little difficulty harvesting bodies. One middle-aged woman, arrested in 1906, had a habit of strolling the boulevards and accosting young unemployed women whom she would engage as housemaids; a few days later they would find themselves shuttled off to whorehouses in the provinces. Larger-scale enterprises sent women abroad, generally operating under the guise of employment agencies that recruited "dancers" and "entertainers" for what were usually described as music hall revues in Argentina or the Cape Colony, on renewable ten-week contracts. Some went straight to brothels, others to dance halls or bars, where they were employed as B-girls, paid strictly on a percentage of the champagne they were able to flog. The influx of women from Paris was such that in those days, "French lady" was the euphemism for whore in Cape Town, "Francucha" in Buenos Aires. Chevalier cites an undated press report regarding a dive on the lower slopes of Montmartre that around 1910 was the principal clearinghouse for the trade:

"Marietta," an anonymous *carte de visite* from a brothel album, 1865

> All day long there hung about characters of an extreme and unusual elegance, with significant nicknames. They were the go-betweens, the suppliers for pimps from around the world. From time to time one of these, just arrived

Three employees of a luxury house, 1930s

CATALOGUE DES PRIX D'AMOUR
de Mademoiselle Marcelle LAPOMPE

TARIF 1915 ANNULANT TOUS LES PRÉCÉDENTS

The price of love on the notional Rue du Chat-Noir, 1915

from Buenos Aires or Cairo or Manchuria, would come in, his fingers heavy with rings . . . to discuss quantity and quality and age, preferably from 16 to 18. The harvesters would work factory exits or the windows of employment agencies where notices were posted. The young women were hauled off to orgies, expertly orchestrated, in some suburban villa.

Sometimes the women weren't given even that much notice. A police raid on a hotel in 1902 netted a whole crew of teenagers bound for the Cape Colony who were fully persuaded that they were joining a dance company, this one as a seamstress, that one as a maker of slippers.

The years just before World War I saw an efflorescence of whorehouses, many of them specialized. Thus Chez Marcelle (on Rue de l'Arbre-Sec) and L'Acropole (on Rue de Hanovre) were only two of many that catered to sadomasochistic fantasies, and Chez Sabine (on Rue Caron) further refined its appeal by indulging slave scenarios—with African women, no less. At Chez Adèle (on Rue d'Aboukir) you could disport yourself in a coffin. Chez Sevoline (on Rue des Rosiers) welcomed couples, while Chez Jeanne de la Grille and Miss Beety—both on Rue Saint-Sulpice, in a neighborhood once known to taxi drivers as "the Vatican"—catered to the ecclesiastical trade. There exists a menu of services, dated 1915, from an establishment run by Mlle Marcelle Lapompe,* supposedly at 69 Rue du Chat-Noir—there is no such street in Paris—which, real or not, perhaps gives a sideways glimpse into the bordello economy: an ordinary hand job cost thirty-three sous, upped to fifty for the additional insertion of the pinky into the anus; fellatio set one back 3.50, or four francs if swallowing was involved (there was apparently no additional charge for the suggested preliminary consumption of a mint lollipop by the woman); the varieties of *soixante-neuf* ranged from 1.75 up to four francs. "Journey to yellow lands" rated 4.90 with the maid or 4.95 with the waiter, while something called

* This turns out to have been one of many pseudonyms employed by the shadowy if prolific Renée Dunan (1892–1936?), a feminist writer with connections to anarchism and Dada, among other things. The menu is presented as the straight goods in Véronique Willemin's *La mondaine* (2009), p. 63.

"pissette sur la quéquette," which sounds as if it might have required use of Edward VII's stirrup chair, in addition to a bucket, dented one's wallet to the tune of 5.45.

Any number of refinements were introduced to the scene after the war, such as a whole spate of houses near the Opéra that fronted as couture houses or jewelers, perfumers, or antique shops. While these might be seen as appeals to the clandestine lure of prostitution, quite the opposite sort of attraction ruled the two major bordellos of the interwar era, Le Sphinx (opened in 1929) and One-Two-Two (1933), which were about as discreet as department stores. Le Sphinx, on Boulevard Edgar-Quinet, in Montparnasse, was noted for its Egyptian Revival façade (still extant) and décor. Its four owners had significant underworld ties as well as healthy connections within the government. In addition to its presiding madam, it employed five auxiliary procuresses who supervised sixty-five women, who each worked three times per day and twice on Sundays. Run along modern managerial lines, it was not only impeccably clean but also notably cheaper than many of the smaller upscale houses around town (a standard thirty francs per visit) and perhaps for that reason drew a clientele that included settled former bohemians, among them Simenon and Hemingway and most of the Montparnasse painters. It was particularly renowned for its erotic spectacles, as refined and choreographed as any top-flight supper club floor show.

One-Two-Two, named after its address, 122 Rue de Provence (which runs behind the Galeries Lafayette), followed the tradition of Le Chabanais in priding itself on its theme rooms: Kama Sutra, Cleopatra, Versailles, igloo, pirates' lair, medieval torture chamber, hayloft, and so on. Its seven floors attracted maharajahs, Hollywood stars, the Aga Khan, Leopold III of Belgium, and suchlike moneyed riffraff; its restaurant, Le Boeuf à la Ficelle, in addition drew many women from the entertainment industry. (Marlene Dietrich seems to have been spotted in every one of these houses.) When the Germans occupied Paris the major brothels lost no time in complying with the wishes of the invaders. After all, hadn't Hitler called Paris "der sogenannte Puff Europas" (the so-called whorehouse of Europe)? Hitler himself was allegedly seen at Le Sphinx, while Chez Marguerite on Rue

The bar at Le Sphinx, 1930s

The reception room of a large bordello, 1920s

Marthe Richard, circa 1946

Saint-Georges was said to be Goering's favorite. Those two, in addition to One-Two-Two, Le Chabanais, and the still-extant Fleur Blanche, were essentially conscripted, and for all four years catered almost exclusively to German officers and the French Gestapo.

That sort of "horizontal collaboration," which during the postwar *épuration* (cleansing) saw many a small-town whore publicly stripped, shorn, and spat upon, was perhaps the major factor that led to the wholesale shuttering, in 1946, of brothels nationwide—1,400 of them, including 180 in Paris. This abrupt break with tradition was the result of a rare joint enterprise between the Communist Party and the Mouvement Républicain Populaire, a Christian outfit, under the aegis of the woman who gave the law its name: Marthe Richard. She was a chameleonic creature who enjoyed a colorful and improbably byzantine career over the course of her long life (1889–1982). She had been a prostitute herself in her youth, first on the street and then in a soldiers' brothel, from which she was allegedly discharged for knowingly transmitting syphilis. Soon, married to a rich man she met in a Paris bagnio, she became a pioneering aviatrix, although she seems to have taken extraordinary measures to counterfeit some significant flight records. Widowed during World War I, she worked as a spy, but along the way got caught up in Mata Hari's orbit and found herself unwittingly used as a double agent—which didn't stop her from being awarded the Légion d'Honneur, nor from writing a heavily fictionalized heroic account of her experiences, which became a bestseller and later a movie, in which she was played by Edwige Feuillère. During World War II she seems to have been one of those many French nationals who rallied to the Resistance very late in the game but thereafter claimed various unverifiable feats of derring-do. In any event, her claims got her elected in 1945 to the Paris Municipal Council, as a representative from the Fourth Arrondissement, and her successful initiative to shut down the houses of prostitution in her district led very quickly to a wholesale national ban.

It seems unlikely that any set of circumstances other than the end of the war and its consequent purges could have led to the devastation of what might as well have been national monuments—as, indeed, the façade of Le Sphinx officially remains—and the sale at auction of their often unbelievable fixtures and furnishings. The outrage was loud and widespread. According to Pierre Mac Orlan, the closures represented "the collapsed foundation of a thousand-year-old civilization," while Arletty, referring to the fact that the French term for brothel is *maison close*, quipped, "It's worse than a crime, it's a pleonasm." There were sundry initiatives to smear Richard, who was accused of jewel theft, among other things, but none of the charges stuck. Although she suggested at the time that the closing of the houses was only the first step toward an eventual eradication of the sex trade, no such thing happened, and the women were simply turned out to try their luck on the sidewalks, inspected on the fly by a "speculum brigade" sent out by the police. Richard spent her remaining three and a half decades variously equivocating and regretting the action to which her name was irrevocably tied.

The *business** was alternately plagued, abetted, and exploited by the police. The *brigade des moeurs*, or morals squad, was first dissolved in 1881 after a commission denounced it as "arbitrary," "inquisitorial," and a "secret police." In its place was founded the *brigade mondaine*, which might be translated as "worldly brigade," the agents of which were called "les bourgeois," and which had the specific mission of rooting out clandestine brothels, those that were neither inspected nor taxed. In 1910 a *section mixte* was added to it, in effect a drug squad. Its tasks were transferred to a *brigade des moeurs* four years later, and that was renamed *brigade mondaine* in 1930—the name changes give the impression of successive veils drawn over a deeply rooted bent for corruption. In 1975 the Mondaine was dissolved and its functions assumed by the *brigade des stupéfiants et du proxénétisme* (drugs and pimping), and then those two aspects were finally split between two squads in 1989. The earliest version of the brigade earned its reputation through such pursuits as a minute surveillance of the adulteries of the prominent, which would seem to be a script for blackmail. Records were kept, for example, of the cash gifts Sarah Bernhardt received from her lovers and of

Fixtures of Le Sphinx being dumped on the street, 1946

* The English word, sometimes spelled *biseness*, has been the French argot term for prostitution since at least the late nineteenth century.

The paddy wagon. Illustration by Théophile Steinlen for Aristide Bruant's *Dans la rue*, vol. 2, 1889

A brothel employee, circa 1860

the visits Zola paid to brothels for his research. Many of the *grandes horizontales*, such as Cora Pearl and Blanche d'Antigny, were systematically tracked by the squad, while others, down on their luck, were recruited as informants.

The squad began seizing pornographic photographs in the 1850s, at the dawn of the medium—Gustave Courbet was cited for possession in 1867—and would periodically crack down on porn whenever public opinion seemed to tilt in that direction, such as the 1930s, when a demagogue, the Abbé Bethléem, made a great show of tearing up publications he found offensive at newspaper kiosks, or the 1950s and early '60s, when, with the encouragement of the prim Mme de Gaulle, the squad regularly seized filthy postcards, which look remarkably tame today, or such mildly risqué magazines as *Paris-Tabou* and *Paris-Frou-Frou*. The activities of the drug squad, too, varied wildly from era to era. Hashish, although consumed by everyone from Baudelaire and Gautier to Apollinaire and Artaud, doesn't seem to have aroused police interest until the 1960s.

Much the same was true of opium until the 1930s—before World War I, a pipe cost less than a drink in a café. However, around that time, cocaine—its argot name back then, *bigornette*, derives from *bigorner*, the root "to kill"—became a problem. It flooded the underworld as well as bohemia; there were open-air markets in Montmartre; various murders were attributed to its effects. After World War I, Laurent Tailhade, who blamed cocaine for destroying the Montmartre bohemia—Tailhade was always mourning the end of something or other, prematurely or not—enumerated the sketchy types who skulked around plying women with the drug, people with names such as Max-la-Bombe and Le Pépère: "restaurant porters, hotel waiters, unemployed barbers, thugs in espadrilles, three-time losers, cashiered madams." Dope was the mortal enemy of pimps, who could easily lose their employees to its effects, and killings of dealers were frequent.

But the facilities were different for the different classes. In 1913, André Warnod wrote:

The pharmacy is heralded by its red and green lights. OPEN ALL NIGHT, says the sign. "Now there's a model pharmacist, who stays up to take care of the injured and relieve the sick," think those who don't know that behind the big red and yellow luminous flasks in the window lies a commerce in forbidden drugs, which opens wide to neurotic women the mysterious gates of the artificial paradise. They come there for their ether . . . Cocaine and other substances are harder to get and often require intermediaries who charge elevated sums for their indispensible services.

Among these was an American, identified only as *le grand* Thomas, who appeared on the scene before the first war—big, well-groomed, debonair, everybody's idea of the rich American— who claimed to be the son of a general, and whose picture had appeared in the *New York Herald*. He had six apartments in Paris, the principal one being a luxury flat on Rue Cambon, where he entertained the bon ton, and he went everywhere in a big car. He claimed to be a supplier of arms to the Italian army, which apparently was true, but he made a lot more money running cocaine, morphine, opium, and hashish, and had a sizeable network of pimps, whores, café owners, and hoteliers in his employ. Scandal broke in 1916 when a little blond dancer called Chiffon was found bleeding out in front of one of his buildings. Before dying she told the cops that Thomas was in the habit of drugging her and then torturing her before an audience of men in dress suits, in a hoodoo ambiance of black drapes and candles around the bed. Finally she had deliberately cut herself, deeply enough to require a trip to the hospital, but instead had simply been tossed out on the street. Thomas was expelled from France as an undesirable alien, but after a brief trip to Monte Carlo he was back, with all the proper documents. He was said to have supplied drugs to Miguel Almereyda, the anarchist who was the film director Jean Vigo's father and whose precipitous decline due to drugs has a familiar late-century ring to it. What became of Thomas seems to be unrecorded. Between the wars the drug supply was intermittent, tossed by the four winds. In 1938 the squad seized one hundred kilos of opium, in 1942 (in the middle of the war) a mere five hundred grams, and then in 1946 all of three kilos. But right around then the Corsican Mafia took over the trade and modernized it, and everything changed.

L'opium à Paris by Delphi Fabrice, 1907

Alumni of the Petite-Roquette: "Whatever happened to the Homebody?" "He's gone wrong, he's taken to blow." Illustration by Aristide Delannoy, from *L'Assiette au Beurre*, 1907

A mid-nineteenth-century "infamous pederast," before . . . and after

A *jésus*, 1887

Homosexuality was also of great interest to the morals squad, who began keeping a register in the 1840s, with photographs when available, that accumulated some twelve hundred names in a decade and was divided into three categories: pederasts, shameful pederasts, and infamous pederasts—the last often wore such sobriquets as "la belle Andrée" or "la petite Colette." Homosexuality was not specifically illegal, although pimping and prostitution of males were, as was blackmail of course, and until the 1980s the police displayed considerable anxiety about links between homosexuality and murder, as if one naturally led to the other. Gay male cruising along certain quais and in the galleries of the Palais-Royal was noted as far back as the eighteenth century, and chickenhawking became the special attribute of the Passage des Panoramas soon after its construction, but with the introduction of the *vespasiennes* (public urinals) under Napoléon III, a special police *groupe des homos* had to be dispatched to curtail trade in what were even then known as "teahouses."

Most traffic between *jésus*, as young male prostitutes were known, and *tantes* ("aunties": their clients) occurred in public places. There were undoubtedly male brothels in the nineteenth century, but evidence of them is scant. It was not until the twentieth that notoriety was achieved by the houses operated by Albert le Cuziat, who had been valet to Prince Radziwill. Most famous was the Hôtel Marigny, on Rue de l'Arcade, behind the Madeleine church; it was seized by the morals squad in 1918. The police inspector noted in his report that in addition to after-hours drinking, every bedroom in the hotel was occupied by a male couple, in each case one of them a minor, who were engaging in "antiphysical debauchery." Among those picked up in preliminary sweeps was Marcel Proust, "*rentier*, 46 years old, 102 Boulevard Haussmann," who later transferred le Cuziat's attributes to his character Jupien. Despite the seizure, in the 1920s and '30s le Cuziat went on to open other such houses, which retained a certain literary allure.

In Pigalle there were crackdowns on sailors, not because homosexuality was illegal per se, noted the police report, but to preserve the morals and the good name of the fleet. Sailors were ever notorious. In his 1924 novel *La lumière noire*, Carco describes a dive on Quai des Orfèvres (right by police headquarters) where women were not welcome:

Chorus boys, 1930s

> Sailors wearing sashes and skin-tight jerseys, their necks bare, made up most of the clientele. They waited near the counter or sometimes danced with one another in hopes that someone would cut in. The waltz is what they liked . . . With every bar of the song, the blue sashes of the sailors seemed to wrap more tightly around their waists so that they comprised a sort of chain, the living links of which flowed together seamlessly. Little by little this chain stretched over to us and drew us into the rhythm of the roundelay, swift and ardent and vertiginous. Foreheads and cheeks glowed with moisture. The pleasure that marked their faces drew them together in a physical expectation that was almost bestial.

But were they even necessarily sailors? The appeal was such that the streets were filled with *faux marins*. In the twentieth

Sailors, real or pretend, 1930s

Partygoers, 1930s

century, anyway, Paris was not lacking in gay nightlife. Before 1914, Bal Wagram, a dance hall that catered to all, had a significant and unabashed gay clientele, of both genders. In the 1920s and '30s there were bars and clubs in Montmartre—Le Roland's, Le Trèfle Rose (the Pink Clover), M. Tagada on the street parallel to the funicular—and the *bals musette* on Rue de Lappe featured not a few that were largely or primarily gay: Le Bousca; Les Trois Colonnes; La Musette, which according to Chevalier featured in its men's room in the '30s a mural by a famous artist (he couldn't quite remember which) of an old man ogling a young sailor pissing. Léon-Paul Fargue wrote, "On Rue de Lappe there were young ephebes with untidy nails, darned sweaters, and rosy cheeks who would deliciously pick your pocket while murmuring 'baby' and 'sweetheart' and 'sugar' to keep you interested." That is perhaps the only thing Fargue wrote that spelled out his homosexuality, although his liaison in the 1890s with his lycée classmate Alfred Jarry was not much of a secret.

Between the wars, Parisian gay life made a public appearance once a year, at the festivities of Mi-Carême, a traditional holiday not unlike Mardi Gras, although celebrated halfway through Lent rather than on its eve. In 1931 and 1932 Brassaï photographed the costume ball at Magic-City, an amusement park (the third built in Europe) on Quai d'Orsay. Its vast ballroom, with a

A mixed *bal*, 1930s

capacity of three thousand, drew a mixed crowd with a large gay component from the 1920s until 1935, when an announcement was made that thereafter the balls would be "in good taste," meaning that men in female drag would no longer be admitted. Brassaï's pictures show elaborate costumes, eighteenth-century shepherdesses and nineteenth-century duchesses, suggesting a well-heeled crowd, although "every type came, faggots, cruisers, chickens, old queens, famous antique dealers and young butcher-boys, hairdressers and elevator boys, well-known dress designers and drag queens."

Brassaï also shot the *bal des lopes*—the sissy ball, you might say—at 46 Rue de la Montagne-Sainte-Geneviève, on Mardi Gras around 1932, as it happens, although the ballroom's activities were year-round. It had been a typical neighborhood *bal musette* for a century, until at some point it changed, the date and the circumstances lost to history. It was sometimes raided by the cops, mostly left alone, and it generally drew mostly people from the neighborhood. The dancers whom Brassaï photographed include many in drag, but also regular people in their regular outfits. As he writes, "once in a while one would see butchers from the neighborhood—rather common in appearance, but with hearts full of feminine longings—forming surprising couples. They would hold hands—thick, calloused hands—like timid children, and would waltz solemnly together, their eyes downcast, blushing wildly."

There were lesbian couples in the crowd, too, working-class women who would have attracted no attention on the street. Paris had always been more accepting of lesbians than of gay men—no doubt largely because of the titillation factor for heterosexuals—so that such foreign women as Natalie Barney and Romaine Brooks were drawn there to live and work. The interwar period brought in new suggestions of emancipation, signaled by such things as the 1922 publication of Victor Marguerite's novel *La garçonne*, the heroine of which is as sexually freewheeling as any man, with partners of both genders. There had long been cafés catering mostly to women, but now explicitly lesbian establishments opened, the most eye-catching being Le Monocle, in Montparnasse—also famously photographed by Brassaï—whose owner and staff, and half its clientele, essentially

A woman at her ease, 1930s

"An evening with the transvestite inverts," 1930s

lived in male drag. Women-only bordellos had been noised about as early as 1907, but apparently there were more than a few in the '30s. There were numerous prominent gay women in the entertainment industry, such as the great cabaret singer Yvonne George, who died young (and broke the hearts of straight men, most famously Robert Desnos, who wrote her some of his most beautiful poems), and the deep-voiced, formidable Suzy Solidor. It was a wide-open era, when the drag performer O'dett (René Goupil) could put on a show at the ABC in 1940 in which he played Hitler as a queen. Naturally that era was ended by the war—although it wasn't so much the Germans who minded, actually, so much as the French collaborationist authorities, who raided bars and swept the *pissotières*, sending those rounded up to German labor camps, with a note that assured them the hardest tasks and worst accommodation.

The "outrage to public morals" laws held well into the 1950s and '60s—they weren't revoked until 1982—leading to a long period of quiet repression. But even as gay life went underground, the Paris-by-night of the tourists included a significant portion of drag, much of it at Madame Arthur's, in Montmartre, where Serge Gainsbourg's father was the pianist and the show was headlined by the internationally celebrated "illusionists" Bambi and Coccinelle. In this as in so many things, Paris continued its reign as the world capital of contradictions, which could be justified as dialectical or shown up as double-dealing.

8

Saint Monday

For centuries upon centuries, drinking in a public place in Paris meant visiting a *marchand de vin*, a wine seller, who generally sold only white and red and perhaps marc, a liqueur made from the lees of wine. As time went by, his successors began to bring in beer from Alsace, rum from the Antilles, absinthe from the Midi, and a great range of eaux-de-vie from all over the country, as well as whiskey, port, madeira, ginever, kümmel, and every other sort of spirituous beverage from abroad. Their outlets ranged from those intended for the rich, which generally served food as well and were known as restaurants (even if the chief interest of their clientele was to become legless), down to the most primitive canteens of the poor.

The barrage of labels given to establishments in the low to middle range over the course of the nineteenth century illustrates how quickly a label would become tainted: by adulterated drink, by a reputation for violence, by standing as a regular police target, by general squalor. Many of these words are barely remembered today: *bibine, boc, bouchon, bouffardière, bousin, cabermon, cabremont, cargot.* A *tapis-franc* was a dive in which everyone present could be assumed to be a criminal, a reputation cemented by its use in Sue's *Mysteries of Paris.* An *abreuvoir* was a drinking trough for horses and cattle, hence a place that entirely dispensed with ceremony; and even farther down the scale was the *assommoir*, a "knock-out" shop, a relatively esoteric term until it was

A family-run *troquet*, circa 1900

A family-run *estaminet*, circa 1910

immortalized by Zola. *Bastringue*, *caboulot*, and *troquet* were perhaps half a step up; *estaminet* a step above that, since the term might actually appear on the front of the building; all four lasted into the early twentieth century, leprous reputations intact. *Cabaret* fell into the same category, although it has been preserved in the language through antiphrasis: it might ironically be applied to a chic establishment, and along the way it acquired an association with musical entertainment. *Bistrot*, from the Russian word for "quickly," was imported by the Cossacks who swarmed through Paris after Napoléon's defeat in 1814; in recent times it has come to signify a restaurant rather than a dram shop. *Brasserie* literally means "brewery," and followed the mid-nineteenth-century rage for bock beer, but was generically applied within a few decades. *Café*, with its roots in the seventeenth-century coffee craze, has been a term of all work for the better part of two centuries. And then there is *boîte*, which can be applied to any sort of outlet, high or low, although its most celebrated usage has been as anchor of the term *boîte de nuit*, a "nightclub."

We lack descriptions of the pothouses of the deep past, have only a handful of names: La Pomme de Pin, frequented by Villon and Rabelais, in the Cité; Le Berceau, on the Pont Saint-Michel; La Corne, on Place Maubert; Le Cornet Fleuri, by Les Halles; La Croix de Lorraine, near the Bastille; La Fosse aux Lions, behind Place des Vosges. We also have names for some of the *tapis-francs* of the mid-nineteenth century, which tend toward the flamboyant: Les Chats en Cage, Le Renard Qui Prêche (the Preaching Fox), Le Boeuf Couronné (the Crowned Bull), La Rose Rouge au Dé (Red Rose and Dice), Le Tombeau du Lapin (the Rabbit's Tomb), La Libre Pensée (Free Thought), Le Pur-Sang (the Thoroughbred). Privat mentions Le Grand Saint-Nicolas as an *estaminet* for the lice-ridden, and he describes a *tapis-franc* called L'Abattoir (the Slaughterhouse) as "a smoky, dark, low, humid, airless cellar that the sun has never been bold enough to visit. Its squalid walls sweat misery and stink; its crippled tables and spavined benches serve as a dormitory for a stunted population of beings no longer conscious of their own existence and who retain no human qualities." In those sorts of places they served whatever rotgut came to hand, poisonous concoctions called *poivre* (pepper) or *camphre* (camphor) or *casse-poitrine* (chest breaker), all of which more or less adhered to the general definition of eau-de-vie. Often, glasses came in three sizes: *monsieur* (large), *mademoiselle* (small), and *misérable* (a thimble's worth).

The most famous cabaret of the time was a place on Rue des Fers (now Rue Berger), which ran between Les Halles and the Saints-Innocents graveyard, and was named after its initial proprietor, Paul Niquet, who may have originated the signal nineteenth-century treat of the poor: cherries (or sour green grapes) preserved in eau-de-vie. The joint was described by both

"Three or four crocks and he's ready to pass out. And he's the one who stood at the altar and promised to protect you." Illustration by Gavarni, from *Impressions de ménage*, 1843

A drinker. Drawing by Bécan (Bernhard Kahn), 1920s

Privat and Nerval, which may have led to its becoming a magnet for slummers, or maybe it was the other way around. It served the marketplace clientele, country folk who started arriving at 4:00 a.m., when their work was done, and it also served the bottom rung of society, hard-core alcoholics, who began to leave when the others arrived. (The drinking joints around Les Halles enjoyed a special dispensation from the normal citywide closing time of 2:00 a.m.) There were two rooms, of which the one in front featured two zinc bars and a long oak bench, while the one in back, accessed from behind the counter and open only to habitués, held three long tables and a complement of benches, which were used more for sleeping than sitting. Fights were frequent, and according to Nerval the place had a novel system of control: waterspouts were turned on the fighters until they calmed down; if they failed to ease up, the water pressure was cranked up until they begged for mercy. Privat describes the crowd as consisting of ragpickers, poets, buskers, cashiered servants—people who never slept, at least not in a bed. "Their life is one long string of todays. The only tomorrow they ever have comes when they are picked up by some security force and thrown into a hospital bed to die."

A tide had turned at the unspecifiable date when eau-de-vie became a staple; another occurred in the 1830s or '40s, when absinthe arrived from the south. Privat attributes this latter innovation to a theater people's café called Le Crocodile: "Our generation . . . is bored, it no longer wants to think, it reaches for obliteration believing it to be diversion." A public hygiene specialist writing in 1900 alludes to an indefinite date when "the toxic powers of manufactured spirits and the essence of absinthe were multiplied by an enormous coefficient" as marking a sharp rise in both alcoholism and juvenile crime. A few years later, Lucien Descaves wrote:

> Michelet said that you have to live in the poor neighborhoods to appreciate how quickly the population renews itself. However, if that great visionary saw the causes for this as stemming from the deadly conditions of the workplace and the adulteration of basic foodstuffs, he could not imagine the future progress of an even more virulent

scourge. It is nevertheless that scourge that within three generations can completely extinguish the lineage of an alcoholic. So it is that many Parisians are, in Paris itself, utterly deracinated. A son is no longer attached to the house, the street, the neighborhood where his people were born but had passed through too quickly to leave a trace. Not having any sense of his roots, it matters little to him to go in this direction or that; he rolls on, a bitter wave. The mists of antiquity, for him, is the lifetime of his grandfather, about whom he knows nothing.

By the early twentieth century, alcoholism was recognized as destroying the social fabric of the working class, leaving its members isolated and impotent. The Bonneff brothers, pursuing their investigations at that time, found absinthe and jug wine (*vin d'Aramon*) sold in laundries, in employment agencies, in places that rented handcarts to market porters. Some dives had whorehouses in their back rooms, some made loans at usurious rates; joints near Les Halles gave overnight credit to market workers, which came due at 10:00 a.m., when the workers were paid. Construction sites imported laborers from the countryside, housed them in unsanitary barracks, fed them slops, and plied them with absinthe, which could not be refused without humiliation, if not beatings.

The drunkenness of the poor became an object of nervous regard by the other half of the city, alternately condemned, fretted over, and rubbernecked. There was always a crowd eager for vicarious degradation. At the start of the twentieth century, Georges Cain took in Les Halles by night, heard the laughter and song at La Belle de Nuit and Le Chien Qui Fume and Le Caveau, and then went next door to L'Ange Gabriel,

"My daddy doesn't drink eau-de-vie!" Public-service poster, 1920s

a notorious bistro, something like the Maxim's of the *apaches*. The gigolettes and the toughs come here to swallow some snails and upend bowls of mulled wine. The big room upstairs is filled with worrisome characters, the heroes of knife fights or confidence tricks, with predatory eyes and thin lips, their girls pale with carmine mouths. All of them are smoking cigarettes, speaking in low tones

At a *bal*, 1930s

Père Lunette's dive on Rue des Anglais, circa 1900

while rapidly glancing to the sides, half listening to some poor devil of a violinist scratching out lugubrious waltz choruses.

Fifty years later, L'Ange Gabriel was brought to the screen, convincingly enough, in Jacques Becker's *Casque d'Or* (1952), as a fairly regular-looking bistro where the gangsters fill a large table, the girls hang around waiting to be noticed, one of the garçons is a police informer, and a party of slummers from points west all get a bit overheated from the excitement of their own daring. A knife fight indeed occurs, but in the alley, decently out of public view.

Considerably farther down the social ladder was Le Père Lunette, near Place Maubert, a venerable dump that managed to draw the tourists, apparently in serious numbers, becoming something like the Sammy's Bowery Follies of its time and place. Part of the reason was that it was ancient—no one knew how old, but dating back at least to Louis-Philippe's July Monarchy. Aristide Bruant sang of it in the 1880s as a place where, long before, you could go hear a singer called La Môme Toinette (the Toinette Kid, that is; like La Môme Piaf) and pay just three sous for the privilege. By 1900 it had declined somewhat. Cain again sets the scene:

> Dirty, stinking Rue des Anglais will soon fall to the pick-axes, and with it will go a notorious dive, a celebrated stage on the official tour of the places of ill repute: the cabaret of Père Lunette. A gigantic pair of spectacles jutting from a narrow red storefront serves as its banner . . . In the back room, as big as a closet, three wooden tables are crowded with drinkers who are more or less drunk, more or less consumptive, equally stupefied, who smoke, babble, rant, or snore while a guitarist tries to sell some romance . . . It smells of vice, misery, thuggery, the lowest kind of crookedness—but nevertheless this ignoble cabaret is not dangerous . . . Le Père Lunette is better than its reputation. As they say in the theater, it's all hype and sham . . . It's less accomplished than the third act of a melodrama, but it makes up for it in stench.

J.-K. Huysmans had visited in the late 1880s and found it already moribund ("a meeting place for malicious urchins and evil grandmothers," enlivened only by the occasional gratuitous murder). The American journalist Richard Harding Davis, in town a few years later and in search of Parisian low life—"In Paris there are virtually no slums at all . . . the Parisian criminal has no environment, no setting"—went there and found the dodge already in effect: the drunks "were as ready to do their part of the entertainment as the actors of a theater are ready to go on when the curtain rises." He had a better time a block away at Le Château Rouge, on Rue Galande—Oscar Wilde also enjoyed himself there—where the bar was filled with sleeping bums and the back room contained a selection of paintings of famous murders.

The entertainment baton was soon taken up with alacrity by the tourist traps of Pigalle, fully stage-managed experiences such as Le Ciel and L'Enfer and Le Rat Mort, which featured elaborately lurid façades, waiters in costume, ordinary beverages given the names of philters and potions, and a lot of haunted house woo-woo.* The professionals had taken charge. No one by then, if ever, was much interested in looking in on low-key everyday wretchedness, of the kind recalled by the poet Jean Follain:

In 1925, many little bars on Boulevard Saint-Michel wallowed in their own misery . . . It was the year of suicides and thefts. That one, the guy they called the boxer, who claimed he was a champion, was in reality no more than a thief of fancy dogs from taxis. One day he was arrested on the street while his friends prepared buckwheat porridge in their garret. In the adjacent toilet a girl who had had all her clothes stolen at an art students' ball and had to make her way back naked under a coat was crying for someone to go fetch her a dress from her aunt's in Grenelle. Later on she gave birth to a child she wanted to feed but who died within a few weeks. One night you could see her drunk and

Le Cabaret des Truands (the Hoodlum Bar), on Boulevard de Clichy, circa 1910

---

* The pioneer of the thematic bar experience was Maxime Lisbonne, who commanded the Saint-Sulpice barricade during the Commune. He came back from the penal colony in New Caledonia after the 1880 amnesty to open first an establishment called Frites Révolutionnaires and then the Café du Bagne ("of the penal colony"), which were appropriately decorated, their servers in matching garb.

Nightclubbing with Léon-Paul Fargue, *Voilà*, 1935

An illegal dive. Illustration from Blaise Cendrars's *Panorama de la pègre*, 1935

bawling, in high mourning on the arms of two students; she had opened her bodice and taken out her swollen breasts. Out on the corner, starvelings conversed in low tones near big white posters with black letters.

At the other end of the social scale, much of what passed for high life was barely less sordid. Everyone wanted to party—*faire la fête*. The Bonneffs explain that there were two basic strategies for realizing this ambition. Method one, the "serious" approach, was to visit a fashionable cabaret after the show, accompanying or meeting a lady, and then dance to the gypsy orchestra, sup in a private salon, and go home at dawn. Method two, the "frivolous" one, was to go up to Montmartre and run through as many cabarets as possible, ordering large quantities of champagne everywhere and offering it all around, with special attention to the ladies—the more ladies surrounding the party hound, the better the party. He would bestow flowers and cigarettes upon them and engage with them in coarse repartee, and then, having emptied the bottles and broken as many of them as he could, he would jump into a cab and have himself driven to another such establishment, where the routine would repeat itself. The most experienced lounge lizard could count on visiting twelve or thirteen *boîtes* in one night. A year later, André Warnod chronicled the aftermath:

All night long there has been a great hubbub of feverish activity, as if it were a factory, and when calm returns in the morning it looks as if a battle has been fought and lost. The last customers depart at dawn. The dancers wrap their coats around their vividly colored dresses; their makeup looks hideous in the light of day. At tables here and there, among empty bottles and dirty dishes, linger the poor girls that nobody wanted. A drunk snickers to himself in a corner. The waiters, the dancers, and the gypsies go home, their job done, exhausted, not with that good fatigue that comes from achieving a task, but rather as if they, too, had dragged themselves aimlessly through the orgy that had just sputtered out only to spark again a few hours thence.

These were the extremes, anyway, always more noticeable and memorable for their emotional violence but not necessarily indicative of the general experience. People had always been drinking in Paris. In a world before timetables and engines, there were fewer hazards to beginning the day with spiked coffee and going on from there. Long before unions fought to shorten the working day and the workweek, it was widely if unofficially accepted that workers would keep the party going into Monday (*la Saint-Lundi*) and would not be available for duty then. Most people drank, in reasonable or unreasonable quantities, in locals where they felt at home and wouldn't be cheated, places that would become extensions of their furnished rooms, where they would come to know the other customers, who would eventually become a sort of prosthetic family.

Cafés developed their own codes, rituals, prejudices, depending on an intricate triangulation of management, location, and clientele. If you were unwelcome you wouldn't know it from the street, and you wouldn't even necessarily know it even when you were inside sitting behind a glass; you might just feel a slight chill in the air if you were sufficiently sensitive. That the place was the exclusive preserve of purse snatchers or monarchists or chicken hawks or anti-Semites might entirely elude you. And such specialization, in a time when there was a bistro on every corner and eight per block, was not only common but essential to the business. As Léon-Paul Fargue noticed in the 1930s, there were

A rustic saloon by a pond, circa 1910

Chez Guignard, on Place Maubert, 1930s

A collector of cigarette butts. Drawing by Gustave Fraipont, 1891

"cafés for unemployed saxophone players, cafés for Armenian tailors, cafés for Spanish barbers, cafés for nude women, for dancers, for maîtres d'hôtel, for bookmakers, for street urchins—even the smallest joint seems to exist to serve drinks to specific professions or else to styles of vagrancy that leave no room for doubt."

Paradoxically, that was also the era described by Richard Cobb as "when the night was still democratic and *à la portée de tout le monde* [affordable by everyone]," when in a café the archetypal faubourg characters "le père la Tulipe and Jojo la Terreur might encounter, at the bar, a noceur, in white tie, a runaway accountant, or a lovesick monsieur décoré, not a flight of fantasy, but an accurate representation of a limitless sociability that did exist, especially between midnight and four in the morning . . ." But then, that was the Paris of the Popular Front, when, however briefly, it seemed as if the barriers of class had been broken down and would remain fallen.

Although the Popular Front government sadly lasted only two years (1936–38), the democratic wind blew at various speeds—and not without a corresponding blowback from the far right—from the worldwide Crash of 1929 until Hitler became an immediate threat ten years later. One of its cultural harbingers was Jean Renoir's *Boudu Saved from Drowning* (1932), in which a bookseller rescues from the Seine an uncivilized free spirit named Boudu, who proceeds to call down chaos upon the bookseller's tidy existence. Boudu, large, hairy, and inarticulate, was probably intended (by René Fauchois, the playwright on whose work the movie is based) as a child of nature out of Rousseau, but the way Michel Simon plays him leaves little doubt as to his social category: even though he doesn't seem to be a drunk, he is inescapably a clochard. This word, the first published use of which was apparently by Aristide Bruant in 1895, derives from *cloche* (bell) and signifies a bum or hobo. There are various theories as to its etymology: that it comes from an argot term for "limping"; that it alludes to the bell announcing the official end of marketplace hours, when scavengers were free to collect unsold produce; that it evokes beggars who rang bells to accompany their pleas; that it summons a memory of when the post of bell ringer at various churches was given to the neediest member of the congregation. My favorite, though, is Jean-Paul Clébert's: that the *cloche* is the sky, and all who sleep under it are its children.

A North African immigrant who became a clochard explained to Robert Giraud in the early 1950s that

> it's easy to become a clochard in Paris. One day you put on a jacket and you say, that's my shirt, and then you put on another jacket and this time you say, that's my jacket, and then you slip on a third—my overcoat. After that you go sit on the quais and you meet other guys like you, also clochards, and with them you smoke some butts and you drink some liters. At night you sleep under the bridges or on top of the sand heaps. When winter comes the clochards die like flies, because it's cold and they don't have on enough jackets, but that's how it goes. In spring others will come and the cycle will start all over again.

The clochard drinks and sleeps, and scrounges or begs or steals or sells junk on Sundays at Saint-Médard or works up schemes or sometimes takes on labor at Les Halles or on the docks. There were old clochards and young ones, mostly men and a few women, quite a few couples—Giraud met a man and a woman who'd been bumming together for twenty-seven years. For that matter he met a grandmother, father, and son, all clochards and happily drinking together. Some were lifers, at it since they were kids. Others had had previous lives, real or imagined. This one claimed he'd been a professor of philosophy, that one was a retired librarian from the Bibliothèque Nationale, another had spent forty years in the Bats d'Af (the Battalions d'Infanterie Légère d'Afrique, the disciplinary corps) and had the tattoos to prove it.

They slept on the quais—those by the Gare d'Austerlitz were particularly commodious and reasonably untroubled, and enterprising clochards built shelters out of crates and planks and maybe car parts. Or in decent weather sometimes they camped in vacant lots. Or else they slept in abandoned houses or sheds in courtyards or maybe empty attics in otherwise occupied houses. If you were bold and discreet you might climb up to the top story

An illustration by Théophile Steinlen for *Les soliloques du pauvre*, by Jehan Rictus, 1897

The racing-form vendor, circa 1910

of some apartment building and start trying doors—you had a good chance of eventually happening upon an unused storeroom. There were innumerable places to sleep with reasonable protection from weather, but you had to really want it. "All those hideouts are impossible for the ordinary piker down below to find, pounding the pavements with his nose in the air. You have to have a vital need, be obsessed with the idea of four walls and a roof, of a shelter from the elements, at the same time that you categorically refuse to be jammed in with others in a barracks." Giraud observed that "a sleeping clochard always looks like a corpse, ideally a headless corpse. Before checking out, as a matter of protection, he wraps his head in a newspaper or a rag, or hikes up his jacket or coat or shirt, whatever he has on. The ostrich, also a biped, does the same." The alternative, for the desperate or in times of police crackdowns, was called *refiler la comète*, "to retrace the path of the comet"—that is, to keep walking all night.

Until they were dispensed with by the city at some indefinable point within the past few decades (sent to whichever atoll or Siberia all the major cities of the Western world exiled their outsiders with the advent of the corporate age), the clochard had no history—or barely any, aside from periodic disturbances such as the edict of 1657, among others, forbidding begging, which dispersed the strongest to the provinces and the weakest to the hospitals. Then there was the life span of the newspaper *L'Intransigeant*, popularly known as *L'Intran*, the selling of which on street corners seemed to be reserved exclusively for clochards. Started in 1880, the paper initially marked the first resurgence of a left-wing press after the fall of the Commune in 1871—its entire staff was made up of former Communards, and it was a sign of hope for those returning to Paris from the penal colonies in New Caledonia after the general amnesty that same year. It was edited for decades by Henri Rochefort, a Communard himself, who changed his spots, however, and rallied in the late 1880s to the cause of the protofascist general Georges Ernest Boulanger, who nearly led a coup d'état in 1889—he lost his nerve at the last minute, and killed himself two years later—and then, in the following decade, broadcast virulently anti-Semitic propaganda during the Dreyfus Affair. *L'Intran*, which lasted until 1940 and managed a brief revival after the war, was viewed for much of its twentieth-century existence less as a journalistic voice than as a way of keeping its vendors alive. Victor Serge, newly arrived in Paris around 1910, made the acquaintance of an ancient vendor of *L'Intran* who was an amateur translator of Virgil and a disciple of Georges Sorel and the anarchist Mécislas Goldberg. Nevertheless, this man lived "in a terrifying world of the most extreme indigence, of willing surrender." He and his kind "descended in a direct line from the first beggars of Paris, perhaps from the lowest rabble of Lutetia . . . The clochard is a terminal being, his inner resources destroyed, who has learned to savor, feebly but tenaciously, the speck of vegetative existence that is allotted him."

The occasional clochard could become a character, appreciated by a wider audience, who bought him drinks for his diverting skills. One of these, although more an eccentric than a drunk, was André-Joseph Salis, known as Bibi-la-Purée (the latter part of his name signifies, basically, "trouble"), an occasional porter, shoe shiner, artist's model, go-between, beggar, thief (of umbrellas, in particular), and police informant, who served as boon companion to Paul Verlaine and was described as his secretary, his duties consisting chiefly of getting the poet home safely when he was blind drunk, which was often. Bibi-la-Purée, known for wearing unpredictable assortments of random clothes, was rendered by Picasso, Théophile Steinlen, and Jacques Villon, and celebrated in poems by Jehan Rictus and Raoul Ponchon as well as Verlaine himself, and even makes an appearance in the French translation of Joyce's *Ulysses* (where he stands in for the original's "Dusty Rhodes"); there were also two movies made about him, in 1925 and 1935. After Verlaine's death in 1896, Bibi-la-Purée made a living selling forged autographs and random found objects as having belonged to the poet; apparently he sold at least ten different walking sticks—"with a heavy heart"—as Verlaine's.

But then Verlaine, for all that he was the Prince of Poets (elected by his peers in 1894), edged awfully near to the status of clochard himself, shuttling from rat hole to public hospital, lying senseless on café banquettes or in doorways, saved from incarceration or certain death innumerable times only by his friends and his prestige. (Allegedly, some police commissioner or other

Bibi-la-Purée

Paul Verlaine on his corner banquette, 1890s

"Idleness." Illustration by Gavarni, 1835

"An original character," Latin Quarter, 1930s

ordained that he was never to be arrested.) In more than just his case, the distance between bohemia and the *cloche* could often seem perilously close. But that had always been the case. "Bohemia," derived from the name of what was believed to be the homeland of the Roma, was employed as a term for people "who lead a life without rules," in the words of the seventeenth-century chronicler Tallemant des Réaux, long before it enjoyed any artistic connotations. A comprehensive accounting of its original compass was provided by Karl Marx in his *Eighteenth Brumaire*: ". . . vagabonds, discharged soldiers, discharged jailbirds, escaped galley slaves, swindlers, mountebanks, lazzaroni, pickpockets, tricksters, gamblers, *macquereaux* [pimps], brothel-keepers, porters, literati, organ-grinders, ragpickers, knife-grinders, tinkers, beggars—in short, the whole indefinite, disintegrated mass, thrown hither and thither, which the French term *la bohème*." The insertion of "literati" into the list should be taken as served.

Most of us know about the origins of bohemia, directly or indirectly, from Henri Murger, who wrote the episodic semi-novel *Scènes de la vie de bohème* in serial installments for a paper called *Le Corsaire-Satan*—Baudelaire was another contributor, although not a friend—that were collected into a book in 1848. In that turbulent and sobering year of upheaval, Murger's sentimental tales of the nobility of art triumphing, if only spiritually, over disease, poverty, and neglect must have struck a chord with people who desperately needed an escapist fantasy version of their troubles. From his perch at the Café Momus, in the pre-Haussmann warren of narrow streets between the Louvre and Les Halles, Murger, a working-class belletrist with no money and many afflictions—purpura gave him a "macabre" complexion, his eyes watered incessantly—wrote stories about idealized versions of his friends. The details of their setting and plot have been worn transparent from passing through so many hands over so many years (Puccini's opera most obviously, and a score of film adaptations): the quest for inspiration, the pawning of possessions, the commodity value of the black frock coat, the knell that sounds as a slight tubercular cough. "Starving artists" has become a trade name for hucksters selling couch art from China in New Jersey motel conference rooms.

Murger's book has both endured and faded because of its

fervent, wholehearted, mulishly determined sentimentality. It branded bohemia, gave it an origin myth—the book is highfalutin pulp, but its premise and story are so elemental they might have fallen from a tree. The myth endures even now in some form or other, and it will probably last even when the actual fact of bohemia has no remaining living witnesses. Murger watered and tended his notion of bohemia, trying to keep it free from radicalism and crime, and from those categories enumerated by Marx. He made it into a sort of secular religion, all noble suffering and unjust persecution. In 1849 he wrote that it was "bordered on the north by hope, work, and gaiety, on the south by necessity and courage, on the west and east by slander and the hospital." Needless to say, while he may have created an enduring myth, he had no influence of any sort on the conduct of actual bohemians, then or later.

But artistic bohemia had already been in effect for a generation by the time Murger sat down to write. Its earliest manifestation may have been hatched beginning around 1818, by the students of Guillaume Guillon Lethière, a neoclassical painter and rival of Jacques-Louis David. Lethière, born in Guadeloupe, the illegitimate son of a French colonial administrator and a local woman of mixed race, lived and worked in a building called Le Childebert, on the street of the same name (now Rue Bonaparte, the house razed long ago in the lengthening of that street). His students, who included Théodore Rousseau and possibly the Johannot brothers, Tony and Alfred,* moved into the building, apparently a slum with crumbling stairs, broken windows, and sweating walls, which a certain Madame Legendre had bought for spare change in some property clearance during the revolution and allowed to slide into decrepitude. Soon they formed one of those tight, shifting, contentious, excitable, fickle, impassioned, impatient, incestuous, untidy coagulations of which students are uniquely capable. They seem to have been the first vanguard of Romanticism in French painting, anticipating the signal works of Géricault and Delacroix by half a decade. They began painting landscapes directly from nature rather than from

An American paperback edition of Henri Murger's *Scènes de la vie de bohème*, 1948

* Privat, the main source for the story, claims Géricault as well, but I have not been able to confirm this.

"Portrait of the creditor." Illustration by Gavarni, from *Clichy*, 1840

idealized classical models, for example, leading hostile critics to accuse them, in a phrase that was to be slung against vanguards for the next two hundred years, of waging a "crusade against beauty."

More significantly, they launched, perpetrated, and then squelched dozens of fads, in a way that feels familiar to us but appears to have had few precedents. There was, for example, a medieval fad, countering the prevailing obsession with Greece and Rome, which began with their reading cheap romances and soon had them wearing satin jerkins and gigot sleeves, carrying around lyres and short swords, and speaking in affected medievalese. They even changed their names accordingly: every Jean became a Jehan, every Pierre a Petrus, every Louis a Loÿs. Then they were on to the Scots (via Sir Walter Scott), the modern Greeks (thanks to Byron), the Turks (by way of Lamartine's *Méditations* and Hugo's *Orientales*), the Spaniards, pirates. They alternately grew their hair to their shoulders, after the English Cavaliers, and shaved it down to a stubble, after the Roundheads. At the theater they made a great show of yawning at tragedies and laughing at melodramas. "A great anxiety haunted them: everything had to be new at all costs."

By the time of the July Revolution in 1830, according to Privat, they had split into two camps: the Bouzingos and the Jeunes-France. While the latter carried on with their doublets and forked beards, the former had moved through the centuries and arrived at the revolution of 1789: they styled their hair after Robespierre, wore waistcoats like Marat's, boiled-leather or red felt hats, and carnations in their buttonholes, and carried cudgels. Not to be outdone, the Jeunes-France soon hit on the formula that Murger eventually made famous: they were dreamy, they were blasé, they brooded, nursed vague longings and inconsolable regrets, cultivated stark white complexions, suggested they were consumptive, turned to assorted religious affectations, such as quietism and Jansenism, and indulged in a "frightening" diet, apparently heavy on cornichons and vinegar. The Bouzingos, meanwhile, dropped the costume drama in favor of materialism and modernity: now they were all about beauty and youth; they drank and danced all night and slept all day. There were other camps as well, although Privat could remember only the Pur-Sangs and the Infatigables; another writer recalled the Badouillards. Somehow all of them faded away around 1838, leaving only a joint hatred of the bourgeoisie, whom they called "grocers." The bourgeoisie nevertheless did their part by converting those fads into consumable objects, in the form of revivalist tchotchkes, which were still turning up at flea markets a century and a half later: "clocks in the shape of cathedrals, Gothic bindings, letter openers in the form of daggers, inkwells and night-lights and innumerable other objects made to look like dungeons or medieval castles with drawbridges, posterns, brattices, machicolations, watchtowers, allures . . ."

Enid Starkie maintained that the Bouzingos and the Jeunes-France were the same group, the name having changed from the former to the latter in 1831. In any case, one or both of these cliques included former members of the Petit-Cénacle, many of whom had taken part in the first art riot, the planned set-to that accompanied the premiere of Victor Hugo's *Hernani* in 1830: Nerval, Gautier, Petrus Borel, Aloysius Bertrand, Jehan du Seigneur (those last three had respectively been christened Pierre, Louis, and Jean), Augustus MacKeat (Auguste Macquet), Philothée O'Neddy (Théophile Dondey), Xavier Forneret, Célestin Nanteuil. The membership overlapped as well with that of the Club des Hashischins. On occasion they drank wine from human skulls, sometimes dispensed with clothing, gave recitals on musical instruments they did not know how to play. Nerval occasionally pitched a tent in his room, or slept on the floor next to a carved Renaissance bed he claimed to be in thrall to. Most famously, he had a pet lobster named Thibault, rescued from a fishmonger's, which he, at least once, walked on a leash. Most of the Jeunes-France went on to respectable careers, although Borel took up an administrative post in Algeria but was driven by shifting political tides to subsistence farming, refusing to wear a hat because "nature knows what it's doing," and died of sunstroke. Nerval, of course, was found hanged with the belt of a woman's apron from the grille of a cabinetmaker's stall on Rue de la Vieille-Lanterne in 1855, wearing a hat, two shirts, two vests, and no coat, and with a tetragrammaton drawn in ink on the left side of his chest.

Henri Murger once told Alexandre Privat d'Anglemont,

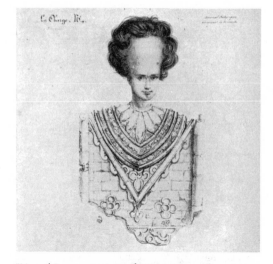

"Hugoth": a caricature of Victor Hugo as a Jeune-France, with appended verses by Petrus Borel, circa 1830

Alexandre Privat d'Anglemont. Woodcut by Écosse, 1857

"Vous n'êtes pas un bohème, mais la bohème"—he was bohemia itself. Privat was born in Sainte-Rose, Guadeloupe, in 1815, son of a freewoman of color and an unknown father. His mother, who was very well-to-do—she was among other things a slave owner—sent him to be educated in Paris, but at some point the family's fortunes declined, so that Privat was left to earn his own living, as a freelance writer. He returned to Point-à-Pitre only once, the story goes, and stayed for just twenty-three hours, this at a time when the Atlantic crossing took between twenty-five and thirty-five days. His primary allegiance was to Paris, and until his death from tuberculosis in 1859, he virtually owned the place, for all that he never had much money. He wore a "style-free" overcoat in all seasons and lived indifferently in furnished rooms, but never spent much time in any of them anyway, since he wrote in bars and cafés and occupied the better part of his days and nights walking. "Like [Louis-Sébastien] Mercier, he wrote his books with his legs," wrote his colleague Alfred Delvau. He seemingly knew everyone in the city, from clochards to Balzac, knew every saloon keeper by name, was esteemed by all. Once, when he was set upon by thieves, he exclaimed, "But I'm Privat!"

During the furor over the use by Alexandre Dumas and others of ghost writers (called, unfortunately, *nègres*), Privat made a case for them as prostitutes of the intellect; since those who were up in arms very likely visited prostitutes, they should understand. After Privat's death it was alleged that he signed his own name to poems actually by Baudelaire, Nerval, and others of his friends, but recent scholarship has raised the question of whether some attributions shouldn't run the other way around, one scholar demonstrating that Baudelaire's novella *La fanfarlo* (1847) was based on a story by Privat called "Une grande coquette" (1842). In a letter to Eugène Sue in 1843, Privat wrote:

> Yes, our literature is etched in acid. Yes, we use blood and fire as others employ tears and warmth. But we were nursed on alcohol, not milk. We have seen in our streets things more terrible and scenes more awful than we could ever describe. We haven't initiated twenty revolutions in forty or fifty years in order to stay where our grand-

parents were. If we deal in the terrible, it's because everything around us is terrible. If we are anxious and ill at ease in our society, it's because the future is there, more terrible and maybe more bloody than the past.

The masthead of *Le Chat Noir*, 1882

The future was every bit as terrible as Privat forecast, but bohemia's engagement with it fluctuated. While bohemians were prominent in the events of 1848 and in the Commune, bohemia more generally was a private and individual subjugation of class to the pure pursuit of art. Social mobility went both ways; an autodidact of humble background could conceivably, if he lived long enough, eventually occupy an armchair at the Académie Française, just as a rising young bourgeois could abandon studies in law or medicine to become an indigent poet, subsisting on café crèmes and whatever he could collect from passing the hat at the Chat Noir. There were, naturally, many more of the latter than of the former. Notice also the pronoun. Women were affiliated with bohemia, either as accessories, such as the original of Murger's Mimi, a maker of lace and artificial flowers named Lucille Louvet; or occasionally as inspirations, such as Marceline Desbordes-Valmore (1786–1859), the only woman Verlaine included in his 1884 anthology *Les poètes maudits*, a great visionary poet who led a life of such unrelieved misery she became known as Our Lady of Sorrows—although you do get the impression that for some bohemians the misery counted for more than the poems. There were also occasional anomalies, such as the adventurous Isabelle Eberhardt (1877–1904), who spent most of her life in Algeria and whose work was published only posthumously. But women did not start to become fully accredited members of bohemia until after World War II—the first widely recognized woman bohemian may have been the indestructible Juliette Greco—and even then their art often seemed to be accompanied in popular estimation by a hovering asterisk.

Juliette Greco, early 1950s

Bohemia, thus, was a kind of priesthood, demanding vows of poverty if not necessarily chastity, with a sideline in mystification. There was a kind of institutional bohemia, exemplified by the Club des Hydropathes, founded in 1878, which became Le Chat Noir, a salon-cum-nightclub as well as a magazine, which in turn lasted until the eve of the twentieth century. It drew tour-

Jules Jouy, 1880s

Les soliloques du pauvre, by Jehan Rictus, cover by Théophile Steinlen, 1897

ists and rubberneckers, and is preserved in popular culture by its trademark haloed feline, designed by Steinlen, but its output and membership ran in every direction. There was always a jocular, bibulous side, represented by its early motto "Wine is a red liquid, except in the morning, when it is white"—the mot is by Charles Cros (1842–1888), a considerable poet as well as an inventor who experimented with color photography and designed a prototype of the phonograph. Its contributors included Verlaine, Mallarmé, and Erik Satie, as well as future Academicians, in addition to, for example, the anarchist and street fighter Jules Jouy; or Édouard Dubus, who died at age thirty of a morphine overdose in a public urinal on Place Maubert;* or Jehan Rictus (né Gabriel Randon de Saint-Amand), who personified the romance of poverty and gave voice to it in his *Soliloquies of the Poor Man* (1897), written in slang and imperishably illustrated by Steinlen; always unworldly, Rictus devolved toward right-wing ultranationalism by the time he died in 1933.

Le Chat Noir wound up an institution on the boulevards, a nightclub and tourist trap decorated with great numbers of pictures of black cats by Steinlen (Richard Harding Davis: "Upon one panel hundreds of black cats race over the ocean, in another they are waltzing with naiads in the woods, and in another they are whirling through space over red-tiled roofs, followed by beautiful young women, gendarmes, and boulevardiers in hot pursuit"). Well before that, it had initiated the bohemian hegira to Montmartre from the Left Bank. Montmartre, up on its heights, was a quiet country village in the late nineteenth century, atmospherically distant from the city below, with tree-lined lanes and old farmhouses and quite a few remaining windmills. Its bars tended to be rustic taverns with names to match: Le Clairon des Chasseurs or Le Vieux Chalet. Le Lapin Agile (which still exists, after a fashion) was an ancient *guinguette* locally known as Au Rendezvous des Voleurs (the Thieves' Hangout); around 1880 the walls were covered with portraits of famous murderers (Lacenaire, Troppmann, Papavoine), after which it was called Le

* His 1886 sonnet "Béatitude," about an "illuminated" drunk who before passing out blows kisses to the moon, which perhaps reciprocates, joins hands with Li Po (701–762) on one side and the American Beat poets of the 1950s on the other.

The Lapin Agile in winter, circa 1910

Cabaret des Assassins. Not long after that the owner hired the illustrator André Gill to paint a sign showing a rabbit escaping from a cooking pot, although it wasn't until 1903, when Aristide Bruant bought it, that it came to be called by its familiar name, which also happened to pun on *lapin à Gill*. And then it quickly became a local for what was shaping up to be the foundational Montmartre crew of the early twentieth century: Picasso, Apollinaire, Utrillo, Carco, Mac Orlan, Fargue, and so on. And they in turn drew hundreds of epigones, who irrevocably altered the place, in what is certainly one of the earliest examples of an artistic vanguard paving the way for commerce and eventual gentrification. Ruefully looking back in 1929, Daniel Halévy wrote, "The Chat Noir was merely a sally, a frothy confection drunk within a few months. But it turned bad, there were disastrous consequences, and it brought to Montmartre the craze that ruined it. First there was the Moulin Rouge . . . and then the innumerable bars and their innumerable crooks.*

   Still, the early bohemians in Montmartre did not have an easy time of it. The Lapin Agile was regularly invaded by *apaches*, and the owner's son was killed in a robbery attempt. Bo-

Little birds of Montmartre struck down by winter. Illustration by Adolphe Willette, 1880s

---

* Halévy is a cautionary example of where rueful nostalgia can lead. Despite the fact that he had been a Dreyfusard—as well as an old-fashioned liberal, an important literary editor, a friend of Proust and Georges Sorel—and that he was of Jewish descent, his misgivings about change ultimately led him to become a public apologist for Pétain and the Vichy Republic.

An alley in Montmartre, circa 1910

The home of a popular singer in Montmartre, circa 1910

hemians were assaulted on the streets by thugs from the Goutte-d'Or and Château Rouge, who put out the gaslights by throwing rocks; some were murdered: "Blond, laughing Pierrot bled to death one night on Rue du Poteau; the ferocious Lagneau was knifed in the back; Mousseron, the deserter, went down on Rue Varon with six bullets in his gut; Critien was killed as he was changing hotels to escape from his enemies; little Pingouin was found hanged, his hands tied behind his back, from the fence-rail on Rue du Mont-Cenis."

And many bohemians themselves wound up in jail, in the penal colonies, or in the Bats d'Af. That was a direct consequence of their poverty, which could be extreme. The young Picasso for a time did not own shoes, and had to borrow a pair whenever he went out; he also didn't have a chair, and had to paint sitting on the floor with his canvas leaning against the wall. Carco stole milk bottles from doorsteps, stole gas from streetlights, roasted meat on the hallway gas jet, sometimes climbed up a lamppost to heat a kettle on the flame, once in a restaurant dribbled gravy on the slate on which his bill was written, then called over the house dog to lick it clean. The artist André Dignimont was skilled at heisting coin machines; a poet named Georges Banneret developed a specialty of stealing photo albums from cathouses to flog the dirty pictures one by one. Many, such as Modigliani, squatted in empty houses; they were usually furnished with furniture stolen from café terraces, and heated with firewood stripped from the wooden pavements of the exterior boulevards.

Anyone who has spent time in bohemia will recognize how responses to difficult material conditions can magically be transformed into fads. The fact that the Montmartre bohemians had no choice but to get their clothes from the Saint-Ouen flea market, and that weird clothes were cheaper there because they were less in demand, led them to try to outdo one another in the outlandishness of their getups. They wore Rembrandt hats, cavalry trousers, sailors' jerseys, Spanish capes, mechanics' jumpsuits, dusters, London coachmen's capes, hooded cloaks, priests' hats, jockeys' caps, lavallieres; the women sometimes unearthed elaborate ballgowns or the short eighteenth-century jackets called *pet en l'air* (fart in the open)—it was as if they were replaying all the fads of the Childebert at once. Since oddball health regimes were

A drinking party in a Montmartre backyard, 1910s

also, almost inevitably, in effect, people went barefoot for reasons of "circulation" and wore colorful turbans that allegedly relieved headaches. Their parties were as loud and disruptive as things could get before the advent of amplified music: firecrackers, animal noises, breaking bottles, obscene songs, target practice with revolvers. In Le Bateau Lavoir, the crooked house (the source of its name remains obscure) on Rue Ravignan inhabited by Picasso, Fernande Olivier, Max Jacob, Juan Gris, Pierre Mac Orlan, Kees Van Dongen, and André Salmon, there were hidden staircases, concealed rooms, something like an oubliette—and one faucet for the entire building. Their famous banquet for Le Douanier (Henri) Rousseau in 1908 was marred somewhat by the fact that the food, ordered from a local hash house, didn't arrive until noon the following day.

The Montmartre bohemia before the First World War remains the gold standard, as much for the luxuriant eccentricity of its trappings as for the fact that so many of its players caught the brass ring. Subsequent manifestations never quite rose to that level of panache. The Montparnasse bohemia of the 1910s and '20s had its own set of weirdos, including a man who dressed in full cowboy regalia and addressed his wife, in Native American duds, as "squaw"; his name was Le Scouëzec and he made a living painting Breton seascapes. That scene is preserved in memory chiefly because of its internationalism, however. La Rotonde, Le Dôme, and La Coupole hosted Lenin and Trotsky

An illustration by Théophile Steinlen for *Les soliloques du pauvre*, by Jehan Rictus, 1897

before 1917 and assorted Americans afterward. Despite the gilded recollections of so many of the latter gang, poverty was as much a feature there as elsewhere. Blaise Cendrars lived in a fleabag called Hôtel des Étrangers, an eighteenth-century house cut up into tiny cubicles:

> You could do everything without having to get up from your narrow bed: wash in the minuscule sink of tarnished and battered tin; cook an egg or reheat insipid vegetables by sticking the aluminum dish on top of the gas jet (which worked only if you fed it a constant stream of two-sous coins through a slot); or open the door, something you rarely did because you had long before abandoned all hope of anyone coming up the stairs and knocking.

The same holds true for the Saint-Germain-des-Prés bohemia after World War II, remembered now for its jazz, its multiracialism, its airless cellar nightclubs, and of course its existentialism, a word that came to mean everything and nothing. But at least as much of that bohemia was happening in the Algerian cafés of Maubert, the clochard cafés of the Contrescarpe, the squats and vacant lots and ruins of the city's fringes. From that other end of bohemia, Guy Debord wrote:

> Paris was a city so beautiful that many people preferred to be poor there than rich somewhere else . . . There was then, on the Left Bank of the river, a neighborhood where the negative held court . . . Those who assembled there seemed to have taken as their sole principle of action, as their public opening gambit, the secret which it is said the Old Man of the Mountain transmitted in his final moments only to the most faithful of his fanatical lieutenants: "Nothing is true, everything is permitted" . . . It was the labyrinth best designed for catching travelers. Those who stopped there for two days never left, or at least not while it still existed . . . Nobody left those couple of streets and couple of tables where the climactic point of history had been found.

9

Show People

The great fairs of the Middle Ages, which could last entire seasons and involved various proportions of commerce and entertainment, were broken up by the revolution. The Saint-Germain fair, which had begun in 1176 and ran from February 3 to Palm Sunday (which could fall anywhere from mid-March to mid-April), was unlike the others in having permanent structures. There is no record of what those buildings were used for the rest of the year, but it is assumed that some sort of shows went on in them at least some of the time; the fair became a year-round covered market in 1818. In the meantime, the whole class of clowns, jugglers, and mountebanks associated with it had migrated out to what was then the edge of the city, the old wall of the Farmers-General near Château d'Eau, the head of Boulevard du Temple. In 1792, when the restrictive laws governing theaters were overturned, a mass of showplaces began opening along that thoroughfare, hastily rigged-up houses that might last for a season or two and then be replaced by something else. The more spectators came, the more the street itself began to fill up with open-air entertainments, food stalls, ambulatory commerce, and, naturally, pickpockets.

The crowds were not only huge, but thoroughly mixed: the bourgeoisie and even the aristocracy came out to see. By the 1820s the boulevard had become a full-service, year-round, seven-days-a-week entertainment district, the first of its kind in Paris. The

Street vendors on the Boulevard du Crime, 1830s

principal theaters, many of them neoclassical affairs with colonnades, stretched principally along the north side of the boulevard in a line that today would reach the center of Place de la République. (Haussmann, who nursed a particular hatred of the boulevard and its culture, not only razed all the theaters in 1862, but, like the Romans plowing salt into the ruins of Carthage, realigned the boulevard so that it would not correspond to that part of its course.) Running east from Porte Saint-Martin were the Ambigu-Comique (the only theater with an illuminated sign), the Cirque Olympique (later the Cirque Impérial), the Folies-Dramatiques, the Gaîté, the Funambules, the Délassements-Comiques, the Petit-Lazari, the Cirque d'Hiver, and the Théâtre Déjazet.* Interspersed were cafés, restaurants, shops, and a wax museum, while a tree-lined allée running down the center of the boulevard sheltered wrestlers' huts, acrobats' tents, shacks containing assorted freaks and dime-museum attractions, magicians' open-air stages, lottery booths, and small shopkeepers' displays. In motion all along the boulevard were acrobats, stilt walkers, sword swallowers, clowns, strongmen, and stongwomen. Buses—horse-drawn *omnibus hippomobiles*, that is—began plying the route in 1828. By some unspoken general accord, the whole carnival stopped abruptly at Rue Charlot.

It was called the Boulevard du Crime (a name devised by the press) not because of its omnipresent pickpockets and purse snatchers but because of its theaters' propensity for histrionic melodrama. In 1836, for example, you could take in *The Horrors of Misery, The Wretched Woman, The Widow's Three Daughters, The Orphans of Pont Notre-Dame, The Spot of Blood, The Tissue of Horrors.* There were other sorts of fads as well; Georges Cain records a week in 1830 when almost every spectacle revolved around Napoléon: *Bonaparte, Artillery Lieutenant; Napoléon in Berlin, or the Gray Frock Coat; The Schoolboy of Brienne, or the Little Corporal;* and *Military Glory in Seven Tableaux,* among others. In the first six months of 1837, to choose a random year, there were 140 plays presented in Paris, three-quarters of them on the boulevard (the remainder were staged in the theaters of

A map of Haussmann's Place de la République laid over a map of what it displaced: the Boulevard du Temple, a.k.a. du Crime. From Georges Cain's *Promenades dans Paris*, 1906

---

* The only institution to have survived is the Cirque d'Hiver, now on Rue Amelot, in a nearby neighborhood where a modest theater district subsequently took root.

"Hoist that rag!" Illustration by Théophile Steinlen for Aristide Bruant's *Dans la rue*, vol. 1, 1889

the upper classes, such as the venerable Comédie-Française and the Odéon). You can get a pretty accurate idea of what the place was like from Marcel Carné and Jacques Prévert's great 1945 film *The Children of Paradise*. The crowds, the chaos, the sideshows, and the rivalries are all there, as is the Théâtre des Funambules, given over to miming because it wasn't certified to present spectacles involving speech. (Many restrictive laws concerning theaters had returned after the revolution.) And while Arletty's character, Garance, is an invention, her four suitors are all based on real people: the actors Baptiste Deburau (played by Jean-Louis Barrault) and Frédérick Lemaître (Pierre Brasseur), the criminal Pierre-François Lacenaire (Marcel Herrand), and Édouard, Comte de Montray (Louis Salou), inspired by the Duc de Morny.

The balcony where the poorest members of the audience sat was indeed sometimes known as the *paradis*, although more often the *poulailler*, the "chicken coop." Just like Bowery theater audiences impatiently yelling, "Hoist that rag!" the crowds here shouted "La toile!" While watching, people ate fried potatoes, sausages, cooked apples and pears, all bought from itinerant vendors outside, and kids enjoyed dropping food and paper remains from the balcony onto the heads of those below. Those did not include the upper classes or the intelligentsia, who preferred the

Actors at the Théâtre Français, 1840s

A photograph by Nadar of Baptiste Deburau's son Charles in his father's trademark costume, 1854–55

loges. Nerval, Gautier, Charles Nodier, the songwriter Pierre-Jean de Béranger, the actresses Mademoiselle Mars and Mademoiselle Georges (of the Comédie-Française and the Odéon, respectively), and the mezzo-soprano La Malibran were all regulars at the Funambules. As the director Nestor Roqueplan told Victor Hugo, "Fashionable people go to the theater the way whores go to church."

The theaters were exceedingly hot and airless in the summer, and generally underlit. That in itself was not a bad thing, since fewer lights meant fewer chances of fire. There were frequent fires, many of them caused by special effects (simulations of fireworks, lightning, explosions, volcanoes), and many involved fatalities. The Gaîté was once devastated when a stagehand threw lycopodium powder (a flash powder made from the dry spores of club moss plants) on a wood fire; nevertheless, it was completely rebuilt in just six months. There was active black market traffic in ticket stubs at the intermissions. The claque (those paid to applaud) was an actual, organized, hierarchical profession that insisted on experience, for all that employees tended to be recruited in local cafés from a social layer just a hair above the criminal underworld. In Balzac's *La Cousine Bette*, Olympe Bijou, a teenage embroiderer newly settled in with the owner of a novelty shop, gets herself seduced by a claqueur. Her mother complains to her friend, the singer Josépha:

> "He's a *loafer*, like all the good-looking boys, a *panderer* of plays, of all things! He's the idol of the Boulevard du Temple, where he works on all the new plays and *eases the actresses onto the stage*, as he says . . . He has relished liquor and billiards since birth. 'That's no profession!' I told Olympe."
> "Alas, it is," said Josépha.

Jean-Gaspard Deburau, known by his stage name, Baptiste, was born Jan Kaspar Dvořák in 1796 in Bohemia. He probably began as a stagehand at the Funambules, and performed there continuously from about 1819 until his death in 1846. Before he became a major star in the late 1820s, he was paid meagerly and lived in the theater's cellar with his dog, Coquette, late of the

Théâtre des Chiens Savants. He was known and universally loved for his character, Pierrot, based on the commedia dell'arte archetype that had gradually shed its roots since its seventeenth-century importation and acquired a Parisian personality. He devised the enduring costume that Barrault wears in the movie, consisting of an oversize white cotton collarless blouse and pants and a black skullcap. (There is a lovely series of photographs by Nadar of Deburau's son Charles in that costume.) He played roles other than Pierrot, but like Chaplin's Tramp, all his roles seem to have been infused with the same spirit. The character, however, was considerably coarser, more knowing, lecherous, vengeful, even malicious than the one attributed to him in posthumous legend, which is the one Barrault presents: tragic, long-suffering, moonstruck. That in turn seems to have been devised by his Romantic admirers, who saw what they wished to see, perhaps under the influence of Watteau's circa 1719 painting of an incongruously sad Pierrot. Gautier, for example, described him as "pale, slender, in colorless clothes, always starved and beaten, the ancient slave, the proletarian, the pariah, the passive and bereft creature who gloomily but slyly takes in the orgies and excesses of his masters." That Pierrot, who would have baffled and disgusted Deburau's core following of street urchins, was the one who proved more useful for the salon, and he was perpetuated in such things as Arnold Schoenberg's 1912 song cycle, *Pierrot Lunaire*.

The theater industry on the boulevard was a cold and unforgiving thing, run like a cartel. In a way that is reminiscent of much later Hollywood practice, plays tended to bear three or four writing credits, not counting the ghosts who presumably did the brunt of the actual work—you sense the hovering shadow of the executive producer. Actors fared just as badly as playwrights, locked into draconian contracts that paid them little and severely restricted their autonomy; there were numerous suicides in both camps. Frédérick Lemaître, who was probably the biggest star the boulevard ever produced, couldn't pay his rent in 1825, when he was already a headliner. Lemaître, who had tried being a *funambule* (a wire walker) but kept falling off, found success in 1823, in a play called *L'Auberge des Adrets*, in which he played a bandit named Robert Macaire. The three authors had intended Macaire as a tragic figure, but Lemaître, finding the

Robert Macaire as a business manager. Illustration by Honoré Daumier, from *Le Charivari*, 1836

Tabarin and company. Illustration by Célestin Nanteuil, 1840s

A rope dancer and a balancing pole. Illustration by J. J. Grandville, from *Fables de Florian*, 1842

language pompous and the melodrama lugubrious, decided to play it for laughs, enlisting the complicity of the actor in the role of Macaire's sidekick, Bertrand. His decision was an immediate and resounding success, and it provided Lemaître with a part he would play for decades (as it did others; there were periods when the boulevard featured three or four Robert Macaire vehicles simultaneously). He kept refining the character, for example basing his wardrobe on that of a figure he spotted on the boulevard one day, a tramp who seemed to imagine himself a dandy. Robert Macaire came to embody his era, in all its cynicism, vanity, and greed—Daumier devoted more than a hundred lithographs to the figure, imagining him in almost every social role—and he was widely deplored by moralists upset at the notion of laughable robberies and clownish murders. He wasn't much liked by the authorities, either; the police interrupted one performance in which Macaire, disguised as a ragpicker, reached into his sack and pulled out the royal crown. Even death couldn't stop him: he stole the keys to heaven from Saint Peter and managed to elude the devil and corrupt all the angels.

Street theater had been around since the dawn of time, probably, most of it unrecorded until the seventeenth century, when Antoine Girard created his character Tabarin, with his brother Philippe playing his crony, Mondor. They were charlatans, which means that they were vendors of quack medicine, who put on a show to attract customers—that is, they were in spirit very much like the presenters of medicine shows who plied the rural United States until sometime around World War II (and their characters sound like the ancestors of Mr. Tambo and Mr. Bones in minstrelsy). They were not the first to engage in this sort of entertainment, but somehow they were leagues ahead of the competition. People of all classes flocked to their makeshift stage on Place Dauphine, where they performed backed by a hurdy-gurdy and viols; Molière and La Fontaine both acknowledged Tabarin's influence. He seems to have influenced the Punch and Judy puppet plays as well, and the name Tabarin became synonymous with a kind of street performance that is longer on wits than on production values. He was, then, the patron saint of all the shows that lined the boulevard and its central allée.

There were the clowns, who had formerly worked the fairs

and who blended physical comedy with dense and rapid word-play: Bobêche, Galimafré, Gringalet, Faribole. There were the *parades*, which were essentially a series of sketches worked out on a bare stage with just a couple of actors, comic and straight man, say, or city mouse and country mouse. There were diverse incarnations of the commedia dell'arte figures: Arlequin, Paillasse (Pagliacci), Polichinelle (Pulcinella), and there was the puppet Guignol, a purely French creation (circa 1796 in Lyon), who nevertheless drew from the same well. There were the funambulists, who worked on a wire, and the *acrobates*, who worked on a rope. Petit-Diable danced on the rope with eggs attached to his shoes, not breaking any; *le beau* Dupuis specialized in languorous, dreamlike dances that made audiences forget he was on a rope at all. Allegedly some grande dame became so passionate about Dupuis that she murdered him in a fit of jealousy; the matter was then suppressed.

A saltimbanque. Illustration by J. J. Grandville, from *Un autre monde*, 1844

Nerval was particularly impressed by the girl who lifted a weight (supposedly sixty pounds) with her hair. The "fireproof Spaniard" took a bath in boiling oil. The *jeune fille électrique* was a Bretonne who emitted something she called an "influx," which could move furniture from a distance. One man would break huge rocks set on the belly of his female partner, who lay on a thin mattress on an outdoor stage. There was the eight-hundred-pound woman, the living skeleton, the magician who would grind up a watch with a mortar and pestle and then miraculously reconstitute it. Then there were the attractions shrouded by canvas walls—"Approchez, approchez," shouted the barkers—the spider who played the trumpet, the offspring of a hare and a carp. One barker would announce, "Here you can see what God himself cannot." Once inside, the marks would find themselves alone with a mirror. "Now you see what God in his majesty cannot see," the pitch would continue, "your equal. God, who is singular and unique, will never see his equal." And then there were "secret museums," although a law of 1841 cracked down on those, prohibiting public exhibitions of "anatomical representations or images of disease." Still, in 1846, Victor Hugo went to see a *tableau vivant*: an English troupe, posed in various attitudes on a wooden disk that slowly revolved, clad in pink body stockings that "covered them from the feet to the neck and

Carnival, 1840s

The Descente de la Courtille, 1840s

were so fine and transparent that you could see not only their toes, their navels, and their nipples, but even their veins and the color of the least blemish on all parts of their bodies. Below the waist, the fabric thickened and you could distinguish nothing but shapes . . . They were poor girls from London. They all had dirty fingernails."

The anarchic spirit of the boulevard spread to carnival, which had perhaps always been uproarious but now became truly unbridled. Carnival lasted from the Feast of Saint Martin on November 11 until Ash Wednesday, which can fall anywhere from early February to early March, and its end, Mardi Gras, was the occasion for balls and parties all over the city. Nowhere was the celebration more vigorous than at the Courtille, an agglomeration of *guinguettes* and other places of amusement that lay just outside the Belleville gate, which was roughly on the present site of the Belleville Métro station. In 1822 a certain Cirque Moderne, the members of which had been roistering in the Courtille, decided to parade into the city on Ash Wednesday at daybreak, just when the *guinguettes* were closing. A huge drunken crowd spontaneously joined the parade, and more and more people thickened the flow as it made its way down to the Hôtel de Ville. Thus was created an instant tradition, the Descente de la Courtille, which lasted three or four decades and has remained proverbial even now.

The furor was intense, and cut across the classes. A liter of wine cost ten sous in the *guinguettes* then (almost nothing), so the crowd was fueled. The rich would compete with one another in bestowing champagne and oysters; the hero of this potlatch was an English peer named Lord Seymour, known to the crowd as Milord Arsouille (Lord Hoodlum), who cuts an ambiguous figure in the literature, more of a provocateur than a benefactor. People threw candy, eggs, eggshells filled with flour, entire bags of flour, cooked apples, raw fruits and vegetables. They yelled insults—at least one manual was published giving instructions on how to insult others without provoking violence. Imagine the crush, the roar, the sudden surges, the invisible eruptions that rippled the crowd from blocks away, the red-faced giddiness always on the verge of becoming something else, the odors. It couldn't last forever, of course—it would eventually have led to riot.

The Fleshy Ox, circa 1910

A fishing float, Mi-Carême parade, 1905

Before the century was out, carnival had been channeled into ritual and commerce. Some of the ritual was ancient, such as the procession of the Boeuf Gras (the Fleshy Ox) on the Sunday preceding Ash Wednesday, which was first recorded in the thirteenth century and is probably much older. (After long lapses in the twentieth century, it was revived in 1998.) The Mi-Carême, meanwhile, had been reserved for the washerwomen since at least the eighteenth century, a day when every *lavoir* would elect a queen and all the employees would parade, merrily borrowing the finest accoutrements that had been left with them for cleaning. In 1891 the city intervened; a committee named a Queen of Queens, who was issued a crown, a robe, and a flower-bedecked carriage in which to ply the streets. In 1898 the city's markets annexed the ceremony, cutting out the washerwomen, and within a few years the title came with sponsorships and endorsements. Until the First World War the queens looked distinctly like laboring women, strong and stout; from 1919 on they looked increasingly like beauty contestants. (The practice died out after 1939, but it, too, has recently been revived.)

Carnival parades, with their ever more extravagant floats and attractions, no longer invited participation; crowds were restricted to ogling from the sidewalk and, of course, spending their money. In carnival season the streets and squares were clogged with booths selling food and drink, games of chance, and all sorts of useless merchandise that caught the drunken eye. Carco gauged the temperature in 1914:

> The whores and hoodlums crowded together in the glare of the acetylene torches, which blazed with a hiss and spread through the booths a harsh light reflected indiscriminately by the red drapes, the ornate mirrors, the gilded moldings, the painted wood shelves, and the jars of English toffee. Rain beat down on the canvas roofs, which the wind intermittently inflated. Water dripped down and puddled. The stilled merry-go-rounds, covered for the night with immense tarpaulins, glowed faintly from afar. A rank odor permeated the place: wet wood, tar, face powder, humidity. Fernande passed from one cluster to another, briefly eager to see how a player was doing at the shooting gallery, then disappointed by the meager thrills of the barrel organs, the photographers' booths, the exhausted jokes of the old clowns. One of these, decked out in green cast-offs and a flat cap, was barking the attractions of a tent of exotic dancers. The locals exchanged smiles, because they knew that the most beautiful of the undressed girls on offer within was none other than Pivoine, whom they all knew and despised. Pivoine, alias Marie-Madame, the object of their derision, fluttered on the threshold of the booth. They parodied her gestures and said cruel things

to her. When the barker enumerated her charms, she displayed them with a pathetic submissiveness.

All the year round there were dance halls, as there had been for centuries. "Before 1848," wrote a contemporary, "you couldn't walk down any street in Paris without noticing, above a wineshop, a pitifully flickering lantern on which was written *Bal*." Some of them were famous, such as the eponymous pleasure spot on Rue de la Grande-Chaumière, originally opened in 1783 by an Englishman named Tickson, which in the early nineteenth century was credited with having popularized the polka and birthed the Robert-Macaire and above all the *chahut*. Inspired by the Andalusian *cachucha*, a dance in which women employed every part of their body, the *chahut* was most famous for its high kick, which got it banned for a while as an outrage to public morals. Even though it wasn't until much later in the century that dancers went as far as "kicking the moon," and even though after the ban was lifted there was always an inspector on hand to see that displays did not become too licentious, the dance still was never considered entirely acceptable in polite company. Along the way it did engender a much greater success: the cancan, a theatrical dance executed by professionals before an audience rather than attempted by customers in a hall.

The *chahut* was also practiced, and the cancan may have been born, at the Bal Chicard, on Rue Jean-Jacques-Rousseau just off Les Halles. Privat thought its name was the source of the word *chic*. He described it as "the most incredible jumble of social nuances, the oddest kettle of fish, faces impossible to reconcile with one another, occult and inexplicable contrasts," and while Privat cheerfully admitted he'd never been there, the idea is borne out by Gavarni's portraits of the clientele, and Gavarni was there every week. Outlandish costumes and wildly stylized attitudes predominate. Its dances were said to be especially unbridled, and small wonder: the orchestra apparently comprised ten solo pistols (or so Privat claims), four bass drums, three cymbals, twelve cornets, six violins, and a bell. To the racket produced by this ensemble the customers perhaps engaged in the waltz, the polka, the mazurka, the *redowa*, the *roberka*, the fricassée, the gavotte, the schottische, the varsoviana, the polichinelle, the hongroise, the

A masked ball. Illustration by Célestin Nanteuil, 1840s

The *chahut*. Drawing by Constantin Guys, probably 1850s

"A dozen oysters and my heart." "On your honor?"
Illustration by Gavarni, from *Les débardeurs*, 1840

meunière, the russe, the *sicilienne orientale*. In that same era the Bal Mabille, off the Champs-Élysées, was the elegant home of "the most transcendent *polkeuses*" (Gautier), but the ordinary stiffs had a great many places of their own to choose from; it was estimated around 1835 that fifty thousand people attended the *bals* every Sunday.

Montmartre was especially dense with dance halls: the Grand Turc, the Molière, the Reine Blanche, the Ermitage, the Château Rouge, the Tivoli (*ancien* and *nouveau*), the Bal Roger, the Rocher Suisse, the Élysée Montmartre on Boulevard Rochechouart, which opened in 1807 and lasted (as a concert hall for its last half century or so) until it was gutted by fire in 2011, and the Boule Noire on the same thoroughfare (founded in 1822 and still running, also now as a concert hall), which was originally the Boule Blanche, but over time the *boule* got dirty. The Goncourt brothers visited and thought it sinister that all the women were dressed in black, while the men looked like hoodlums and the dances were animated by a "bestial" joy. There was the Folies Robert, also on the boulevard, the habituées of which included dancers with such monikers as Chicardinette, Élisa Belles-Jambes, Le Bébé de Cherbourg, Bertha le Zouzou, and one Jeanne d'Arc, so called because "she was burned by the English, which in those days was another word for creditors."

There was the *guinguette* and dance hall at the Moulin de la Galette on Rue Lepic, a beloved Sunday outing destination depicted by nearly every Impressionist (the windmill still stands, although now a private residence). Down the hill, on Boulevard de Clichy, on the site of the ancient and "rotting" Reine Blanche, was and remains the celebrated Moulin Rouge. It was primarily a music hall, a showcase for revues, rather than a dance hall proper (at least after 1900); it was explicitly intended for the slumming rich; and the cancan was already old news by the time it opened in 1889, for all that it has ever since claimed to be its birthplace. Still, the Moulin Rouge is worth noting for the quality of its terpsichoreans, many of them painted by Toulouse-Lautrec: Jane Avril, La Goulue (the Glutton), Grille d'Égout (Sewer Grate), La Môme Fromage (the Cheese Kid), Nini Pattes-en-l'Air (Feet in the Air), Rayon d'Or (Golden Ray), Sauterelle (Grasshopper), Clair-de-Lune, Cha-tu-Kon, Cléopâtre,

The resident troupe at the Bal Tabarin, circa 1900

Cascadienne, Cri-Cri. La Goulue (Louise Weber; 1869–1929), whose most celebrated male dance partner was Valentin le Désossé (the Boneless), enjoyed and endured a career of extremes. From inhabiting the *hôtel* owned by La Païva, mistress of Napoléon III, on Avenue du Bois, she went to jail "after some lark," then became a lion tamer in a traveling zoo, then a laundress, "then nothing," and spent her last years drinking in the Zone.

The Bal Bullier, Boulevard de Montparnasse, circa 1910

The dance halls of Montmartre were by that point primarily known as showcases for prostitution, but there were dance halls in most other neighborhoods. In Montparnasse, the venerable Bal Bullier, on the site of the original Closerie des Lilas, was the preserve of such names as Nina Belles-Dents (Nice Teeth), Peau de Satin (Satin Skin), Bouffe-Toujours (Keep Eating), Henriette Zonzon, Isabelle l'Aztèque, Canard. In the Marais, the Bal des Gravilliers, opened in 1863, was at first a homey place where the music was provided by a couple of Italian *pifferari* on harp and violin, and where the house provided china and cutlery, although they didn't serve food: clients would bring their own or buy from purveyors on the street. After 1900, however, it became a *bal d'apaches*. According to André Warnod, those gentlemen were "persuaded of their superiority because of the attention accorded them by writers . . . They might be dressed like any other bourgeois, but you could spot them right away, because of . . . their hands, their big, thick stranglers' hands, their short-fingered hands." Nearby was the Bal Charlemagne, known as the Bal des Moutons, since *moutons* (literally "sheep") then signified police informants, who were prominent among the clientele. In Charonne stood the Bal des Lilas, known as the Bal des Punaises (cockroaches or bedbugs), which had, tucked away behind the orchestra, a bench reserved for women too drunk to dance, and those who lacked shoes. On Rue de la Gaîté was the Bal Grateau, "where the dances were nothing but battles, fisticuffs, quadrilles, obscenely swaying women unbuttoned down to their waists, hiccuping drunks." The area around the Contrescarpe was home to the Bal de la Cave ("a stinking hell"), the Bal du Vieux Chêne ("paradise for ragpickers and fifteen-year-old hoodlums"), and the Bal des Vaches ("a bandits' roost"). On the other side of town, by the Quai de Javel, endured the "ignoble" Bal

Le Bal des Puces, a novel by Aristide Bruant, 1910

des Singes (monkeys), where the women smoked pipes and the whores "threw themselves into disgusting saturnalias."

Rue de Lappe, near the Bastille, was the center of the Auvergnat population, who in the mid-nineteenth century went "to the musette, the Auvergnat dances, and never to the French [*sic*] dance halls, because the Auvergnats . . . remain isolated like the Hebrews in Babylon." They danced to their own music, played on the musette, a bagpipe smaller and higher pitched than the Scottish or Irish model. At some point, though, probably in the late 1880s or early 1890s, while the non-Auvergnat dance halls still mostly featured trumpets and violins, the musette slowly began to be replaced by the accordion, an instrument imported by Italian immigrants. As that occurred, the music itself began to change, the Auvergnat strain compounded by the Italian, with a dose of Parisian song, the result becoming known as musette, so that by 1900 a *bal-musette* would have been increasingly unlikely to feature the original instrument. Not everyone approved, of course. Addressing his compatriots in 1896, the head of a league of Auvergnat musicians warned that "where the accordion and the violin have replaced the musette, and the *chahut* has overtaken the bourrée, there, too, openhearted laughter has been replaced by the knife." He had a point, since the familial atmosphere of the Auvergnat dance hall, open only on Sundays, was rapidly giving way to a seven-day bacchanal heavily infested with *apaches*. But it was a moment of syncretic change in popular music the world over, and musette was developing in parallel with jazz in New Orleans, tango in Buenos Aires, *danzón* in Cuba, paseo in Trinidad, and *biguine* in the French Antilles—all of them hybrids that bridged nations and continents, the music of diaspora.

Anyway, not all was violence and dissolution. A typical hall on Rue de Lappe, seen by Warnod:

> It's free to enter, but generally you pay for every dance with tokens bought from the cashier, four or five sous apiece. Right in the middle of a waltz or a polka the music stops, then the manager gets up on a stool and yells, "The coin, let's have the coin!" and the dance doesn't resume until everybody has ponied up . . . Maybe the crowd is

A dance hall, 1930s

sloppily dressed, but you know right away you're among good people. The women are solid, strapping broads with black hair and ruddy complexions who dance with spirit and laugh out loud. The men wear caps, but there are righteous caps, too: the caps of workers, of artisans, of railroad employees. Soldiers, on leave or quartered in Paris, undo their tunics; some are in shirtsleeves. Everybody dances, has a great time with big laughs and salty jokes, red wine or bottles of beer. The musician announces the next number, and the couples begin to sway. PROPER ATTIRE REQUIRED, say signs posted everywhere, and we've even seen these words painted on a wall: JAVA PROHIBITED. The java is the dance of the moment among a certain less desirable crowd, and this prohibition is enough to keep out the desperadoes who foregather every afternoon at the Petit-Balcon dance hall down the street.

By that time, 1922, dancers were abandoning the prewar repertory of the tango, the maxixe, the cakewalk, the *craquette*, while the fox-trot, *le fox*, was just starting to catch on. The java seems to have been something on the order of a modified mazurka, with a sliding step perhaps borrowed from the Argentinian *milonga*, while its name, which some claimed alluded to *javanais* (an underworld argot in which the syllable *av* is placed between every consonant and its succeeding vowel in a word, e.g., *havôtavel*), more likely derived from *dchjava*, the imperative of "to go" in the Roma language. Anyway, there was nothing inherently low-life about the dance, but it happened to have been claimed early by the *apaches*, and so for decades it was associated with criminals and shunned by the upright.

But if the squares stayed away, all the more reason for fashionable slummers to flock, to rub elbows with the whores and the hoodlums and savor that frisson of danger and perdition. The summit of high-low thrills was manifested in a dance hall called La Java, in the Faubourg du Temple, with its red lacquered walls and, hanging from the ceiling, that new and brilliant nightlife fixture: the mirrored ball. You could observe the bad boys and the fallen girls and the *noceurs* arrived by limousine from points west in their party clothes, but also something au-

The java: sheet music for Fréhel's "La vraie de vrai," 1920s

"A couple of pure ones," circa 1910

The accordionists Frédo Gardoni and Dino flanking the singer and actor Jean Cyrano, 1930s

thentic and pure, local teenagers who were trying on the styles, who might later slide into a pimp-and-pro relationship or just go on to become regular folks. He would be wearing a sideways cap tilted back, a bandanna around his neck and a larger one around his waist, espadrilles on his feet, and a handkerchief drooping from his breast pocket with his embroidered initials showing; she, in black and red, with his initials tattooed in the crook of her left elbow. It was at La Java that Francis Carco observed a boy, his mouth agape, staring at a sensational girl, waiting until she lit a cigarette, whereupon he lit one, too, and proposed to her that they exchange gaspers, which they did, and then they took to the dance floor.

But by 1931, Carco was already writing the *bal-musette*'s epitaph: "It's nothing but a banal, newly painted waiting room where travelers of all classes mingle, expecting a train that doesn't arrive." Such are the perils of being early on a scene; you peak early as well. Certainly Brassaï's pictures of *bals-musette* from the following years show vivid and populous action—it was the war, if anything, that killed it. Furthermore, in the 1930s the music itself was only becoming richer and more complex. The primal scene had occurred in 1913, when Charles Péguri, a second-generation Italian accordionist from Marseille, married the daughter of Antoine Bouscatel, the premier Auvergnat bagpiper in Paris, thus formally merging the two strains. Soon there were Auvergnat accordionists in addition to Italian, Belgian, and native Parisian players. In the 1920s the bandoneon came in with a craze for all things Argentinian. Accordions found their way into the *chanson réaliste*; Gus Viseur and Adolphe Deprince accompanied Piaf and Damia, respectively. And by 1930, when Péguri hanged himself, musette had been thoroughly infused with swing. The dance hall accordionist, at one time alone up in his aerie, or accompanied at most by a violin or a harp, gradually became the leader of a full band, with clarinet, saxophone, piano, banjo, string bass, drums. Guérino, Tony Muréna, Charley Bazin, Jean Vaissade—all at various times played with Django Reinhardt, the great Roma jazz guitarist. Musette, a mongrel creature that drew elements from all over the globe, had become the quintessential sound of Paris.

Another prime source of popular entertainment was the café-concert. There had been music in cafés for a long time; the *café-chantant* (a singer warbling in a corner, maybe backed by guitar or violin) dated back to the early eighteenth century, and from late in that century until 1867 the Palais-Royal featured the Café des Aveugles, with its impassioned orchestra of the blind. The café-concert, born of the Second Empire, was another sort of enterprise. It was generally much larger than the ordinary café, for one thing; more significantly, at a time of increasing and pervasive repression, it was the voice of the crowd. Smoking was permitted, where it was not in theaters, and varyingly discreet prostitution was allowed to occur on the fringes, usually up in the loges, if there were any. The cafés-concerts often featured an orchestra of fourteen to twenty pieces and a whole variety show's worth of performers in evening dress: a tenor, a baritone, a contralto, one "strong," one "trilling," and two "light" chanteuses, and three male and two female comic singers, who would all lounge around on the stage, waiting for their turn in the spotlight. Performances usually ran from seven to eleven most evenings, stretching from two to eleven on Sundays and holidays. An army of waiters and bartenders (as many as sixty) attended to the audience, which indulged especially in those populist favorites of the time, bock beer and cherries in eau-de-vie. The waiters, with their 5 percent share of the take in addition to tips, could earn as much as the conductor—twice as much as the singers and four times what a musician could net.

The first cafés-concerts were outdoor affairs, mostly in the then-wide-open spaces of the Champs-Élysées, with the stage set at the rear of a garden laid out with tables. But although the most successful of these, Café Morel, went on to a long career as the Alcazar d'Été, by the mid-1850s the new places were rooms the size of theaters, mostly along the boulevards: the Alcazar d'Hiver, the Eldorado, the Alhambra, the Cigale, the Éden-Concert, the Scala, the Ba-ta-clan; later the Folies Bergère, the Concert Mayol, and La Pépinière (which had a clientele consisting mostly of domestic servants); and the very toney Ambassadeurs, a seasonal place near the Élysée Palace, memorably depicted by Degas. Eventually the form spread out to many smaller outdoor joints along the quais, and to cabarets and music halls all over the city. Performance was general and mutual; the crowd

A singer-accordionist in a café. Illustration by Théophile Steinlen, from *Gil Blas*, 1897

was there not merely to take in the entertainment while getting a snootful, but also to put itself on display. As Alfred Delvau observed:

> To live at home, to think at home, to eat and drink at home, to die at home—we find that annoying and uncomfortable. We need to be out in public, in the open, in the street, in the cabaret, the café, the restaurant—so that, for better or worse, we can be seen . . . We love to pose, to be the center of attraction, to have an audience—a crowd—as witnesses to our lives.

The haut monde had always enjoyed this indulgence, displaying itself at the opera and the races in its new clothes and adornments, creating an arena in which everyone was simultaneously spectator and spectacle. The café-concert in unprecedented fashion extended that ability to the other classes—although the different classes did not necessarily see one another. Divisions remained in force, as Huysmans noted of a humbler spot at Point-du-Jour:

> The audience is divided into two categories that brush against one another but do not merge. Above are the people, in silk caps or American caps with straight bills, a few hatless women, children on laps, and clay pipes and chaws. Below is the petite bourgeoisie of shopkeepers, spotless families in their Sunday best, bowlers, and black frock coats so free of creases they might as well be made of wood, with collars that go up to the ears, that all but advertise their department store origins. The clay pipes have given way to briar pipes and meerschaums, if not quite to cigars.

But even if the mingling of classes extended only as far as "an agreement to listen to the same songs," there were many who were alarmed by the sheer existence of contact, such as the reliably reactionary Goncourt brothers, here describing the Eldorado in 1865:

> A big circular room with two rows of loges, gilded and marbled; blindingly bright chandeliers; a café on the prem-

An unidentified singer in a boulevard café, 1920s

ises black with men's hats, the bonnets of women from the slums, military headgear, military caps on children, a few hats belonging to whores on the arms of shop clerks, a few pink ribbons on the women in the loges; the visible breath of the whole crowd, a cloud dusty with smoke.

In the rear, a theater with footlights; there I saw a comedian in a black suit. He sang incoherently, with clucking sounds, barnyard noises, epileptic gesticulations—a St. Vitus' dance of idiocy. The crowd was delirious with enthusiasm. I don't know, but I feel as though we are on the verge of revolution. The people have been corrupted by stupidity, their laughter so unhealthy that we need a great upheaval, a bloodletting, to clear the air and cleanse even comedy.

The Moulin de la Galette in Montmartre, circa 1910

The most successful performers were indeed those who spoke most directly to the people, who interpolated argot into their lyrics, who gestured to the crowd and addressed them in asides and alternated lyrical swoops with bursts of patter. Thérésa (née Emma Valladon, 1837–1913) was such a star that she may have been the first in France to endorse commercial products. She got her start burlesquing popular songs, and made her mark with low comedy and the broadest sort of wordplay. She was also among the very first *diseuses*, which is to say that her singing was interleaved with spoken monologues; it was a style that was to dominate the fin de siècle. Paulus (Jean-Paulin Habard, 1845–1908) was her male counterpart, a performer in continual motion who employed the whole breadth of the stage and made endlessly inventive use of his hat and cane as props. He toured as far as Russia and the United States, but he also hitched his wagon to the cult of the protofascist conspirator General Boulanger, and never quite recovered from the collapse of that enterprise.

Paulus and Thérésa were hardly subversive, but many others tested the limits of the permissible. The pioneer was in fact the very first star attraction of the café-concert, Joseph Darcier (Joseph Lemaire), who as early as 1848 wrote and sang his "Song of Bread" ("You cannot quell the grumbling / Of the crowd when it says, 'I'm hungry'"), which may not sound very radical today but nevertheless was rapidly shut down by the censors; he also wrote the music to Rosa Bordas's epochal "La canaille." There were

Thérésa, caricatured by André Gill in *La Lune*, 1867

Sheet music for "Folichon-Polka" by Paulus, 1880s

"The censor." Illustration by J. J. Grandville, from *Oeuvres complètes de P.-J. de Béranger*, 1835

also those singers, both during the Empire and after the Commune, who evaded censure by playing on words—for example, enjambing an end rhyme so that the first syllable of a word sounded like one thing whereas the completed word meant something quite different.* And make no mistake: there were many in Paris who considered censorship a necessity; for example, Maxime du Camp, writing in 1879:

> After every revolution, censorship collapses, and the reigning power thinks it can win popularity by eliminating it. But you only need to see what happens then to understand that it is far from useless: the stage immediately becomes a platform on which smut, to say the least, is impudently displayed. When it comes to government, everything is linked: to permit God to be insulted is to jeopardize the gamekeeper . . . Theatrical works heard by the masses, who in the process are subjected to something like electric shocks, have a rapid and contagious influence far more profound than any book or newspaper, which can only ever act on the individual reader.

Indeed, in 1872 the minister of education had blamed the Commune at least in part on popular songs. And du Camp, to drive home his point, took the measure of the entertainment industry in Paris in 1879: 41 theaters, 180 cafés-concerts, 238 dance halls, and (he alleged) 25,000 drinking establishments. Anyway, the laws governing cafés-concerts were hardly limited to censoring song lyrics. A law of 1859, for instance, established a conventional pitch, which was enforced at all musical performances. And the theater lobby, wary of competition, saw to it that the café-concert was limited to a single stage set at all times, with no costumes, no props, no effects, and no renditions of opera or comic opera airs.

Despite it all, songs led lives of their own, passing from mouth to ear behind the backs of the authorities. There was indeed smut; Gustave Habrekorn, who for a time owned the celebrated

---

* You can gauge this effect, for example, in Fréhel's "Dans une guinguette" (1934), in which the line "il faut des compartiments de dames seules"—"you have to have train compartments for single women"—breaks after the first syllable of the fourth word, so that you initially hear "il faut des cons"—"you have to have cunts."

Divan Japonais in Montmartre, was known for his "sensual" songs, which included "Your Rump," "I'll Drink Your Saliva," "I'll Have You Whole," and "Your Feet in My Mouth." These were sung by Flavy d'Orange and illustrated onstage (by now we're in the looser 1890s) by a chorus line of young women in body stockings. By then there was also a full repertory of anarchist ditties. There was the "Mad Cow Tango"—(long before the phrase denoted bovine spongiform encephalopathy, to eat one, hypothetically, indicated starvation): "There's no bread at our house! / There's some at the neighbor's! / But it isn't for us!" After the execution of the anarchist Ravachol, who set off two bombs that injured no one, people sang: "Let's do the Ravachole / Hooray for the sound, hooray for the sound / Let's do the Ravachole / Hooray for the sound of explosion." There were many verses to the saga of Père la Purge (Father Enema), the "Pharmacist of Humanity," and his daughter, Equality, who in their shop kept everything needed to "marinate" the oppressors. And Carco recalled:

"The other day at La Roquette / They were up early guillotining," croons a singer in his most foppish manner, "When suddenly I notice a head . . ." This head reminds him of someone, some person whose name he can't quite call to mind. He's perturbed, gestures to the executioner to wait, to give him time to put a name to this not-unfamiliar face. But "Chop! The blade comes down." And the chorus goes off with a "tralala."

For some thirty years, beginning in the early 1880s, the undisputed king of popular song was Aristide Bruant (1851–1925). He began at the Chat Noir, and when its owner, Rodolphe Salis, moved it to the boulevards, he took over the Montmartre location and renamed it Le Mirliton. One night early on, when he found his audience consisted of just three people, he began to insult them individually. Word spread, and soon people were lining up to be insulted by Bruant. He had a particular genius for publicity. He insisted on being referred to as Le Chansonnier Populaire, as if he were the only one, and his chutzpah was such that the title actually stuck. The posters he commissioned from

Les bas-fonds de Paris, an installment of a serial novel by Aristide Bruant, 1902

Toulouse-Lautrec cemented Bruant's fame, and indeed they remain ubiquitous to this day in reproduction, so that many people who have never heard Bruant sing can instantly call to mind his wide-brimmed black hat, his red scarf, his enormous head, his flowing hair. He published an irregular newspaper named after his cabaret, and an argot dictionary in installments, several serial novels, a number of plays in collaboration, and five volumes of his song lyrics and monologues—many of these appeared under his own imprint. And he recorded the majority of his songs late enough in the development of gramophone technology (1909–10) that they have survived in reasonably vivid shape, every number introduced by him in the manner of the time, giving the title and his name: "'À Batignolles,' chanté par Aristide Bruant."

Richard Harding Davis visited the Mirliton, "a tiny shop, filled with three long tables, and hung with all that is absurd and fantastic in decoration," where "there is a different salutation for everyone who enters the café, in which all those already in place join in the chorus." The repertoire was all Bruant, although many of the songs were delivered by two or three young men dressed like him. "Every third number is sung by the great man himself, swaggering up and down the narrow limits of the place, with his hands sunk deep in the pockets of his coat, and his head rolling on his shoulders. At the end of each verse he withdraws his hands, and brushes his hair back over his ears, and shakes it out like a mane." The music was not really the point; his songs all seem to have more or less the same melody, or maybe there are two or three templates that reappear with minor variations. They proceed resolutely in a singsong up-and-down cadence, all in the same walking tempo. They have a certain military air to them, emphasized on record by trumpet flourishes. But their appeal was all about the words, which described social conditions familiar to everyone, with no rhetorical grandstanding but large doses of mordant irony and no small amount of tenderness, with a lot of argot and everything pronounced with the slurred and elided syllables, the drawled and spat and melismatized vowels of the Parisian populace.

He had a particular line in songs about the people's neighborhoods, all of them simply titled by those names preceded by *à*: Batignolles, Bastille, La Villette, La Chapelle, La Glacière, Place

Maubert, Goutte-d'Or, Saint-Ouen, Montparnasse, Montmartre, Montrouge, Grenelle, and of course Belleville-Ménilmontant (his home base) along with the prisons and the disciplinary corps: Saint-Lazare, La Roquette, Mazas, Biribi, Bats d'Af. Most of the songs are portraits, in some cases summing up entire lives in six or eight verses; in others, written from the point of view of the subject. In "À Saint-Lazare," for instance, a prostitute sentenced to a cure for some sexually transmitted disease writes to her man, worrying about him since she can't provide him with money: "To think of you like that, without a dime, makes me ache. / You're likely to do something stupid, it eats me up. / You're too proud to go picking up cigar butts, / The whole time that I'll be spending at Saint-Lazare." And just like that he makes you see the shape and nuance and dynamic of the relationship—the songs are short stories, the least of them vignettes, rendered in the (sadly untranslatable) everyday language of his subjects, who were also his ideal audience. His star power, his flamboyance, his roaring good health did not represent a paradox for his constituency; those were not just his due but also a kind of token of luck to be passed on.

The vast majority of Bruant's heirs were women. In a woman's voice, his songs were stripped of their irony, their tragic

"Belleville-Ménilmontant," by Aristide Bruant, illustrated by Théophile Steinlen, from *Dans la rue*, vol. 1, 1889

"À la Roquette," by Aristide Bruant, illustrated by Théophile Steinlen, from *Dans la rue*, vol. 1, 1889

core fully exposed and bleeding; "À Saint-Lazare," for example, was covered dozens of times by female singers. Among the first women to sing Bruant's repertoire was Eugénie Buffet (1866–1934), who was also the very first to be called a *chanteuse réaliste*. She dressed in the short jacket, long skirt, and apron of the street prostitute, a *pierreuse*, and her powerful chest voice, with its reverberating vibrato, owed nothing to vocal convention but instead evoked the cries of market hawkers. Her "Sérénade du pavé" was an enormous hit in 1892, and it remains indelible today; you can hear Piaf sing it in Jean Renoir's 1955 *French Can-can*. Buffet was so popular that police barriers were put up automatically to contain the crowds whenever she was to appear—and the cops sang along with the fans. And she took her role seriously, singing in the streets for the poor and for striking workers and, until the end of her career, appearing at every possible benefit. She was in fact a right-wing populist activist, whose first act upon hitting Paris in 1889 from her native Algeria was to shout "Vive Boulanger"—referring to the conspirator—at the passing carriage of the president of the Republic, which netted her a term in jail. She was later appointed an honorary sergeant in the Croix-de-Feu, the veterans' organization that became a virulently rightist and anti-Semitic street-fighting unit during the Popular Front 1930s.

Her immediate heir, in turn, was Fréhel (1891–1951), born Marguerite Boulc'h in Paris to Breton parents, who first called herself Pervenche (Periwinkle) but later took the name of Cap Fréhel in Brittany. She began as a street singer, hawking sheet music, when she was still a child. Barely into her teens, she was onstage at the Pépinière, soon moving up to the tavern at the Olympia music hall, where she became a favorite of the *grandes horizontales*: Cléo de Mérode, Liane de Pougy, La Belle Otéro. Her recording career began, with a single and isolated two-sided date, in 1909. She was *plus belle que belle*, according to her most consistent boyfriend of those years, the equally young Maurice Chevalier; there were scores of other lovers, from millionaires to boxers, including Jack Johnson. She gave birth to a child who died in infancy, attempted suicide, and in those prewar years, when access to drugs was easy as well as legal, fell under the spell of cocaine and ether, in addition to alcohol. An invitation to sing

Eugénie Buffet and her accompanists performing in a courtyard, 1895

in Russia in 1914 coincided with the start of the war; unable to make it back to France, she spent the duration in Bucharest and then Istanbul, where drugs became her life.

She didn't get herself repatriated until 1925, and her reappearance was a shock to everyone who'd known her before—she'd grown enormously fat and was aged beyond her years. By her own estimation she looked like "a stallholder at Les Halles, puffy-faced and truculent." But that did not stop her from resuming her singing career, this time around as "Madame Sans-Gêne" (Shameless), the incarnation of the streets, whose greeting to her audiences was "Shut your traps so I can open mine." As ostentatiously free of illusions as she was of makeup and styling, she assembled a repertoire that merged Bruant's style of social realism with the torch song. Her songwriters pitched lyrics aimed squarely at her image and her life, such as "J'ai l'cafard" (I'm depressed; Jean Éblinger, 1928): "I've taken tons of things, / Ether, morphine, cocaine, / Evil drugs / That lure women, / All the better to crush their brains, / Even as I know that every drop / Of that disgusting poison / Drags my body / To its death." In her earthy, raucous voice, impeccably musical nevertheless, she sang about the Zone and its pleasures, about prostitution, about criminal lovers sent off to the penal colonies or guillotined at La Roquette, and about nostalgia—about the fortifications being leveled and the old houses of Montmartre razed in favor of bank branches. She who had been a rising star at the close of the Belle Époque and now staggered through life as if it were one long hangover was perfectly positioned to evoke the lost youth of the generation that achieved its fullness of maturity in the 1930s.

Her charisma and strength of personality, in addition to the map of her life in her face—her big eyes and full lips remaining as proof of lost beauty under the palimpsest—got her cast in movies, sixteen of them, mostly in the 1930s. She never had a starring role, but she was impossible to overlook. In *Coeur de lilas* (Anatole Litvak, 1932) and *Pépé le Moko* (Julien Duvivier, 1937), she played opposite Jean Gabin (the son of a café-concert singer and himself the most convincing male claimant to the *réaliste* mantle), with whom she sang raucously in the first and regretted lost chances in the second. But she never reformed. After her death, an anonymous woman wrote to the newspaper *Ici Paris*:

Fréhel, "Queen of the *Apaches*," 1930

Fréhel and Jean Gabin in Anatole Litvak's *Coeur de lilas*, 1932

Fréhel as Pervenche, 1908

One afternoon in 1938, outside the Anvers Métro station, I stopped short at the feet of a big woman, probably drunk, crumpled at the base of a tree. A police wagon soon arrived to pick her up and take her away. But she faced down the cops. She yelled: "Leave me alone! I'm Fréhel, yes, Fréhel the singer." . . . They hesitated for a minute, and I managed to whisper in her ear, "Sing! I beg you, sing!" Then, hands on hips, suddenly sober as if by magic, she started in on "La java bleue" with as much force as in her prime. Soon a crowd had formed, agog at having witnessed an authentic miracle.

In her last years, she sold vegetables on the street. Her landlady said, "She scared me. She was like a bull." In 1950 a group of young admirers that included Jacques Yonnet and Robert Giraud got her to perform one last time, in an old ballroom in the Contrescarpe, before an audience of clochards and ancient bohemians, but that was the end. A year later she was dead in a miserable *hôtel de passe* in Pigalle.

The realist style, which flagged somewhat during the First World War and during the intoxicated *années folles* of the 1920s, returned in full force in the 1930s, during the worldwide financial crisis and, locally, a decade of strikes and factory occupations and enormous and often violent street demonstrations. The style was not political as such, its singers not especially *engagées*, the only major exception being Marianne Oswald (née Sarah Alice Bloch, 1901–1985), the daughter of Polish Jews resettled in Lorraine. Her voice was beyond unschooled; it was altogether indifferent—her mode was *Sprechstimme* (talk-singing), and she had both a great deal of soul and a perceptible analytic intelligence. She started out as the major French interpreter of Kurt Weill and Bertolt Brecht, later had songs written for her by Jean Cocteau, Jacques Prévert, Hanns Eisler. On her last record, in 1957, the liner notes were by Albert Camus.

Mistinguett (née Jeanne Bourgeois, 1875–1956) had no particular voice, either, but that did not stop her from becoming the single greatest singing star in the period between the wars, virtually personifying Paris itself. La Miss, as she was invariably known, began as a comic singer at the Eldorado before the turn of the century, became a very early screen comedienne (she made no fewer than forty-five silent films, but only two sound pictures), and was often partnered onstage by men who carried the melody, most memorably Maurice Chevalier, with whom her offstage partnership lasted a decade. Despite her general-audiences sheen, Mistinguett could nevertheless chirp the masochistic tango "Mon homme" (1920), which Carco saw as emblematic of java culture: "He beats me up, / He takes my money, / I'm at the end, / But despite it all, / What do you want? / He's so far under my skin."

There were numerous other women in those same years who sang of Paris and the streets, of hunger and prostitution and the guillotine. There was Berthe Sylva (1885–1941), who anticipated Fréhel in many ways but lacked the latter's impeccable taste in material. There was Yvonne George (1896–1930), who inspired dozens of poems by Robert Desnos, and of whom Janet Flanner wrote, "She was ephemeral. She could magnetize only small groups; before the great audiences of the Palace, the Olympia, and the bigger music halls, she failed—usually magnificently." Although she was a heavy user of opium and cocaine, what killed her early was tuberculosis. Her recordings are exceedingly hard to find today, even in their single CD reissue, but they are worth seeking out.

There was Emma Liebel (Aimée Médebielle, 1873–1928), who made a great many records but has been unjustly forgotten because of her death just before the big realist surge—either from tuberculosis or from having her throat slit by a lover, depending on which account you read. There were Marie Dubas, Germaine Lix, Lucienne Boyer, Lucienne Delyle, Nitta-Jo, Yvonne Printemps, La Palma, the deep-voiced and broad-shouldered Suzy Solidor, and Lys Gauty, whose hit "Le chaland qui passe" was slapped onto the soundtrack of Jean Vigo's *L'Atalante* (1934). There was Florelle (Odette Rousseau, 1898–1974), who was better known as a movie star than a singer, but who was nevertheless a remarkable singer. She was Kurt Weill's choice to play Polly Peachum in the French version (in the early sound era they often made versions of movies in different languages, often with different casts) of G. W. Pabst's film adaptation of *The Threepenny Opera* (1931), over the director's initial reservations—and no wonder, since her voice has grit reminiscent of his wife Lotte

Mistinguett at the Eldorado, circa 1900

Florelle, circa 1930

Lenya's. Much like her characters in many movies, she is trilling and flirtatious on the surface, but has a rough, deep bottom range. Her "Pirate Jenny" can stand with the best of them. She first appeared onstage at the age of four, had speaking parts at fourteen, made movies for forty years. She was capable of playing romantic leads well into middle age—no small achievement for the time—for example, in Jean Renoir's *Le crime de Monsieur Lange* (1936), where she plays the quintessential Parisian washerwoman with an extraordinary combination of sexual knowingness, calculating intelligence, and openhearted generosity.

And then there was Damia (Marie-Louise Damien, 1889–1978), perhaps the greatest singer of them all. A native-born Parisian, she ran away from home in her early teens, was saved from starving by the kind ministrations of a street prostitute, passed from theater extra to music hall attraction in a blink. She was cast as the typical *midinette* (shopgirl) in her simple black dress, ran with Fréhel when the latter was still known as Pervenche, and indulged in all the drugs and excesses of the time. Then, in the 1920s she reinvented her persona, transcending the street in her visual expression and sometimes in the content of her songs. She kept the black dress but cut it down to a simple sheath, darkened her eyes with kohl and accentuated her extraordinarily wide mouth with red lipstick—scuttlebutt had it she also whitened her arms with flour—and stripped the stage and took the lighting down to a single spot, sometimes colored, depending on the specific song.* She made only the most minimal, stark, expressionistic gestures, suggesting the words rather than describing them. "Her face and arms often foretold what her voice would say—the same theatrical technique employed by Maria Callas." Many of those decisions later became commonplace for torch singers, but no one else was employing them at the time. Damia was unquestionably a diva, with a significant gay and lesbian constituency; Jean Genet in fact acknowledged

---

* One of her lovers—she had many of both sexes—was Loïe Fuller (1862–1928; born Marie Louise Fuller in Fullersville, Illinois), who, initially a failure as a dancer after her arrival in Paris in the early 1890s, had an epiphany "inspired by the nuances dropping from the great rose windows of Notre-Dame upon her handkerchief, spread (since in her discouragement she had been weeping) upon her knees to dry" (Flanner, p. 40), which led her to experiment with colored lights.

her as the model for Divine, the transvestite protagonist of his *Our Lady of the Flowers* (1943).

She was also an auteur, which is to say that her interpretations of songs were so definitive, so lapidary that it was as if she had written them herself; if they had previously been sung by others, she utterly transformed them. She could go the populist route, with accordions and lyrics about *guinguettes* and mussels and beer, but her primary note was classical and tragic—not for nothing was she called *la tragédienne de la chanson*. She was no intellectual, but her taste was unassailable, as was her intuition. She commissioned music to "La veuve," a poem written in 1887 by Jules Jouy, anarchist contributor to *Le Chat Noir*, about the guillotine (the widow). "Stretching her long red arms, / Pretty and freshened up, / She awaits her new husband— / The widow . . . Because her lovers, voracious, / Killed on their very first turn, / Only sleep once with / The widow." She sang about drowned sailors ("Les goélands"); about a madman who kills a child, told from his point of view ("Le fou"); about a woman whose sailor husband is on his way to Tahiti and who prays to the Virgin that, rather than let him be seduced by the native women, She cause his ship to be dashed upon the rocks ("La mauvaise prière").

Perhaps her single greatest number is a fatalistic love song, "La chaîne" (L. Daniderff, E. Ronn)—not exactly banal in its essence but also not untypical of its time—which starkly illustrates how completely she could transform her material. First of all, she pays no attention to the time signature as written; she stretches some words and phrases out well past their allotted beat and ruthlessly clips others, depending on their emotional weight. She proclaims some phrases and slips others into parentheses, launches an attack at the start of some measures and lets others trail off. She slides and slurs her intonation for emphasis, employs her rolled *r*'s like a sort of castanet percussion. She continually destabilizes the listener, forcing attention to every word, pitching her craft on emotionally storm-tossed seas, manufacturing a kind of suspense that's not in the lyrics. She uses the nasality inherent in French as a mournful continuo; her slurred notes are kin to Billie Holiday's. And even in her darkest songs she can make a rising inflection transcend all the bitterness and sorrow

Damia at her peak, early 1930s

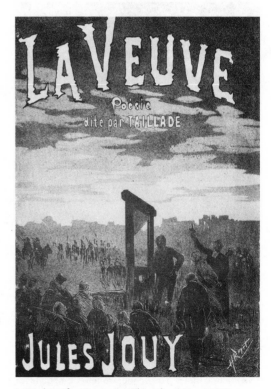

Lyric sheet for "La veuve," by Jules Jouy, 1887

and squalor, as if she could see over the horizon into some better world. She lived to a very old age, although she barely recorded or performed after the Second World War.

Part of the problem was a young upstart, La Môme Piaf, later Édith Piaf (Édith Giovanna Gassion, 1915–1963), a generation younger than many of these women, who emerged seemingly from nowhere in the late 1930s and, unlike any of them, became an international star. Her mother had been a singer who sang at the Chat Noir and other Montmartre joints of the fin-de-siècle and on the streets, but who had let herself go; according to the few who heard them both, Édith inherited her mother's voice. She began singing on the streets when she was fifteen, accompanied by her half sister and alter ego, Simone Berteaut; had a child at seventeen who died two years later; was discovered on a corner by the club owner Louis Leplée in 1935. Leplée groomed her, gave her her name (*piaf* is argot for "sparrow"), assembled a repertoire for her (she had primarily been singing Fréhel's songs). Less than two years later Leplée was murdered, possibly by a trick—the case was never solved—but Piaf, who had already released her first record, was on her way. She had immediate and extraordinary luck in finding collaborators, in particular the lyricist Raymond Asso (who wrote, among many other things, "Mon légionnaire," an enormous hit for Piaf that was also recorded by half the singers in Paris) and the composer Marguerite Monnot, who wrote the music to "Mon légionnaire" and thirty other songs for Piaf, stretching the whole length of her career. Piaf wrote the words to eight of these, making Monnot-Piaf the very first female composer-lyricist team in the history of French popular music.

In the beginning Piaf was unsurprisingly raw and unsophisticated, and her repertoire of the 1930s showcases her breathlessness, her naïveté, her street urchin credentials, even as it cannot help emphasizing her huge debts to Fréhel, Damia, Berthe Sylva, Marie Dubas, and others. Simone Berteaut's biography* has the author upbraiding Piaf, her half sister, for her lack of polish:

Sheet music for "C'était un jour de fête," by Édith Piaf and Marguerite Monnot, 1941

---

* One of the great showbiz bios of all time, written in addictive, headlong street prose you can imagine issuing from its source as a monologue in machine-gun tempo. (I can't vouch for its English translation.)

I'll tell you what she's doing there, Marie Dubas. If you talk to her about Baudelaire she doesn't ask you for his phone number so he can write her a song. If a man kisses her hand she doesn't slap him with it right after. If you serve her fish she doesn't eat the bones or spit them out on her plate because she doesn't know what to do with them. If you introduce her to a cabinet minister she doesn't ask him, "How's business?"

Piaf as packaged for the American market, early 1950s

But she learned as she went along, at least as a musical artist. Her private life—which was barely private, not even so much because the press hounded her as because she herself continually broadcast every passing emotion as if it were a historical watershed—was a succession of infatuations, sprees, breakdowns, jags, detoxes, crises, illnesses, tragedies; the death in 1949 in a plane crash of the boxer Marcel Cerdan, perhaps the love of her life, as he was coming to meet her in New York, was the single darkest item. By the time she died at forty-seven of liver cancer she looked seventy.

Her music, meanwhile, grew past the confines of Belleville, of Paris, of France—when the American public, ordinarily not given to much patience with anything in a foreign language, accorded her its imprimatur after the war, it crowned her as a world star, among the very first not to have been processed through the Hollywood mill. But then, in her prime, her voice told you all you needed to know about the contents of a song. Her singing may have lacked some of the artistry of Damia or Billie Holiday, but her genius lay in her lack of boundaries: between herself and the song, and herself and the listener. As Léon-Paul Fargue wrote, "The subject of the song has to roll around in her voice like a body in a bed." While her voice never lost its cutting *réaliste* vibrato, descended in a direct line from Eugénie Buffet, it was internationalized by her willfulness; in her later recordings she is clearly addressing her intimate concerns to a vast arena, a thousand times bigger than the Palace or the Olympia. The jazzy syncopation of her first worldwide hit, "La vie en rose" (1947), certainly didn't hurt; nor the ultra-Parisian shtick of "Milord" (1959), which, through the brilliance of Marguerite Monnot, manages to telescope the rhythms and intonations of everything from Offenbach to the Moulin-Rouge

Sheet music for "Y'a pas d'printemps," by Édith Piaf, 1944

to the tourist traps of Place du Tertre into its suave four minutes. By the time we get to "Non, je ne regrette rien" the following year, we are approaching the new world order of the franchised musical, of *Man of La Mancha* and *Les misérables* and the works of Andrew Lloyd Webber. It was certainly not Piaf's fault that when she died, Paris was on the verge of becoming the trade name "Paris." If she was an accomplice, it was both because she contained her city within herself and because she couldn't help projecting herself outward. In addition to being a nonpareil vocalist who encapsulated and apotheosized an entire tradition, she was the point of a prism.

10

Mort aux Vaches

The Parisians have long had an equivocal attitude toward crime. Theft was often just a matter of making ends meet, after all, and brawls certainly happened and sometimes turned out badly. This is not to imply that most Parisians have been criminals, in any era. It's just that even the law-abiding could often appreciate a well-played hand on the dark side, or at the very least could find solidarity in opposing and undermining the *sergents de ville*, who were mere instruments of the upper classes and whose job was to make everyone's life miserable, not only those of thieves and killers. Celebrity criminals have been a feature of every society in the world—bandits among the peasantry, toughs in the cities—but perhaps the Parisian model had more style. In any account there is no getting around François Villon (1431–c. 1463), who was one of the very earliest modern poets and recognized for his gifts even in his time, but who was also a brawler and a thief. At the very least he is known to have killed a priest and participated in the burglary of five hundred gold écus from the sacristy of the Collège de Navarre, as well as being implicated in many smaller larcenies and any number of assaults in tavern set-tos. His rap sheet never impinged upon his literary esteem.

Two and a half centuries later there was Cartouche (Louis Dominique Garthausen, 1693–1721), the "beloved bandit." He was a cutpurse, burglar, and highwayman who from a very young age commanded a gang of men and women that seems never to

François Villon

have numbered fewer than a hundred and at its peak was perhaps two thousand strong. Legends abound of his gallantry, derring-do, and redistribution of wealth. One night, allegedly, he broke into the *hôtel* of a duchess and demanded not money but an intimate supper with champagne. The food was acceptable, but not the wine, he told her, and left; the following day a case of very good champagne arrived at her door. In 1719 he is said to have stopped a man from jumping into the Seine. It turned out his problem was overwhelming debt, and Cartouche instructed him to tell his creditors to come the following day to a tavern in the Cité. Cartouche was indeed there with a sack containing twenty-seven thousand livres, and paid off the creditors. Then his confederates jumped them on Rue de Glatigny and took the money back. More significantly and verifiably, Cartouche's band made off with 1.3 million livres in shares from the coffers of the state-appointed swindler John Law, which certainly did not damage his popularity with the many citizens who had suffered directly or indirectly from Law's schemes.

But it had to end, especially since Cartouche had cohorts in high places who worried about being unmasked and implicated. He was arrested twice and escaped; a third time he was given away by a barking dog. He denied everything and refused to speak, even after having his legs crushed in the method of torture known as *les brodequins*. Finally, maybe because he was disappointed not to have been freed by his gang, he made a complete confession before the judges. More than 350 arrests followed, and the sum of the consequent trials took two years. His admissions did not save him, however. He was broken on the wheel and roasted alive before a large crowd on Place de Grève, after which thousands paid admission to see his remains, exhibited in a nearby shack for days. And that illustrates another aspect of the historical Parisian fascination with crime: the general interest in public executions, which began in the mists and lasted until the practice was abolished in 1939.

If crime is a constant in Parisian history, it also marks the boundary between the old world and the modern. Until the second or third decade of the nineteenth century, crime was exceptional, or at least something that happened to other people. If you regularly transported jewelry by coach between the city and

A dime novel about Cartouche, 1907

Versailles, you might expect to be held up on occasion; and if you frequented certain dives in the Cité, you did not go there unarmed or alone. For the ordinary citizen, though, the night held no terrors. Chevalier points out that Mercier's nocturnal wanderings in the eighteenth century were conspicuously lacking in danger; the same was true of Restif's. "On the whole it was an unhealthy and brutal city, its faubourgs inhabited by a primitive population, but it wasn't menaced by crime or haunted by fear; it was crowded with unfortunates, but not with criminals." By 1830, however, a pair of journalists could write:

> Those who have something to hide come to Paris. They see the labyrinth of its streets and the depravity of its morals, and they plunge into it as if into a forest. Paris must change. Its current makeup is a grave wrong. Statistics of crime demonstrate that it numbers twice as many thieves as any of the other royal courts in France. The almost 900,000 people crowded there are prey to twice as much corruption as the 31 million who surround it.

An ambush by an *apache*, 1890s

Despite the authors' seeming belief in an inherently criminal mind-set—they were hardly alone in this—the principal factor was overcrowding, the chief difference the contrast between the demographically stable population of the ancien régime and the enormous influx that occurred after the revolution and especially during the Restoration after the fall of Napoléon. Although many commentators were content to fulminate along general preacherly lines, the demographic equation did not escape attention, and crime was employed as an argument against unchecked immigration, then almost entirely from within the Hexagon but especially the south, whose natives were sometimes considered to be almost a different species. And, naturally, overcrowding bred joblessness, poverty, disease, and every other affliction that might drive people to crime. In 1845 George Sand wrote, "There are no poor people in the streets anymore. You have prohibited them from begging out of doors, and the man without means begs at night, knife in hand."

Fear was in the air by then. That was in part a consequence of how the city was laid out, with the streets of the poor and the streets of the rich entangled together everywhere in the center.

"Bell ringer." Illustration by Théophile Steinlen for Aristide Bruant's *Dans la rue*, vol. 1, 1889

No journey from point A to point B failed to involve crossing class boundaries. Navigation involved among other things a sense of physical nuance as finely tuned as that of any experienced forester; every Parisian pedestrian was Natty Bumppo alert to the snapping twig and the interrupted birdsong. Balzac presents the landscape in *The History of the Thirteen*:

> In Paris there are streets as dishonored as any man guilty of infamous deeds. There also exist noble streets, and merely honest streets, and young streets the relative morality of which has not yet been determined by public opinion. Then there are murderous streets, and streets older than the oldest dowagers, and reputable streets, streets that are always clean, streets that are always dirty, laboring streets, diligent streets, mercantile streets. The streets of Paris possess human qualities, and as a consequence of their physiognomy they impress certain ideas upon us against which we are defenseless.

Rue Pierre-Lescot. Illustration by Honoré Daumier, 1840s

There was, for example, the old Rue Pierre-Lescot, erased by Haussmann, which, lying very near the side of the Palais-Royal that opens onto Rue Saint-Honoré, metaphorically acted as "a sort of drain, a type of canal into which flows all the trash on the surface of the water." Its other end was clogged with heaped debris from construction work on the Louvre, and its desolate emptiness "rendered it favorable to all the crimes and ignominies that require silence and darkness. There thieves held their nocturnal parleys; there the ignorant child, the obscene monk, the old man devoured by sterile lust all came to seek shameful satisfaction of their impure desires; there theft and murder were so to speak endemic . . . The history of Rue Pierre-Lescot can be summed up in four words: murder, theft, poverty, prostitution. Did the street ever enjoy innocence?" More than sixty years later, well after Haussmann's revisions, the same area was still subject to similar sorts of criminal conventions: "In the summer the gardens of the Palais-Royal are the site of meetings of dangerous prowlers who chase away honest folk. It is there that advantageous burglaries of nearby jewelers' shops are planned, there that those fearsome gangs of 'wall borers' are organized each year."

A similar criminal genealogy could be drawn up for Porte Saint-Denis, where "it is not so much that the most crimes have been committed in that neighborhood as that in every era, perhaps more in the first half of the nineteenth century than in our day, crime has been more frequent there than in most parts of the city . . . Its criminals are petty, the riffraff of crime, disorganized and penurious, with no money or plans, not criminal by nature but driven to criminality by their laziness, stupidity, or bad luck." On the nearby boulevards, meanwhile, were always gathered "the greatest number of youths desirous of wrongdoing and of learning its means, as well as of the less young eager to instruct them." And a bit farther south was the Plateau Beaubourg, where "most of the dives shelter the lowest rung of the Parisian underworld, the sole occupation of which appears to involve fingering greasy cards and handling slimy stacks of dominoes. Much of the money earned from thefts, from rolling johns, from small-time swindles is spent there; some of the nastiest tricks in Paris are planned in their back rooms."

Rolling a drunk, 1870s

Given that all these places lay within a few blocks of more favored streets—Rue Pierre-Lescot was in spitting distance of the Banque de France, for example—you would think that observant Parisians would have had some idea of who those criminals were, and might have taken general note of their habits. But whether they were deluded by their fear or influenced by the Manichean outlook of religion or the stratifying inclinations of society, they were unable until sometime past the middle of the nineteenth century to see how crime was the result of material conditions, and how much of it was desperately opportunistic and hastily improvised. Instead, even people as clever as Balzac and Hugo—even the pioneering detective Vidocq, who had begun as a criminal himself—seemed to think of crime as an organized alternative society. While it is true that criminals had their own language to an extent—it was shared with hucksters and street performers and market workers and many others who were not necessarily dishonest or violent—and also true that some specific branches, such as that of pimps, maintained a form of internal government, writers in the early nineteenth century tended to vastly exaggerate the organizational and hierarchical aspects of crime. Balzac wrote that "thieves are a separate nation

Men of the *milieu*, 1930s

The police prefecture before Haussmann's demolition, 1850s

within the nation . . . [They] comprise a republic with its own laws and customs; they do not steal from one another, scrupulously hold to their oaths . . . Thieves even have their own language, their own leaders, their own police." Above all, writers were fixated upon the idea that criminal society, just like theirs, had its different classes, its high and low orders. If ordinary footpads were dangerous nuisances, how much more lethal were the aristocrats of this society! Jules Janin explored the conceit in an 1827 novel:

> One day I saw a man in rags, horrible to see, enter a little pothouse on Rue Sainte-Anne; his beard was long, his hair a mess, his whole person filthy. A moment later I saw him emerge decently dressed, his chest bristling with medals of honor, his face venerable. He was on his way to dine with a judge. This sudden transformation frightened me, and I thought tremulously that perhaps it was thus that the extremes of society were linked.

While this fiction, which Chevalier qualifies as a *"parodie sérieuse,"* may be fantastic, rooted in ambient fears and worries, it was probably also inspired by the career of Eugène François Vidocq (1775–1857). Vidocq was an incomparable shape-shifter, with a penchant for disguises, who slipped easily from one side of the law to the other. He came from a relatively bourgeois family in the Pas-de-Calais, and enjoyed a picaresque early career, high in color, filled with duels, daring escapes, wide-ranging travels, amorous interludes, battlefield action, and prison time—it is impossible to gauge how much of it actually occurred, since the only source for most of it is Vidocq's *Memoirs* (1828), which itself was written mostly by ghosts. In any event, Vidocq was arrested in 1809, faced a long stretch in prison from accumulated previous sentences, and made a deal to become an undercover agent; freed two years later, he initiated a plainclothes force he named the Brigade de la Sûreté, which Napoléon certified in 1813 as the Sûreté Nationale, which still exists. Vidocq quit the force in 1827 owing to a changed political climate, and a few years later opened the Bureau de Renseignements, which may have been the world's first detective agency. He went to prison one last time, for fraud, in 1849. His story, and his proclivity for hiring ex-cons in his various enterprises, seems to have inspired the character of Jean Valjean in *Les misérables*. He definitely inspired his friend Balzac's character Vautrin—in his youth he apparently was nicknamed Le Vautrin (local patois meaning "Wild Boar"). Vautrin first appears in *Le Père Goriot*, where he is unmasked as the escaped convict Jacques Collin, and reappears in *Illusions perdues* in the guise of the priest Carlos Herrera, who saves Lucien de Rubempré from drowning and makes him his ward. In *Splendeurs et misères des courtisanes* he gives himself up in exchange for the exculpation of two of his former associates, destined for the guillotine. The deal involves his becoming an undercover agent; we learn in an aside that he headed the Sûreté for fifteen years.

Janin's fantasy had another issue, direct or indirect: a long line of evil geniuses in popular literature, including Ponson du Terrail's Rocambole (nine novels, 1857–71), Colonel Bozzo-Corona in Paul Féval's *Les habits noirs* (eleven novels, 1844–75), and Erik, the Phantom of the Opera, in Gaston Leroux's 1910 novel. The apotheosis of this tendency, though, was Marcel Allain and Pierre Souvestre's Fantômas (thirty-two novels, 1911–13; in addition to eleven by Allain alone [1926–63]; as well as five films by Louis Feuillade in 1913–14, numerous other adaptations, radio and television series, a song cycle by Kurt Weill and Robert Desnos, a long-running Mexican comic strip, and much more). Fantômas is the consummate genius of evil, virtually an invisible government unto himself, a one-man conspiracy. Whereas Vidocq and Vautrin could fully incorporate both sides of Janin's character, the terrifying wild man and the venerable sage in one, Fantômas merely impersonates benevolence, albeit with such success that he can insinuate himself into every realm of power and undermine it from within as well as attacking it from without.

He kidnaps a king and holds him in a cell under Place de la Concorde, his cries from below causing the fountain to sing. He methodically strips the gold from the dome of the Invalides. He replaces the contents of department store perfume dispensers with sulfuric acid, and he causes an enormous chandelier to fall on the clientele. He makes a Métro car vanish at the point where the number 2 line goes underground between Barbès and Anvers.

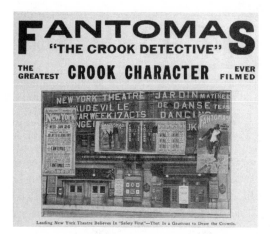

Fantômas comes to Times Square, circa 1914

Le cercueil vide (The empty coffin), Pierre Souvestre and Marcel Allain's twenty-fifth Fantômas novel, 1914

His confederates crash a city bus through the wall of a bank. He nearly blows up the reservoirs in Montmartre, flooding the city. The books, indifferently written and absentmindedly plotted, are somewhat less than the sum of their parts—the set pieces are everything. Nevertheless the scale and daring of those set pieces succeeded in tunneling directly into the subconscious of their readers, and the slapdash construction of the novels may actually have assisted in the process by erasing the distinction between reverie and literature; they were authentically oneiric. Feuillade in his film adaptations could not hope to replicate the more grandiose spectacles, but on the other hand he could situate the action in real locations, immediately identifiable by Parisian viewers: the henchmen plot in La Villette, the prostitute Joséphine rides the *métro aérien* running west toward Montmartre, Fantômas and police inspector Juve stage their gun battle among the casks in the wine depot at Bercy. The terror, the movies said, lived just outside the door.

Since Souvestre and Allain were writing in the years before the First World War, they supplied Fantômas with accomplices that included two gangs of *apaches*, the Ténébreux (Shadowy) and the Chiffres (Numbers), both of which were headquartered in dives in the Nineteenth Arrondissement. The popular imagination was already then luxuriating in fear of an "army of crime"—the phrase coined in 1890 in a tract of the same name

A bunch of *apaches*, or possibly actors, circa 1910

by one Ignotus (Félix Platel) that employed blood-and-thunder rhetoric to argue against the abolition of the death penalty. There had of course always been gangs, but the novelty of the *apaches* was in large part an invention of the press, the term itself coined in 1902 by a journalist, either Arthur Dupin or Victor Morris. The Native American tribe of that name—in actuality a complex of tribes that did not necessarily have much in common apart from the structure of their languages—surrendered to the U.S. Army in 1886; by 1902 their leader, Geronimo, had become an attraction at fairs around the country. The French had long had a fascination and wishful identification with Native Americans, initially spurred by the popularity of Fenimore Cooper's novels, which led, for example, to Alexandre Dumas's dull and interminable *Les Mohicans de Paris* (1854). The *apaches*, though, caught the imagination of the wider world, resulting in such miscellanea as a 1912 book by Alfred Henry Lewis confusingly titled *The Apaches of New York*—it was a collection of reported pieces on gangsters—and the "Apache dance" (a sort of tango, with the male, invariably wearing a striped jersey, a neckerchief, a flat cap, and espadrilles, sometimes with a rose between his teeth, dragging the female, in low-cut black, around the floor), which you could still witness at supper clubs in disparate locations as late as the 1960s.

The item that made the Parisian *apaches* jump from local *faits-divers* to a worldwide sensation was the story of Casque d'Or. In January 1902 a corpse was found on Rue des Haies, southeast of the Père-Lachaise cemetery, loaded down with two high-caliber revolvers, a knife with a ten-inch blade, a switchblade, and a hatchet; his cap bore two bullet holes. An inquiry led the police to a man of Corsican origin named Leca, in the hospital with two bullets in his side, who, however, wouldn't talk. A visitor was observed, a woman named Amélie Hélie, known to be a *gigolette*, who sported a crown of strawberry-blond hair. She told him that their enemies, a gang called Les Orteaux, led by someone called L'Homme—the rivalry between the gangs was said to be "hereditary"—were lurking in wait behind the *mairie* (the borough hall) of the Twentieth Arrondissement. Leca told her to gather his troops, Les Popincourts, and to hire a coach. Hélie, familiarly known as Casque d'Or (Golden Helmet), was

Actors playing *apaches* in a Gaumont film, circa 1910

Amélie Hélie, alias Casque d'Or, circa 1902

Simone Signoret in Jacques Becker's *Casque d'Or,*
1952

to board the coach, with the Popincourts dissimulated within. Sure enough, the Orteaux emerged; one jumped on the carriage step; knives and guns flashed and barked; Casque d'Or fled.

She had met L'Homme, whom she knew as Manda, four years earlier, at the Bal des Vaches on the Left Bank, but his job as a brass polisher proved insufficient to support her in style, so he became head of Les Orteaux. But then Casque d'Or fell in love with Leca, who apparently was more handsome. She told him that his mistress, La Panthère, was having an affair with L'Homme, and then laughed in his face at his inadequacy. The next day, the battle was joined on Rue des Haies. Not long after the carriage incident, Manda located Casque d'Or, who told him they were through. He was on the point of leaving for England when he read in a newspaper of her impending marriage to Leca, and decided to massacre everyone in the wedding party, but the police caught wind of the plan. Under arrest, Manda/L'Homme turned out to be Joseph Pleigneur, twenty-six. The charges didn't stick, but as soon as Manda was released the war resumed, climaxing in a battle in a café on Place de la Bastille that left two dead. Leca fled to Belgium.

Casque d'Or immediately became a celebrity. She acquired an impressive wardrobe; postcards were published bearing her image; a portrait of her by a certain Depré was exhibited in the Salon; she was engaged to perform in a revue, *Casque d'Or et les Apaches,* at the Bouffes du Nord. However, when she made her singing debut at the Cabaret Alexandre, the two gangs showed up and battled, whereupon the police prefect banned the revue and had the portrait taken down. Manda, who testified in court that his criminal career was due to love, was sentenced to forced labor for life, Leca to eight years in the penal colony, and the two served side by side in the *bagne* on the island of Saint-Martin-de-Ré, although they never quite made up. Casque d'Or milked her notoriety for a few years, passing through a succession of wealthy lovers, then became an animal tamer in a circus. By the time she died, in 1933, she had been so completely forgotten that no obituary appeared, and the date became known only when her husband, fifteen years her junior, lodged a complaint against Jacques Becker's 1952 film. It's hard to see what he could have faulted, since Simone Signoret invests the title role with an epic sexuality, as if playing

Aphrodite rather than a small-time whore. Claude Dauphin is a reptilian Leca, and the young Serge Reggiani a very moving and credible Manda. The story is simplified and considerably romanticized, but then, it may as well have been designed for that purpose. It is all but impossible not to cry at the end.

The *apaches* were modern gangsters, which is to say that they were violent poseurs, fully attuned to the image they cut, on the street and in the press. They were poor, and their clothes were lousy (shapeless jackets, workmen's blouses, patched trousers), but they invested whatever profits they accrued in exquisite handmade yellow boots. Chevalier quotes a retired criminal addressing a class of apprentice *apaches* in a café called La Guillotine, near Place de la République: "A man uses a knife, not a revolver. Guns and such are fine for women. Women can produce their weapon from their sleeve or from under their skirts—a revolver for society dames, acid for everybody else. But you have to have blood. A gun makes a barely visible hole, sometimes without a drop of blood. And only blood is for real." Besides knives, the *apaches* made use of *savate*, a form of kickboxing that had been around for centuries and was exclusively identified with guttersnipes; the word also means an old, broken-down shoe. And they were experts in *le coup du Père François* (the garroting of someone from behind with a scarf).

The *apaches* were also pioneers of tattooing. Gangs had their own distinctive marks. The man who tattooed Manda, who claimed to be the inventor of the *apache* tattoo, was interviewed on the subject. "The Hearts of Steel? Oh, they're just ragpickers, despite the flaming heart on their left wrists. And the Linked Hearts? They're on their way out, just like the Beauty Marks, who had a mole tattooed under their lower lip. Now those were genuine tough guys." When fifteen members of a gang called Les Tatoués were arrested in 1902, they all turned out to be completely covered with designs of every sort: guillotines, hearts pierced with arrows, the words "Child of Misfortune"—and also portraits of Paul Kruger, who led the Boers against the British in South Africa from 1899 to 1902, because Anglophobia was very much alive in the streets. *Apaches* tended to sport a blue dot under their left eye. Many gangsters bore the initials P.L.V., meaning *pour la vie* (a vow of commitment for, rather than an affirmation of, life),

Le coup du Père François, circa 1900

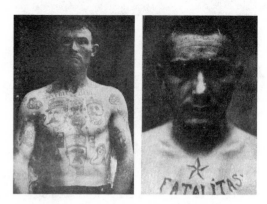

Prison tattoos, circa 1910

A police raid, 1930s

The cover of Auguste le Breton's autobiographical novel *La loi des rues* (The law of the streets), 1955

and many had a dotted line around their necks, to guide the blade of the guillotine. Three stars signified service in the Bats d'Af; three dots between thumb and index meant *mort aux vaches* (the equivalent of "death to the pigs"), although many simply inscribed that phrase. Five dots—four in a square and the fifth in the center—meant solitary confinement. And then: Reserved for the Ladies. Faucet of Love. Long Live Love. Born Under an Evil Star. Fatalitas. No Luck. Hatred and Revenge.*

After the war, the *apaches* gave way to a new criminal world, the *milieu*.† The term apparently had its origin in Francis Carco's play *Mon homme* (1920; its title derived from the Mistinguett song), the story of an ex-*pierreuse* who hangs around the *bals* on Rue de Lappe and falls for a bad boy in a felt hat and spectator shoes. Its look and operational methods came direct from Chicago. Al Capone, tommy guns in violin cases, the St. Valentine's Day Massacre—those things burrowed deep in the Parisian imagination, not just its criminal subset. The term followed suit, spreading rapidly through movies, newspapers, novels—Fréhel's 1928 song "Il n'est pas du milieu," for example—out to the streets to stay, until at least the 1950s. Carco wrote, "By 1925 the hard men from the Bastille, the hairy beasts, the *vrai de vrai*, the pimps, the flat-capped crooks were all knights of old. The underworld [*la pègre*] had given way to the milieu." In many ways the milieu was the same old honor-loyalty-virility guff dressed up in new suits and fedoras, a classic instance of gentrification. They didn't roll their own cigarettes anymore, but insisted on tailor-mades, frequently American. They still liked knives, but they didn't appreciate blood so much now that they were modern executives, so they worked clean or—what the hell—went for the roscoes. Their old neighborhoods were for chumps; they moved en bloc to Pigalle, Anvers, Place Blanche—Montmartre, the center of the left-hand universe. They spurned public transport, had to have the latest flivvers, also frequently American. They were organized now; they had *caïds* (from the Arabic for

* And then "Mon légionnaire" (words by Raymond Asso, music by Marguerite Monnot): "He was covered with tattoos / That I never quite understood. / His neck said: 'Not seen, not caught.' / His heart said: 'Nobody.' / His arm said: 'Discuss.'"
† Someone claimed that Zola first used the term, but I've been unable to confirm this.

"governor") and lieutenants, in addition to knife artists, spear carriers, and background muscle; they were now students of management.

And whereas the *apaches* had generally limited their activities to keeping a string of two or three whores on the sidewalk and mugging pedestrians late at night, the new men owned *maisons closes*, ran contraband liquor and cigarettes, eventually took over the cocaine trade from the Germans, who had been the principal importers since long before the war. They did robberies, too, but street crime was beneath them; nothing less than a bank or a warehouse would do. They were less feared than the *apaches* by the general population, because they killed only one another. They enjoyed socializing at *bals*, many of which, such as the Petit Jardin, on Avenue de Clichy, designated special days for them and their top-earning girls, from which ordinary customers were barred. The social aspect of these gatherings was always secondary to their business component—new girls were passed in review, new product lines discussed, the take from recent jobs cut up and distributed. It was all very correct. The trend-setting *caïds* would not tolerate the presence of any man not wearing a necktie or walking around in imperfectly shined shoes.

The cast of characters shifted a few times. The top-ranking

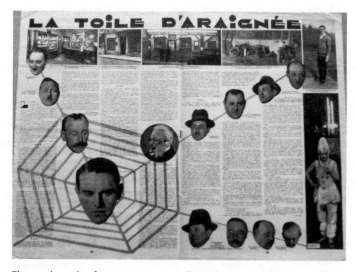

The spiderweb of crime, in a typically striking centerfold layout from *Détective*, 1930

gangsters of the 1920s were Parisians, such figures as Alphonse Lecroq, a.k.a. Miroir, "the best-looking man in Paris"; Émile Jacquot, a.k.a. Charlot Leather Coat, hijacker of *maisons closes*; Eugène Charrier, who owned the Bal des Gravilliers; Maurice Jalabert, who owned the Chabanais; Charles Codebo, who owned the Moulin Galant. But right around then there began a major surge of immigration from points south: the Corsicans had arrived. There had long been plenty of Corsican pimps in Pigalle,* but now Montmartre was called the "capital of Corsica." Important gangsters moved to Paris, including the people who effectively owned Marseille, and they brought along, as muscle, illiterates who a month earlier had been tending sheep in the hills. There were two strains, the Corsicans from Corsica and the Corsicans from Marseille, the former led by Ange Salicetti and including the Preri, Morazzani, Santi, and Stephani families; the latter headed by Philippe Graziani and dominated by the Nicolai and Morganti clans. Despite their free-spending habits, the Corsicans were not necessarily appreciated by the locals; for one thing, they conversed in their own dialect rather than argot. A war between the two strains broke out in 1936, having principally to do with cocaine trafficking—Graziani was killed the following year by Salicetti, who himself would be cut down in 1950. After World War II they battled over the cigarette trade, and two decades later they fought over the heroin business that came to be known worldwide as the French Connection.

It was not the Corsicans, however, who were the prime beneficiaries of the German occupation of Paris—not that they minded it, since many of them owned cathouses requisitioned by officers, from which they made out very well. But the black market was run by Parisian gangsters, the same people who operated as the Carlingue, the French Gestapo. Equipped with official papers, they were free to roam the city and beyond, to manufacture and sell documents of all sorts, to collect and market the contents of apartments belonging to Jews, and to torture and kill Resistance members in the cellars at 93 Rue Lauriston. After

Police detectives at the scene of a jewelry store robbery, 1930s

* Chevalier claimed he couldn't find a single patronym from the island in the municipal arrest records between 1900 and 1910, although he must surely have noticed Leca—unless he, too, was really named Dupont.

D-day, many made last-minute attempts to change their spots and join the Resistance themselves; in any case a startling percentage of them managed to evade the postwar cleansings, official or otherwise, and went right back to business. Jo Attia, who seems to have played a double game during the war, acting on behalf of both sides, was arrested by the Germans and would have been executed if his Carlingue pals hadn't stepped in. Upon being released from Mauthausen he reunited with his former colleagues Pierre Loutrel, Abel Danos, and Georges Boucheseiche, all of them active at Rue Lauriston, and formed the Front-Wheel-Drive Gang, named in honor of their favored Citroën 15 Six. They specialized in serious armed robbery: banks, armored cars, freight trains, factory payrolls. They did very well for about a year and a half, operating at a rapid clip, until Loutrel went out of control. Known to newspaper readers as Pierrot le Fou, he was France's first Public Enemy Number One, an alcoholic given to psychotic violence, first distanced by his gang and finally dumped by the milieu. He operated on his own until one night in 1946 when, following a failed break-in at a Paris jewelry store, he accidentally shot himself in the bladder while drunkenly stowing his gun. After his agonizingly slow death, his colleagues buried him in secret. He was routinely pinned for seemingly any unsolved crime until his body was finally found three years later by the police. The picture circulated by the police to prove their identification of the remains, a photo montage of Loutrel's skull laid over a portrait taken in life, is an image of criminal destiny more potent than any tattoo.

Had he been caught he would have been guillotined. Dr. Joseph-Ignace Guillotin (1738–1814) intended the device to relieve the sufferings of the condemned by ensuring them a quick and painless death, and to impart capital punishment equally, without class distinction. It wound up serving for not quite two centuries, and provided the nation and the world with a nonpareil graphic representation of fatality. Before that, on Place de Grève, where executions were held for five hundred years, the means were sloppier and defined by class. Plebeians were hanged, the gentry were decapitated by ax or sword, and criminals guilty of lèse-majesté were drawn and quartered. From the sixteenth century to the revolution, brigands and murderers were

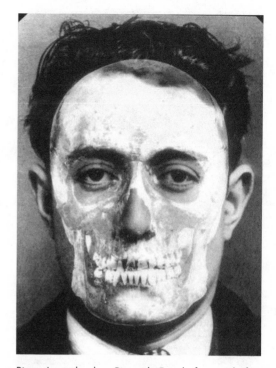

Pierre Loutrel, a.k.a. Pierrot le Fou, before and after death, 1946

An eighteenth-century guillotine

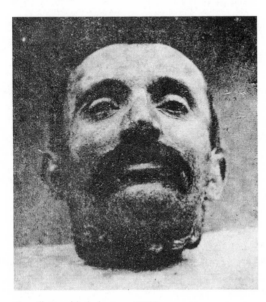

A guillotined head, circa 1900

afforded the martyrdom of the wheel, which is to say that they were strapped to a rough St. Andrew's cross; the bones of their arms, legs, thighs, and chest were broken with iron bars; and then they were attached to a large horizontal wheel, their broken limbs tied under them, their faces turned to the sky. They remained there for as long as the deity saw fit to keep them alive. The phrase *coup de grâce* originally referred to the mercifully terminal blow the executioner could administer with the iron bar. Executions were always holiday occasions, and indeed they were frequently held on June 23, St. John's Day and the eve of the solstice, when the festivities would be topped off by a feast and a dance. In the sixteenth century, additional entertainment was provided by burning cats alive, in a sack or a barrel.

Dr. Guillotin did not invent the instrument named after him, which was perfected by Antoine Louis and Tobias Schmidt—the latter, a German engineer, proposed the angled blade. Its first victim, in 1792, was Nicolas Jacques Pelletier, who assaulted and robbed people on the street; its last, in 1977, was Hamida Djandoubi, a killer who tortured his victims. (He was guillotined in Marseille; France abolished capital punishment in 1981.) There were a total of nine headsmen after the revolution, seven of whom were officially designated national executioners, an office whose top-hatted tenant was often referred to as Monsieur de Paris; Louis and Anatole Deibler, father and son, between them served for sixty years. The Widow was moved from Place de Grève to the Barrière Saint-Jacques in 1832; to the front of the Grande-Roquette prison, on Rue de la Roquette, in 1851; to the front of the Santé prison, on the corner of Rue de la Santé and Boulevard Arago, in 1909; and finally to an inner courtyard of that prison after 1939. To go to the guillotine was to marry the widow, to go to the barber's, to sneeze in the sawdust, to be shortened by thirty centimeters, to stick your head out the window, to get yourself photographed—the executioner's aide who positioned the victim's head in the lunette was called "the photographer."

Louis-Ferdinand Céline called the guillotine "the Prix Goncourt for murderers." That would have applied especially well to Pierre-François Lacenaire, played by Marcel Herrand in *Children of Paradise* with exactly the right combination of wit and menace, even though his actions in the picture are all fictitious.

Lacenaire, born in a suburb of Lyon in 1803, was a brilliant but unruly student expelled from a string of schools for insubordination. He wanted to be a famous writer, or maybe a lawyer, but after moving to Paris in 1829 he soon lost all his money gambling, and contemplated suicide.

> I sat on the parapet, considering my options. Drowning? No, the pain would be too great. Poison? I don't want to be seen in agony. The blade? Yes, that must be the sweetest death. Since then, my life has been one long suicide. I was no longer my own master; I belonged to the blade. But instead of a knife or a razor I chose the great ax of the guillotine. I wanted it to be a vengeance. Society would have my blood, but I would have the blood of Society.

He decided on a scheme to lure a bank messenger, kill him and take his money, then remove the corpse to the countryside, dismember it, and cook the pieces so that no trace would remain. Since he couldn't find a promising accomplice, he had himself arrested so that he could recruit in prison—he stole a carriage and fenced it so ineptly that he was caught at once and sentenced to a year. He passed through the Dépôt, La Force, Bicêtre, and finally the suburban prison of Poissy, where he met Pierre-Victor Avril, who was to be his inseparable companion (and who also turns up as a character in *Children of Paradise*). When they both got out in 1834, word got to them that someone they had known in prison, a swindler named Chardon, known as Tante Madeleine because of his *moeurs particuliers*, who dressed as a priest and preyed on the pious and stupid, had threatened to inform on them. They killed him with a triangular file and an ax, and then Lacenaire beat Chardon's aged mother to death. Lacenaire then sought to lure a bank messenger to his room by means of a forged draft on a Lyon bank, but when the messenger eventually showed up he caused such a ruckus that Lacenaire was forced to flee. Two months later, he was arrested for forgery. Eventually brought before a judge, he dismissed the charge as a trifle and admitted to killing Chardon and his mother. Over the following eight months, before and after his trial, Lacenaire finally achieved

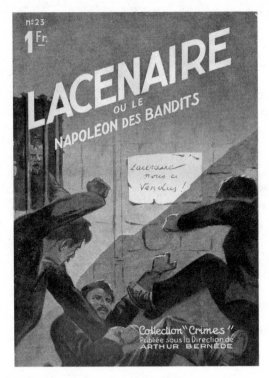

A dime novel about Lacenaire, 1931

Liabeuf's weapons and handmade spiked armlets and braces, 1910

the glory he'd sought. He wrote his memoirs (which have never gone out of print) as well as songs and poems, and word got around in Paris concerning his philosophy of crime and his epigrams. The infirmary at La Force became his salon; duchesses and literary arbiters came to call and succumbed to his mesmeric sway. Finally, on January 9, 1836, he inserted his head in the lunette, but the blade was misaligned and got stuck on the way down. Lacenaire then had a chance to turn around and watch the blade as it fell the second time.

Literature had been awaiting Lacenaire. He was the romantic criminal, a role that many had wishfully claimed for themselves, but he was the first to turn his words into deeds. He is inescapable in French literature thereafter, discussed or alluded to by Stendhal, Balzac, Hugo, Gautier, Baudelaire, Laforgue; absorbed and recast by Isidore Ducasse in the sixth of the *Chants de Maldoror*. He is included in André Breton's *Anthology of Black Humor*, and Breton described Bonnelier and Arago's prison interviews with him as "an illustration of thought in the nineteenth century." Breton also wrote, famously, that "the simplest Surrealist action consists of going into the street, guns in hand, and shooting at random into the crowd," an allusion to Lucien Morisset, a law clerk in Tours fired for theft who did just that, in 1881—one dead, four wounded—explicitly under the influence of Lacenaire. (He was sentenced to forced labor for life.) It is necessary to recall that this was something that hadn't been done before, and was rare for a long time after.

Jean-Jacques Liabeuf may never have heard of Lacenaire, much less read him, but he carried out an act of vengeance upon society that Lacenaire would have understood. Liabeuf was an apprentice shoemaker from Saint-Étienne who kept getting into minor scrapes with the law, racking up stints in jail, and then was sentenced to serve in the Bats d'Af. Upon his release in 1909 he moved to Paris, where he fell in love with a young prostitute, Alexandrine Pigeon, whose pimp was a police informant. Very soon he was arrested for pandering by two vice cops who had seen him with her. His lawyer failed to show up at his trial, and Liabeuf was given three months in prison, followed by an *interdiction de séjour*; caught on the street in Paris after his release, he was sent back to serve another month. He swore that he would exact revenge upon the police for framing him. On January 8, 1910, three days before his twenty-fourth birthday, he walked through the parish of Saint-Merri armed with a revolver and two shoemaker's blades and wearing, under a short cape, leather armlets and shoulder braces of his own manufacture bristling with sharpened steel points. In a dive on Rue Aubry-le-Boucher he yelled, "I want to take out two cops!" and rushed outside, where he was immediately set upon by a passing patrol. They quickly released him, their fingers bleeding. He stabbed one of them in the chest and shot another before being brought down with a saber thrust in the hallway of the hotel next door.

He was sentenced to death in May, the execution set for July 1. In the meantime the story circulated, and his cause was taken up by the combined forces of the left. A journalist called his case "the Dreyfus Affair of the working class." The militant socialist newspaper *La Guerre Sociale* wrote that Liabeuf gave "a lesson in energy and courage to the mass of ordinary folk, and to us, revolutionaries, he set an example"; for this the editor was sentenced to four months in jail and a thousand-franc fine. Miguel Almereyda, Jean Vigo's father,* warned that there would be more blood around the guillotine than under it. Tens of thousands of people, protesters and curiosity-seekers, massed around the Santé prison on the night before Liabeuf's execution:

Execution. Drawing by Jacques Wely, 1900

> Excited couples came straight from the *bal-musette*: a whore and her mack, somewhat sinister themselves, the girl a bit too happy, her eyes enormous with makeup, the man making a throat-cutting gesture with his hand. Some came by taxi from the nightclubs, in evening dress, plumes in the hair of the *poules de luxe*—hisses and threats were tossed their way . . . Militants from every faction were there, driven back by lines of black-clad police. Rioting erupted when the wagon bearing the guillotine arrived, escorted by a cavalry squadron. The pitched battle lasted for hours, charging police driving us into the darkness of the side streets and then the crowd surging back a minute later. Jaurès was spotted at the head of one wedge

"The police charge." Illustration by Félix Vallotton, 1893

* His real name was Eugène Vigo.

and nearly killed. Almereyda tried in vain to force his way through the barricades. There were many injuries and some blood—one cop was killed. At dawn, fatigue overtook the crowd. When the blade fell on the furious head, still protesting his innocence, an impotent delirium took hold of the twenty or thirty thousand protesters and became one long roar: "Murderers!"

As Victor Serge notes, Liabeuf died still shouting that he was not a pimp. On the scale of one-person insurrections, he and his betrayed innocence lie at the opposite end from Lacenaire, the romantic fatalist, *acte-gratuit* aesthete, and pioneer of suicide by cop. Directly in the middle falls Jacques Mesrine, dead now for thirty-five years but still an unquiet symbol and cause of contention in the Francophone world. Mesrine,* born in Clichy to a bourgeois family in 1936, separated himself from his upbringing very early, started hanging around Pigalle as a teenager, signed up for the military, and served in Algeria; he was decorated for valor by de Gaulle. The experience, by his own admission, formed him, and likely unhinged him. Although he dispatches the subject of his military service in about five fairly bland pages of his memoirs, he is said to have participated in summary executions of civilian prisoners, and at some point joined the Organisation de l'Armée Secrète. Back in civilian life he became a thief, carried out burglaries in Spain and Switzerland as well as France, was jailed twice, then was arrested in 1968 when he tried to hold up a couture house in Paris. He managed to flee to Canada with a girlfriend, and it was at that point that he went from small-time crook to major media spectacle, eventually becoming Public Enemy Number One.

He robbed factory payrolls, robbed an armory, robbed the Deauville Casino, undertook various kidnappings for ransom. He claimed in his memoirs to have killed thirty-nine people. He appeared indestructible and uncontainable. He evaded several sweeping manhunts and escaped from prison three times, including from maximum security—although he failed in two

"Mesrine Gunned Down," *Qui? Police*, 1979

---

* The *s* in his name is silent, although television and radio broadcasters seemed to make a point of sounding it, perhaps to make the name appear foreign.

attempts to break into prisons to free inmates—and fled the courthouse during one of his own trials, taking the judge as hostage. In the course of another trial, in 1977, he loosened his necktie, removed a clutch of handcuff keys from the knot, and flung them at the judge as evidence of the pervasive corruption of the system. In 1979 he kidnapped a tabloid reporter, took him into the woods, stripped him, and shot him in the cheek and the arm "to keep him from talking . . . and writing bullshit," and in the leg "for pleasure." The reporter subsequently found an informant who gave up the location of Mesrine's hideout, in the Eighteenth Arrondissement.

On November 2, 1979, Mesrine's car was stopped at Porte de Clignancourt, behind a truck whose bed was covered with a tarp. Suddenly the tarp lifted, revealing a line of gunmen from the anti-gang squad. Twenty-one shots were fired at Mesrine's car; eighteen bullets were found in his corpse. Another took out one of his female companion's eyes. Witnesses were unanimous: there was no warning issued before the firing started. Mesrine's memoirs, *The Death Wish*, written in prison, are terse and novelistic, clearly influenced by the Série Noire style. They mostly avoid self-pity and stick to what seem to be forthright admissions: "I have chosen revolt, and the rebuffs of society mean nothing to me. I have violated its laws with pleasure and have lived outside them. I have accorded myself the right to take . . . I am an outlaw. Society has lost all power over me and has made me impervious to punitive sanctions." In France he is a folk hero the way Jesse James or Pretty Boy Floyd were in their day in America; possibly no figure is cited more often in French hip-hop and hardcore. He is an image of resistance to power at a time when active political resistance has fallen to an unprecedented low. The moral of his book—that criminals are made by the penal system—resonates profoundly among France's youth.

La Santé, from the maximum-security block of which Mesrine made his last break, is the only prison remaining within Paris, which now depends primarily on a network of penal institutions in the suburbs. The city has had a great many prisons and houses of detention over the centuries, the most widely famous the Bastille, built in the fourteenth century as a fortress and turned into a prison by Cardinal Richelieu three centuries

The Santé prison. Photograph by Charles Marville, circa 1867

The revolutionary crowd attacks the Bastille, 1789, as imagined in the 1840s

The Maison de la Force, early nineteenth century

later. It had eight towers, walls six feet thick, a dry moat with a drawbridge, but its maximum capacity was a mere forty-five. Voltaire was interred there twice in his youth; the Man in the Iron Mask (it was velvet, actually) died there in 1703; the Marquis de Sade spent five and a half years. The crowd seized the prison on July 14, 1789, but it was a private contractor who began to demolish it the following day, turning some of its stones into miniature replicas of the edifice, which were sold to collectors. Far older than the Bastille was the Grand Châtelet, which originated as a wooden fort in the ninth century and was turned into a prison beginning in 1190. It richly deserved its reputation as the most sinister building in Paris, possessing all the horrendous features that lore later ascribed to the Bastille: secret lockups, oubliettes, and a place in the cellars called "the ditch," into which inmates were lowered by pulley. The ditch was a sort of inverted cone with a low ceiling, making it impossible to stand or lie down, but then, the floor was six inches deep in mud and shit. The average life expectancy there was two weeks; prisoners might be eaten by rats, or drowned when the waters of the Seine rose. While the Bastille's inmates were freed by the revolutionary crowd, the Châtelet's last 214 prisoners were massacred by it instead, in 1792.

The Maison de la Force, built as an *hôtel particulier*, became a prison in the 1780s. Its men's wing was intended for debtors; its women's side was where fathers could consign daughters, and husbands their wives. In 1790 the reform-minded duke of La Rochefoucauld-Liancourt, who observed rampant scabies, ringworm, and scrofula there, wrote, "It would be less evil to let the human race die out than to preserve it with such lack of consideration." In the nineteenth century, when it was expanded and became a general prison, it derived considerable notoriety from its use by novelists, such as Eugène Sue in his *Mysteries of Paris*, and Balzac, who had Lucien de Rubempré hang himself in his cell there.* The Maison de la Force was demolished in 1845. Mazas, which replaced it, was constructed as a model prison, the biggest in France, with a panoptic design of six three-story buildings arrayed around a central tower from which all the

* When Oscar Wilde was asked to name the saddest event in his life, he replied that it was the death of Lucien de Rubempré.

wedge-shaped cells could be seen. Rimbaud was briefly locked up there, as were Victor Hugo, Félix Fénéon, and the future prime minister Georges Clemenceau. It was razed in 1900, to spare visitors to that year's Universal Exposition from having to see it when they exited the Gare de Lyon, across the street. Sainte-Pélagie, built in the seventeenth century as a home for former prostitutes and made into a prison a century later, was by turns a confinement for royalists, highborn sexual offenders, debtors, and political prisoners. Sade, Vidocq, Proudhon, Nerval, Béranger, Daumier, Courbet, Jules Vallès, Aristide Bruant, Communards, and anarchists all spent time there. It was torn down in 1899.

Most ordinary arrestees in the nineteenth century were taken to local holding tanks familiarly called *violons*. If they were not released after questioning they were temporarily moved to the Dépôt, in the police prefecture, which was equipped with eighty-three cells for men and seventy-six for women; the cells were shared, and were reserved for inmates who needed to be isolated from the general population. All others were stuffed into two common rooms, the *salle des habits noirs*, for those "conventionally attired," and the *salle des blouses*, for the proles; there was also a common room for children. For a good part of the century, female detainees were taken to the Salpêtrière, which was also an insane asylum, and for a time some were taken to the former convent of the Madelonnettes, which in addition took up from La Force the function of lodging women committed by their families. Prostitutes were consigned to Saint-Lazare, formerly a leprosarium, the oldest part of which dated back to the twelfth century; it became a prison during the revolution. For most of its term, Saint-Lazare was a hospital prison; prostitutes reported there for their required annual checkups, and those who turned out to be carrying or afflicted by sexually transmitted diseases were held as long as they displayed symptoms. Its second wing lodged prostitutes who were being held for crimes, and later in the century it expanded to take in a general population of female prisoners; Louise Michel and Mata Hari were both inmates. There was also a section reserved for young girls removed by reformers from families of ill repute; somehow it was believed that sequestration would preserve their moral fiber. Saint-Lazare was closed in 1927.

Mazas prison in 1871

"Entry and exit of the royal prison." Illustration by Honoré Daumier, from *Le Charivari*, 1834

The exercise yard at the Salpêtrière asylum, circa 1900

The two prisons of La Roquette were built in the 1830s. The Grande Roquette was the Dépôt des Condamnés—its inmates were either on death row and destined to be guillotined on the street outside or else awaiting shipment to one of the penal colonies. After numerous protests over its conditions, it was closed in 1899. The Petite Roquette was a juvenile detention center, for boys ages fourteen to twenty, built on a semipanoptic model, its inmates spending their days in a "chapel school" where they were isolated in booths open at the front and top. Alfred Delvau described the pair as "one the antechamber of the other, the prologue facing the epilogue, the exposition in view of the dénouement, the tree nursery on the step of the forest." Then, from 1935 until it closed in 1974, the Petite Roquette was the city's last prison for women.

La Santé, built in the 1860s and doubled in size following the closure of the Grande Roquette, was the signal prison of the twentieth century. Its high, featureless walls impart a Gothic gloom to its neighborhood in the Fourteenth. It looks impregnable, and yet quite a number of escapes have been made; you can see a convincing one in Jacques Becker's *Le trou* (1960), based on the admirably claustrophobic novel by José Giovanni. Jean Genet, who was first incarcerated at age fifteen in the Petite Roquette, spent time at La Santé in addition to a number of penal institutions outside the city. Other alumni include Guillaume Apollinaire, when he was accused of stealing the *Mona Lisa*, as well as Maurice Papon, Manuel Noriega, and Ilich Ramírez Sánchez, a.k.a. Carlos the Jackal—it remains the number one celebrity lockup in France. For a time in the late twentieth century its four blocks were divided up ethnically: one for Western Europeans, one for North Africans, one for sub-Saharan Africans, and one for the rest of the world.

For several centuries, those judged guilty of infractions deemed too severe for ordinary prison time but not quite deserving of the death penalty were sent to the *bagne*, which has come to mean "penal colony." As its etymology would suggest—from the Latin *balneum*—its origins were nautical, and indeed the *bagnes* were at first literally galleys, exclusively so until the mid-eighteenth century; the practice survived until steamships began to dominate in the mid-nineteenth. In the intervening century,

"Île de Ré: convicts leaving for Guyana," circa 1910

dry-land *bagnes* were built near French ports, the most important at Toulon, Brest, and Rochefort. For reasons that included security and reduction of costs, they began to be moved offshore and overseas around 1840.* The island of Saint-Martin-de-Ré, in the Bay of Biscay, was the transshipment point for the *bagnes* in Indochina, Madagascar, French Guyana, and New Caledonia. The Cayenne complex in French Guyana achieved worldwide notoriety as a result of the cases of Alfred Dreyfus and much later Papillon (Henri Charrière), both of whom were confined to Devil's Island, which in turn was just one part of the *bagne* of the Îles du Salut; the entire complex comprised four *bagnes* and twenty-four inland camps. The New Caledonia *bagnes*, in particular the immense one at Nouméa, became associated with the Communards who were sentenced there in 1871, some remaining for many decades afterward. (Francis Carco, whose father was an administrator, was born there in 1886.) But as brutal as these civil *bagnes* were—and there is a vast literature of torture and escape, concerning Cayenne in particular—they pale compared with the military *bagnes*.

Both of the military *bagnes* were in North Africa; confusingly, one of them, Tataouine, was a single installation in Tunisia, while the other, Biribi, was a large complex of far-flung camps: five in Algeria, three in Tunisia, and one in Morocco. Biribi, which achieved notoriety as a result of Georges Darien's 1890 novel of that name, Aristide Bruant's song "À Biribi," a special issue of *L'Assiette au Beurre* in 1905, and many other things, took its name, in common parlance if not quite official, from a version of the shell game. The great reporter Albert Londres called Biribi "hell on earth"; his book on the subject was titled *Dante Never Saw Anything* (1924). Biribi began at an uncertain point before 1845 and was not shut down until the early 1970s, despite its being known to one and all as a place of torture, where the means of discipline included chaining prisoners to a horizontal bar and leaving them open to the elements for an indefinite period (*la barre*), binding hands and feet together behind the prisoner's back and then leaving him exposed (*la crapaudine*),

* There was a precedent for this. In 1797 the Directoire sentenced sixty-five deputies to what was termed the "dry guillotine," deporting them to Guyana.

Institute of Correctional Education for Children, called "Petite Roquette," circa 1910

"Cayenne: prisoners from Madagascar breaking rocks," circa 1910

Biribi, discipline militaire, by Georges Darien. Cover illustration by Théophile Steinlen, 1890

and putting the bound prisoner into a small tent with his head out and a pan of water just out of reach (*le baillon*). The military *bagnes* were intended for military discipline, comparable to, for example, the "brig" in the U.S. Navy. A disproportionate number of the inmates in Biribi, however, came from the Bats d'Af, formally the Bataillons d'Infanterie Légère d'Afrique. Originally a colonial military division of no special distinction, the Bats d'Af began at some indefinite point in the late nineteenth century to be employed as a punitive measure for young urban miscreants, and that was cemented by a law of 1905 specifying the sorts of convicts to be sent there, which included pimps, con artists, and sexual offenders. Naturally, the corps became an extension of the French underworld; the function of the *caïd*, for example, originated there and was exported to Paris. In their day, the Bats d'Af were also notorious for the open and unabashed pursuit of homosexual practices among their ranks, engaged in by at least two-thirds of conscripts, by a conservative estimate. The battalions were not finally dissolved until 1972.

Overseeing all incarcerations were the police, formally established in 1667, organized under a prefect in 1800, and given uniforms in 1829, when cops in Paris began to be called *sergents de ville*. There were 85 of them that year, 480 in 1849; reorganized under Napoléon III and now called *gardiens de la paix*, they numbered 7,756 right after the Commune, and more than 8,000 in 1892, following a further reorganization in the wake of anarchist bomb scares. There were 17,000 in 1938, and there are about 15,000 today. Traditionally they were attired in pelerines, short hooded capes, and for a century these were topped with the cylindrical *képi*, which gave way to caps in 1985.* The police were hated by the poor, even the most law-abiding; they were not viewed as protectors or justice seekers but as agents of power, at best a nuisance, at worst a menace. In a small item in *L'Endehors* in 1893, Fénéon reported seeing in a music hall in the Twentieth Arrondissement the following notice: BY ORDER OF THE PREFECT: SONGS CONTAINING THE TERMS "POLICE OFFICER" OR "CONSTABLE,"

---

* Contrary to a persistent belief in the Anglo-Saxon world, they are not *gendarmes*, that term being reserved for the rural and exurban constabulary, roughly equivalent to state troopers in the United States.

OR REFERENCES TO ANY OTHER KEEPER OF THE PEACE, ARE STRICTLY FORBIDDEN; he suggested that there were many synonyms to choose from. And indeed the police were collectively known as *la poulaille* (poultry), *la renifle* (the snort), *l'arnaque* (the scam), and many other terms not easily translatable, and individual cops were mannequins, pedestrians, penguins, snails, slugs, *flics*, and for a very long time *vaches* (cows), which began as a general term of abuse but by the late nineteenth century had come to be applied to all forces of order, most usually the police. Steinlen's frontispiece drawing for the second volume of Aristide Bruant's *Dans la rue* (1895) shows a young couple, the girl looking on shyly while the boy carves something in a wall. The last page of the book shows a couple of cops in pelerines inspecting the result, not a heart pierced by an arrow, but MORT AUX VACHES.

A fascination with crime, its players, its circumstances, its props and effluvia, was something that cut across class lines. Although this prurient interest dated back to antiquity, it was not really exploited by the press until a paper called *Faits Divers* appeared in 1862, soon followed by first the *Petit Journal* (1863–1944) and then the *Petit Parisien* (1876–1944), which initiated and cultivated the enduring national fascination with the *fait-divers*. There is no real equivalent in English for this term, which can be rendered literally as "sundry fact." It is usually a brief news item, comparable in size to the filler item but not simply used to fill up column space; frequently *faits-divers* are stacked together under a rubric. More generally they are the sort of thing that tabloids have traditionally been devoted to, crimes and local disasters and instances of grotesque misbehavior; the term can encompass continuing stories, with the proviso that they be complete unto themselves, with few if any reverberations in the wider world. As Roland Barthes put it, "Take a murder: if it's political, it's news; if it isn't, it's a *fait-divers*." The term effectively defines a broad category in French thought, only partly intersecting with the English *anecdote*. The germ of *Madame Bovary* is a *fait-divers*, for example, although that cannot be said of *Les misérables*, for all that it contains numerous *faits-divers* in its voluminous folds. Some of Balzac's shorter works are decorated *faits-divers*, while Georges Simenon's *romans durs*, his non-Maigret novels, are pure *faits-divers*, perhaps more than any other body of

Police rampage. Illustration by Félix Vallotton, 1893

"Mort aux vaches." End plate by Théophile Steinlen for Aristide Bruant's *Dans la rue*, vol. 2, 1889

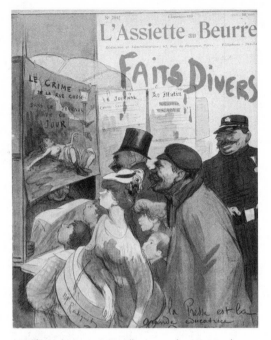

"Les faits-divers." Cover illustration by Max Radiguet, from *L'Assiette au Beurre*, 1906

"The execution of Jean-Baptiste Troppmann." Broadside print, 1870

Cover of *L'Oeil de la Police*, 1914

literary work, if you except Fénéon's daily factual contributions to a *fait-divers* column in *Le Matin* for six months in 1906. The essence of the *fait-divers* is that it involves a voyeuristic fascination with other people's miseries, a taste for the lurid and the scabrous—ideally stories of passion and violence with implied scenery, although mere morbidity and squalor will do in a pinch—and of course the ability to consume such things in the safety of one's armchair.*

Le Petit Journal made its bones in 1870 with its comprehensive coverage of the Troppmann case—a young German immigrant murdered eight members of the Kinck family in Pantin and was caught carrying their papers and jewelry, about to board a steamer to America—which virtually defined the *fait-divers*. It got a further jump on the competition when it began to feature an illustrated supplement in 1884, and then, as of 1890, illustrated covers in full color. Parisians were able to feast their eyes every week on tabloid-size artists' renditions of train wrecks, *apache* brawls, crimes of passion, anarchist bombings, and dramas in the

---

* A law of 1884 prohibited the hawking of counterfactual news reports on the street, which shut down a brief frenzy of sheets headlining such things as an explosion in the Chamber of Deputies and the suicides of Sarah Bernhardt and Louise Michel.

colonies. Although *L'Oeil de la Police*, a more specialized publication employing similar cover art, attempted to refine the market in 1908, its impact was ephemeral. It was not until twenty years later that a weekly entirely devoted to crime properly galvanized the nation.

Détective, a tabloid with full-page photographic front and back covers and aggressively jazzy layouts, was launched in 1928 by Georges Kessel and his brother, the novelist and reporter Joseph Kessel, under the surprising imprint of Gallimard, the most august of Parisian publishers. The paper succeeded in having it both ways. Early issues ran in-house ads labeled "How They Read It," with photographs of *Détective* being studied on café terraces by flat-capped hoodlums, *midinettes*, sailors on leave. At the same time, it drew the bourgeois intelligentsia with—besides its layouts—contributions by significant writers, including Carco, Mac Orlan, and Jean Cocteau; major reporters such as Joseph Kessel and Géo London; the Bonnot Gang affiliate Eugène Dieudonné, who had escaped from Devil's Island and wrote a series on the penal colonies from his new home in Brazil; and the young Simenon, who as Georges Sim wrote puzzle stories: prizes were awarded to readers for the most ingenious solution to the mystery. By its second year its circulation had shot from 250,000 to 800,000; above its masthead ran the line "The largest circulation of any illustrated paper in the world."*

It was not alone in its field. Besides lesser epigones such as *Police Magazine*, there was, for example, the short-lived *Scandale: Revue des Affaires Criminelles* (1933), which sumptuously aestheticized the subject, with nudes and Hollywood stars alongside bloody crime scenes and staged gang photos by Brassaï. And there was *Le Crapouillot*, which began as a frontline paper in World War I (the name means "trench mortar," as well as being a slang term for "penis"), mutated into an art magazine in the 1920s, and then in the late '30s brought a fine connoisseur's eye and scholarly

Scandale: Revue des Affaires Criminelles, with Joan Crawford on the cover, 1933

---

* And, well, it still exists, sort of. In the later 1930s its layouts got stodgier and its literary quality dropped off; after the war it became simply formulaic. In the '70s it featured cover photos of bikini-clad models accompanied by shock-horror headlines, and in the '80s it featured unaccompanied shock-horror headlines in four-inch letters, white on black. Now, as *Nouveau Détective*, it looks like a typically busy supermarket tabloid, but with pictures of victims and monsters instead of stars. It's very big on murders of children, retailed with disconcerting anatomical specificity.

"New Year's Day on death row at the Santé prison."
Détective, 1930

documentation to the disinterested study of crime and vice, knowingly situating the horrors of the moment in well-upholstered historical context.

But none of these was as purely symptomatic as *Détective*, which in its prime exemplified all the ambiguities of the Parisian bourgeois attitude toward crime: its vicarious perch on the dotted line between order and disorder, its amused tolerance for mayhem at a safe distance, its epicurean consumption of the sordid in decorously presented canapé form, its fatalistic preoccupation with foredoomed and extreme mentalities and behaviors, its appreciation for the promiscuous mingling of louche glamour and grim terminal depravity, its supposition that barbarity begins just outside the door, making the *foyer* (the hearth) the capital of reason. Also, it implied a view of class in which you, the reader, proved your aristocratic bona fides by virtue of your ability to encompass high and low with equal sangfroid. Even cops and grocers were invited to join the elect for as long as they could cock an eyebrow, exhale a smoke ring, and forget that they were cops and grocers.

11

Insurgents

In a sense, the revolution that began in Paris in 1789 never really ended. The uprising of the population against its rulers, which overthrew feudalism and absolutism, produced the Declaration of the Rights of Man that same year and then proclaimed a republic in 1792, failed to achieve its stated goal of liberty, fraternity, and equality. The Constitution of 1793, passed overwhelmingly by popular vote (universal male suffrage), was never implemented. In 1794, in the wake of the Terror, the army besieged and defeated the sansculottes in the Faubourg Saint-Antoine, summarily terminating any hope of a classless state. The following year, the Directoire replaced universal male suffrage with a vote based on property, handed the economy over to speculators, brought back the monarchists, and paved the way for Napoléon Bonaparte. And after Napoléon's defeat the Bourbons immediately came back, first the feeble Louis XVIII and then the vile Charles X.

Nevertheless, the Parisian population would not fold its cards. The Parisians have historically shown an extraordinary willingness and even eagerness to fight authority in the streets. The first half of the nineteenth century in particular can seem like a continuous blur of riots and skirmishes and full-scale insurrections, ranging from the strictly local and obscurely motivated to the world-historical and reverberating. Even today, when the city is generally far outside the means of even the middle class, and its

The mob piles on. Drawing by Théophile Steinlen, circa 1900

221

social problems have been exported to the *banlieues* and the provinces, it continues to serve as a theater for every sort of demonstration and strike, on a regular basis, often to the exasperation of visitors from more placid or repressed societies. Friedrich Engels sounded like a particularly appreciative nineteenth-century tourist when he wrote that the Parisians "join, as no other people have done, a passion for enjoying life with a passion for taking historical action." A century later, Walter Benjamin speculated that "Paris is a counterpart in the social order to what Vesuvius is in the natural order: a menacing, hazardous massif, an ever-active hotbed of revolution. But just as the slopes of Vesuvius, thanks to the layers of lava that cover them, have been transformed into paradisal orchards, so the lava of revolutions provides uniquely fertile ground for the blossoming of art, festivity, fashion."

The decades that passed between the demise of Napoléon Bonaparte's empire in 1814–15 and the coup d'état undertaken by his nephew, Napoléon III, in 1851, are a confusing welter of incidents that account for nearly every year of that span. What they had in common is that they were all directed against authority, generally royal authority, although they took many different forms. There were riots by liberals,* and there were riots by students defending professors who had been expelled from their chairs because of their liberalism. There were anticlerical riots—the Church, after all, was the First Estate, above even the nobility in its power. There were riots by Bonapartists, including, in 1822, the brief uprising that resulted in the execution of the Four Sergeants of La Rochelle, once so famous that cafés were named in their memory. The sergeants were Carbonari, members of a Masonic secret society that exerted enormous influence throughout Europe, notably in the reunification of Italy. The Carbonari—the name derives from its original function as a guild of charcoal makers—in turn inspired a great number of secret societies with diverse goals, such as the later revolutionary cabals: the Society of the Seasons, the Society of Families, the Society of Avengers. The first of these attempted its own insur-

* "Liberal" in a sense not far removed from the one it now has in the United States, as opposed to its current meaning in Europe, where it signifies a proponent of laissez-faire capitalism.

rection in 1839, out of the blue, which failed because its potential allies were caught unprepared; all three societies were active in the thwarted revolution of 1848. Secret societies in any case held a cloak-and-dagger appeal that covered the political spectrum. In his *History of the Thirteen* (1833), Balzac, who was fascinated by occult fraternities and attempted without much success to found a secret lodge of writers, laid out the seductive promise of the ring:

Disabled veterans. Illustration by Célestin Nanteuil, 1840s

> In Paris under the Empire, thirteen men came together who were equally possessed by the same idea, all of them endowed with sufficient energy to be faithful to the same principles, sufficiently honest with one another not to betray the cause even when their individual interests conflicted, so deeply prudent as to keep hidden the sacred bonds that linked them, strong enough to position themselves above all laws, tough enough to undertake all that was required, and so lucky that they almost always succeeded in their schemes. They had run great risks but veiled their defeats; they were impervious to fear and had never trembled in the presence of the prince, nor of the executioner, nor of innocence itself; they accepted one another for what they were, despite social prejudices; they were undoubtedly criminals, but they also displayed some of the qualities that mark men as great; they only recruited among the elite. Nothing is lacking in the dark and mysterious poetry of this story: these thirteen men remained unknown, for all that each of them had realized the most bizarre ideas that imagination might conjure based on the fantastic powers falsely ascribed to a Manfred, a Faust, a Melmoth—and today all of them are broken, or at least dispersed.

The other effect of the fascination with conspiracies is of course a tumble in the direction of pure fantasy, leading easily to the evil-genius criminal template. Nevertheless, the cabal model was more than idle playacting when it came to revolutionary plans arising from the elite—from power, money, or intellect— since royal Paris was small enough that its prominent citizens

The insurgents seize the Louvre, 1830

could be minutely scrutinized by the forces of order, who had spies in every drawing room.

Revolution in that period could come from the top or the bottom, and even sometimes both at once, as happened in 1830 and briefly in 1848. The bourgeoisie had suffered under the yoke of the Old Regime, and they suffered again under its compromised revival. Nevertheless, their concerns were rather different from those of the poor, and they had more leverage to turn things their way. And once their needs were met they generally had little interest in helping out anyone else. The July Revolution of 1830 is often known as the Trois Glorieuses because it happened in just three days. It seems like a model revolution, stirring and noble—the uprising's enduring icon is Delacroix's tableau of bare-breasted Liberty hoisting the tricolor to encourage the People, in top hats and rags, over the barricades strewn with their dead—and at the same time efficient. The people got their tricolor and the bourgeoisie got their constitutional monarch, in the form of a member of the house of Orléans with a famously pear-shaped head: Louis-Philippe. It wasn't a republic, but on the other hand the prospect wasn't another Bourbon with a view to regaining absolute power, either, so maybe things would work out. Which they didn't, of course.

If the July Revolution has endured in memory for any single thing, it is the style in street fighting it presented, not entirely novel but rather distilled and refined from long experience and providing a model for the rest of the century and the rest of the world. The barricade as a means of improvised defense dates back, at least in Paris, to 1588, during the wars of religion, when a "day of the barricades" focused the combat between the relatively tolerant Henri III and the Duc de Guise and his Catholic absolutist Holy League. Barricades had recurred here and there over the centuries, although they barely figured in the 1789 revolution. In 1830 they were central. Some of the fundamentals of guerrilla fighting were invented in those three days, and they hinged on the existence of neighborhoods, in the tight blocks of medieval Paris, which, through the use of barricades, could be transformed quickly and cheaply into fortresses. Anything would do in a pinch: furniture, crates, bedding, even ropes strung across a street could give an advantage to the barricade's defend-

The barricade on Rue Dauphine, 1830

ers. Some of the most successful barricades used omnibuses—horses unharnessed, passengers let out—turned over on their roofs, which effortlessly blocked a street and could be made nearly impregnable with just a few more meters of additional impedimenta and perhaps an outer wall of paving stones; it seems that "the 4,054 barricades . . . were made from . . . 8,125,000 paving stones." The fortress analogy holds; not only were the windows of the outward-facing houses nests of sharpshooters, but as would have been the case in a medieval castle defense, perhaps even more destructive action came from their roofs. "Fewer were felled . . . by bullets than by other projectiles. The large squares of granite with which Paris is paved were dragged up to the top floors of the houses and dropped on the heads of the soldiers." The royal troops on the ground, trained for traditional combat involving fields and straight lines, were not at all prepared.

The insurrection of June 1832 also lasted three days. Its precipitating cause was a report by republicans that inventoried gains and losses for their side in the two years since Louis-Philippe became king—overwhelmingly the latter—and it warned that a counterrevolution was well under way. The news spread rapidly, and the opposition was further galvanized by the funeral of the republican general Jean Maximilien Lamarque, who had died in the cholera epidemic that was then waning. But the rebels were quickly crushed, at a cost of 166 dead and 635 wounded, and the uprising would have fallen into relative obscurity had it not been for Victor Hugo, who made it the climactic centerpiece of *Les misérables*. Writing long afterward but drawing on ample documentation as well as his own experiences of fighting behind them (in 1851, after the coup d'état of Napoléon III), he gave the world a determining view of barricades.

> In less than an hour, 27 barricades had sprung up in the neighborhood of Les Halles alone. At the center was the famous house at number 50, the fortress of Charles Jeanne and his 106 companions, which, flanked on one side by a barricade at Saint-Merri and on the other by one across Rue Maubuée, commanded three streets, Rue des Arcis, Rue Saint-Martin, and Rue Aubry-le-Boucher, which it fronted. Two barricades at right angles stretched out, one

Louis-Philippe, "past, present, and future." Illustration by Honoré Daumier, from *La Caricature*, 1834

from Rue Montorgueil to the Grande-Truanderie, the other from Rue Geoffroy-Langevin to Rue Sainte-Avoye. That without counting the innumerable barricades in twenty other neighborhoods of Paris: in the Marais, on the Montagne Sainte-Geneviève. On one of them, Rue Ménilmontant, you could see a porte-cochère torn off its hinges; another near the little bridge off the Hôtel-Dieu was made from a horse cart, unhitched and overturned, this just three hundred feet from the police prefecture.

But these horizontal barricades were merely roadblocks. The novel's great barricade rises up as a towering symbol.

The Saint-Antoine barricade was monstrous, three stories high and seven hundred feet across. It sealed off the vast mouth of the faubourg from one corner to the other, comprising three entire streets. Furrowed, jagged, notched, hacked up, crenellated with one enormous rip, buttressed with piles that were themselves bulwarks, pushing out peaks here and there, powerfully braced by the two great promontories of the faubourg houses, it loomed like a cyclopean levee at the far end of the formidable square that witnessed the first July 14. Nineteen barricades rose in tiers down the depths of the streets behind the mother barricade. Just by looking at it you could feel that the faubourg's immense agony had reached the point where distress shades into catastrophe.

And then he stages the heroic death of Gavroche on the Saint-Denis barricade, allowing him the full movie-star treatment: he is shot but immediately stands up, a trickle of blood running down his face, and starts to sing; then another bullet finishes him off.

There were more barricades erected in 1834, and again in 1839, during the brief and unexpected attempt at insurrection carried out by the Society of the Seasons; and then once more in 1848, when the Saint-Denis barricade included an entire locomotive, dragged there from the shop where it was undergoing repairs. It was on that barricade that Hugo saw a woman, young, beautiful, wild-haired and wild-eyed. This woman, a prostitute, lifted her dress up to her waist and shouted to the national guards . . . : "Cowards! Shoot the belly of a woman if you dare!" . . . The guards didn't hesitate. The shots of a whole squad knocked her over. She fell with a loud cry. There passed a silent moment of horror, on the barricade and among the attackers. Suddenly a second woman appeared, even younger and more beautiful, barely seventeen; she, too, a prostitute. She lifted up her dress, showed her belly, and shouted, "Shoot, you thugs!" They fired, and she fell, riddled with bullets, across the body of the first.

On Rue Saint-Martin the barricade was dominated by five women, one of them a widow in weeds, armed with sabers and halberds requisitioned from the prop shop of the adjacent theater. There were sixty-eight barricades on Rue Saint-Antoine, built with felled trees and carts filled with paving stones. Neverthe-less, the iconography of the 1848 barricades yields one primary image: Meissonier's painting of a street in which a scatter of paving stones is nearly obscured by the clot of corpses.

The wily professional revolutionary Louis-Auguste Blanqui, head of the Society of the Seasons, who had fought in the streets in 1830, 1839, and 1848 (and who in 1871 was elected president of the Commune, although he languished in prison for its entire du-ration), had learned from those experiences, and while in exile after escaping from Sainte-Pélagie in 1865 he wrote a manual of guer-rilla warfare, *Instructions for a Show of Arms.** Among other things, he gave precise directions for the construction of barricades: built from paving stones mortared with plaster, the rampart should be twelve meters wide by three meters tall by two meters thick, fronted at a distance of six meters by a counterguard of the same dimen-sions, with a glacis extending a further four meters at its deepest.

Did anyone ever follow those directions? None of the barricades that were photographed during the Commune quite answers to

The Barricade, Rue de la Mortellerie, June 1848. Painting by Ernest Meissonier

A rough barricade during the strikes in Limoges, 1905

---

* Interestingly, Thomas-Robert Bugeaud, a field marshal, wrote a counterguerrilla manual, *The War of Streets and Houses* (1849), based on the same experiences viewed from the opposite direction.

The Rue Royale barricade, 1871. Photograph by Hippolyte-Auguste Collard

The barricade on Place de la Concorde, 1871. Photograph by Alphonse Liébert

the description, although some of the central ones, such as those on Rue Royale, Rue de Castiglione, and Rue Saint-Florentin, engineered by Napoléon Thiébault and built with paving stones and sandbags, look absolutely formidable, especially the last of these, in which the ramparts rise up in tiers, fifteen or twenty feet tall, with ditches, projecting buttresses, and inserted snipers' nests. On Place Blanche was a "perfectly constructed" barricade, built and guarded by a battalion of 120 women. Nevertheless, some of the biggest defenses, such as the one on Rue de Rivoli that protected the Hôtel de Ville, proved porous at the crucial moment. But the barricades in the outlying faubourgs, among which were some of the last to fall, were another matter, improvised from the same detritus as their predecessors. A photo of Boulevard de Puebla (now Rue des Pyrénées) shows paving stones piled haphazardly about four feet high, fronted by the metal grates that to this day protect the bases of trees (and to this day, when rioting appears imminent, the city removes and stores those grates). Louise Michel tells the story of Élodie Richoux, a very proper restaurant owner, who oversaw the construction of the Saint-Sulpice barricade out of the largest statues she could find in a nearby religious paraphernalia shop. When she was arrested and made to account for herself, she said, "The statues were made of stone, and those who were dying were made of flesh."

Life during an insurrection could sometimes appear weirdly normal. Hugo:

> Outside the insurgent neighborhoods, nothing is more strangely calm than the face of Paris during a riot . . . People shoot at each other on corners, in arcades, in culs-de-sac; barricades are taken, lost, and taken back; blood flows, house fronts are riddled with grapeshot, stray shots kill people in their beds, the sidewalks are choked with corpses. And a few streets away you can hear the clicking of billiard balls in the cafés.
>
> Rubberneckers talk and laugh two feet from those streets full of war; theaters are open and hosting vaudevilles. Carriages roll along; people go off to dine at the restaurants—sometimes in the very neighborhoods where

fighting is taking place. In 1831 an exchange of gunfire was halted to let a wedding party pass through.

He notices a street vendor, an old and sickly man, pushing around a cart topped with a tricolor from which he sells coconut water, calmly serving first one side and then the other. In 1830 the entertainments on the Boulevard du Crime proceeded as usual, while fighting was kept to the side streets. In 1834 the agitator Guillard de Kersausie, who made a habit of meeting his coconspirators on that boulevard, where the noise and the press of bodies would shield them from surveillance, met his fate the same way. When he was grabbed by three undercover cops near Porte Saint-Martin, he yelled, "Help me, republicans!"—to his cohorts a warning rather than a request, but also an appeal to the crowd—but he was drowned out by the hubbub of the fun-seekers.

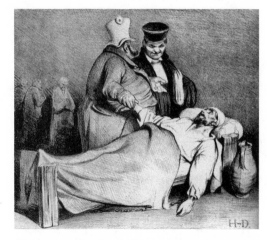

"This one can be freed. He's no longer dangerous."
Illustration by Honoré Daumier, from *La Caricature*, 1834

The events of 1834 were brief and might have been ephemeral—the rioting was at least nominally prompted by a ban on neighborhood news criers—but when news of Kersausie's arrest spread, it led to street fighting around Saint-Merri. At some point an officer was wounded by a shot that was believed to have come from a house on Rue Transnonain (now Rue Beaubourg), next to a barricade, whereupon soldiers rushed into the house and massacred everyone they found. The inhabitants had all been huddling in the back rooms, away from the fighting. The famous lithograph by Daumier shows four corpses in a bedroom, at its center a man in a nightshirt whose body is crushing that of a baby. The picture was, amazingly, allowed to pass by the censors, perhaps because it had spread so far so fast, perhaps because it made no rhetorical claims.

In 1830 the revolution was declared over once the flag had been changed and the Orléanist king installed, and the republicans were invited to go lick their wounds. That king, Louis-Philippe, proved unpopular almost at once—he trampled on freedom of the press, for example, and soon swapped his ministers, most of them active in the events of 1830, for a more conservative set.* A united republican front had gained momentum by

Rue Transnonain, April 15, 1834. Illustration by Honoré Daumier

---

* Over the course of less than fifteen years he was the target of no fewer than ten

February 1848, when a series of mass events was delayed by rain. Weighing his options in view of the fact that the National Guard refused to fight the crowd, the king threw the opposition a sop by dismissing his widely hated minister of foreign affairs, the historian François Guizot, who was the de facto head of state. In the ensuing festivities an impromptu youth parade was halted by the military, one of whose guns discharged accidentally. The soldiers then fired into the crowd, killing between fifty and a hundred. The mood changed immediately; the king abdicated and fled; crowds rushed into the Tuileries palace, seized the throne, and burned it on Place de la Bastille.

However, with the addition of a socialist journalist and a metalworker, the provisional government was otherwise the same as the old one. It agreed to certain socialist demands: the establishment of state-run workshops for the unemployed, the right to unionize, the ten-hour day, universal male suffrage, and the abolition of debtors' prisons. But when a crowd of one hundred fifty thousand demanded the withdrawal of troops, the government lied and said they were already gone; the socialist deputy went along with the lie. When the crowd demanded that elections be postponed, to allow time for the largely illiterate population to absorb the facts and make an educated choice, they were refused. The upshot was that the socialists came in a weak third, far behind even the monarchists, while the liberal moderates declared victory. Two weeks later, socialist leaders, backed up outside by fourteen thousand unemployed workers, entered the constituent assembly under a pretext; once there, they declared the assembly dissolved. Instead, the leaders and four hundred supporters were arrested, and the workshops were eliminated.

That broke the coalition cleanly across class lines. The liberals sided with the monarchists, and soon moderate figures such as Lamartine and Tocqueville could be heard urging radical

The army takes the barricades on Rue du Petit-Pont, June 23, 1848

---

assassination plots or attempts, their authors ranging across the entire political spectrum, from Bourbon legitimists to anarchists. In 1835, on the fifth anniversary of the revolution, Giuseppe Fieschi deployed an "infernal machine," made from twenty-five rifle barrels that were supposed to fire a coordinated salvo. It only winged the monarch but killed eleven and wounded forty, many of them high-ranking military figures. A year later, Louis Alibaud, who had just seen a play about Fieschi (who became a staple subject at theaters and in wax museums), fired at the king with a cane in which a rifle barrel had been inserted; he missed.

means of crowd control. The government created the Mobile Guards, manning its ranks with disaffected working-class youths. Karl Marx, who spent a month in Paris during the lull between Louis-Philippe's abdication and the election, was moved to define a new demographic category for members of the working class who would shoot their own: the *Lumpenproletariat*. War in the streets broke out in June, with awful scenes. Cannons were placed between the sickbeds in the Hôtel-Dieu to fire on the Left Bank barricades; hand-to-hand combat went on indoors and out and demolished store aisles. Within three days the government forces had overpowered the rebels. But the violence continued after their surrender: the last holdouts of resistance in the Faubourg Saint-Antoine were massacred; the Mobile Guards set up kangaroo tribunals, passing death sentences that were carried out on the spot; those rounded up were shot on bridges, shot on their way into jails, thrown into the river. At least five thousand people died overall. Six months later Louis-Napoléon Bonaparte was elected the first president of the French Republic. Five months after that, universal male suffrage was revoked and voting was once again restricted to property owners. Then, in December 1851, two years after he was elected, Louis-Napoléon staged a coup d'état. He brought in troops to seize the major printing presses and round up republican leaders, and papered the city with notices announcing that he was henceforth emperor. The liberals, aghast, tried to raise an insurrection, but few of the workers they had betrayed two and a half years earlier were inclined to join. Instead they watched from their windows as the bourgeois fought and died, some four hundred of them, on their own barricades.

Eighteen forty-eight was to have been a historical pivot, and its failure led to a general demoralizing of the population. The more prominent losers of '48 and '51, such as Hugo, went into exile. The city was reconfigured with, among other things, a view toward eliminating the barricade-fortress strategy of civilian defense. A quantity of bread and circuses was proposed as a palliative distraction. It was the era of the café-concert, of the *fait-divers*, of elaborate whorehouses and socially prominent courtesans, of Nadar's portraits, of Offenbach and Rossini, of the *Flowers of Evil* and *Madame Bovary* trials, of the birth of haute

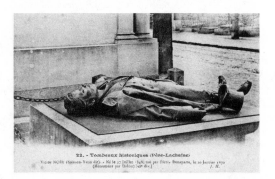

The tomb of Victor Noir, Père-Lachaise cemetery

couture, of streetcars and the belt railway. The city was hugely expanded. The poor were pushed out of many parts of the city center, but many more became Parisians by fiat as their formerly peripheral villages were annexed. It was also a time of repression and surveillance; the press had little freedom, and dissidents were regularly arrested. Matters were not improved by the 1858 assassination attempt on Napoléon III by Felice Orsini, who believed that the emperor was the single major obstacle in the course of Italian unification. (He had a point; Bonaparte did in fact favor restoration of the Papal States.) His three bombs killed 12 and wounded 144, but the imperial couple, on their way to see Rossini's *William Tell*, were unscathed. Although the incident did manage to sway Napoléon on the subject of Italy—he met Camillo Benso, Count of Cavour, in secret and promised his aid in exchange for Nice and Savoy—it only redoubled the intensity of his repression of dissidents.

The sole significant public show of opposition to the regime occurred in January 1870, when the violently truculent prince Pierre Bonaparte, a cousin, killed the journalist Victor Noir over an obscure matter involving Corsican newspapers. The prince was acquitted, although forced to pay damages—he was hated by the emperor, who forbade him to use his full name, Pierre-Napoléon—while Noir's employers were prosecuted for provocation. Victor Noir was not widely known in life, but in death he became a symbol of militant opposition. Some two hundred thousand persons attended his funeral; people took the horses off their traces to pull the hearse themselves. Some urged that the occasion be made the spark of an insurrection, but members of the International Workingmen's Association counseled patience instead, anticipating a more propitious opportunity later, since the empire was showing signs of tilting askew, thanks to its overreaching ambitions. They did not have long to wait.

The emperor, already beset by a string of foreign policy miscalculations, and with a predilection for letting himself be outmaneuvered by rivals at home and abroad, allowed himself to be swayed by hawkish elements in his court. On July 19, 1870, he declared war on Prussia. A hyperventilated frenzy took over Paris, with torchlight parades and hysterical speechifying. Zola catches the flavor in the closing pages of *Nana*. As his heroine lies dying of smallpox in the Grand Hôtel, a metronomic chant keeps drifting up from the boulevard: "À Berlin! à Berlin! à Berlin!" By this point, Nana has come to incarnate the empire:

> Pustules had swarmed over her whole face, one boil closing in on the next. Withered now and with a grayish tone like mud, they looked like a fungus on that shapeless pulp, its features indistinguishable. One eye, the left, was already sunk in the purulence; the other, half-open, was foundering, like a gaping black hole. The nose was still suppurating. A reddish crust stretched from one cheek to invade her mouth, fixed in an abominable rictus. And atop that horribly grotesque mask of nothingness, her hair, her beautiful hair with its solar blaze, tumbled down in a shower of gold.

The emperor, hugely outmatched by the Prussians, tried in vain for a glorious death in battle, but finally capitulated at Sedan just six weeks into the war. Two days later, on September 4, crowds broke into the Palais Bourbon; the empress fled to England; the cabinet proclaimed a republic; a Government of National Defense was formed. The Prussian army surrounded the city on September 19. Adolphe Thiers, who had held government posts almost continuously since 1830 and now functioned as a kind of minister without portfolio, proposed an armistice, but Parisian resistance to the ineffectual government rapidly gained momentum. On October 31, National Guards under Gustave Flourens seized the Hôtel de Ville with the intention of proclaiming a Commune, but the occasion was premature. Meanwhile, although battles took out various suburban towns, the Prussians declined confrontation with the city itself, where the mass of able-bodied citizens potentially outmatched their army in numbers (fifty to one) if not in training or equipment. They were content to starve them out.

The Siege lasted four months. Supplies of nearly everything were exhausted within the first month. The Bois de Boulogne was soon firewood, followed not long after by the Bois de Vincennes and then by the trees of the Champs-Élysées. Butchers' meat ran out early in October. Horses, donkeys, dogs, cats, and

"Germans crowning themselves with laurels in the Tuileries Gardens," 1870

"A funeral during the Siege," 1870

rats were eaten grudgingly at first, but by November commanded extravagant sums. Various menus have been preserved that list such epicurian fancies as consommé of horse, dog liver brochettes, carpaccio of cat, filet of dog shoulder, salmis of rat, and so on. The anarchist Victorine Brocher-Rouchy recalled that she saw a vendor on the boulevard unload a large quantity of canned goods. It was gone instantly; she bought a can herself. Back home, she spread the contents on crepes, but the baby began to cry right away. "It was a paste made of mouse meat, and they hadn't even removed the skins, which gave it an awful taste." The zoo animals of the Jardin d'Acclimatation were sacrificed in inverse order to their popularity: yaks, zebras, and water buffaloes in late October; antelopes a week later; in mid-November boars, reindeer, the kangaroo, the cassowary, and the rare black swan; finally, at the very end of that month, the two beloved elephants, Castor and Pollux. They all wound up on bills of fare at the finest restaurants. The great cats had meanwhile all died of starvation. Fresh vegetables had long before ceased to exist, and cheese likewise, but there were black market purveyors who could produce fingernail-size portions of gruyère for incredible sums. Although the good bakeries had shut down in late September for want of butter, bread was not rationed until mid-January. What bread there was between those two points contained increasing amounts of sawdust and straw.* Gas for lamps ran out in November, replaced by hazardous and unreliable petrol; street lighting in any case ceased, and the city plunged into total darkness at the fall of night. The only staple in bottomless supply was wine. The overall death rate had more than tripled as compared with the same period a year earlier.

In early January the Prussians, losing patience, began shelling the city. On January 22 an attempt was made to proclaim a Commune. After a brief firefight that left six dead on the Communard side, the attempt was quashed; many arrests ensued, and newspapers were suppressed. On January 26, France formally surrendered to Germany, signing an armistice that included spe-

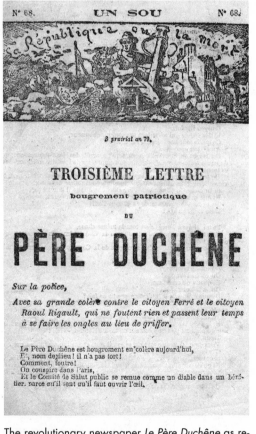

The revolutionary newspaper *Le Père Duchêne* as revived during the Commune by Eugène Vermersch and Maxime Vuillaume

* A souvenir print commemorating the Siege was published two decades later, with elaborate graphics surrounding a mounted cube of this bread. You can see an example in the Musée Carnavalet; the bread, now over one hundred forty years old, looks much as it must have when freshly baked.

cial provisions for Paris: it would not be occupied, and local units of the army and the National Guard would not be disarmed. Those dispensations did not impress the Parisians, who took a dim view of the armistice and swore a fight to the end, had it been up to them. The restriction on disarmament was anyway not for the convenience of the people, but for the protection of the interests of the powerful—guns were needed to stop looters. On February 8 the constitutional monarchists overwhelmed the republicans two to one in the national elections; nevertheless, on February 17, Parliament elected Thiers, a republican, president. Thiers was a man of the future: an expressionless manager. In the broader French political landscape, he was rather to the left: a republican, a Deist, an exile (briefly) after 1848, an opponent of the Franco-Prussian War. In the city, on the other hand, he functioned strictly as a security guard for the interests of the propertied classes.

A detachment of Communards on Place de l'Opéra, 1871

On March 1, inaugurating a long tradition, Prussian troops marched down the Champs-Élysées. Meanwhile, the city held some four hundred obsolete cannons, paid for by public subscription, deployed in defensive positions on the heights—meaning Montmartre and Belleville, working-class neighborhoods. On March 17, Thiers ordered the army to seize the cannons. On March 18, the army took control of the cannons in the Buttes-Chaumont and other parts of Belleville, but in Montmartre the National Guard would not let the army touch them. They won the standoff. The first barricades started going up late in the morning, as the army retreated from Montmartre, and then in short order Thiers, the government, and the army all relocated to Versailles.

On March 26, 227,000 voters elected 90 representatives. The following day, 200,000 people surrounded the Hôtel de Ville and sang "La Marseillaise." Gabriel Ranvier, a porcelain painter and member of the central committee of the National Guard, proclaimed the Commune. Képis were flung, red flags waved, handkerchiefs fluttered. There were twenty-five laborers among the new officials; the rest were office workers, accountants, doctors, teachers, lawyers, and at least twelve journalists. They faced an enormous administrative task. Not only was the city embattled and barely recovered from the effects of the Siege, but Thiers, on

"The insurgents seizing the guns," March 18, 1871

his departure, had ordered all services shut down and their employees dismissed, thus affecting, for example, street lighting, road maintenance, markets, tax collection, the telegraph system, and six thousand patients in the city's hospitals. The delegates opened soup kitchens, distributed tickets redeemable for bread, halted all evictions for nonpayment of rent, remitted all rents for the period of the Siege, and continued the postponement of commercial debt obligations to keep small shopkeepers from bankruptcy. They abolished the death penalty and effected the separation of church and state. (For one thing, the Church had, and after the Commune continued to have, until 1905, a monopoly on primary education.) They halted sales and prolonged terms of loans indefinitely at the *mont-de-piété,* the state-run pawn shop that functioned as the bank of the poor. What they failed to do was to seize the assets of the Banque de France, which was barely defended, except by ingrained fear and prejudice. Instead, the Commune periodically sent delegates, hat in hand, to request loans, eking out its existence from day to day like a penurious household. Twenty years later, a member of the Commune wrote that "the central committee presented the bizarre spectacle of a victorious revolution—well armed, well equipped, and having at its disposal capital of roughly a billion francs locked up in the vaults of the national bank—furnishing its ill-equipped, resourceless, penniless enemy with hundreds of millions so that it could come and cut its throat. Such stupidity is unparalleled in history."

The Commune was a leaderless revolution, not quite by choice and not entirely to its profit. Blanqui possessed all the qualities for leadership—long experience, intellectual clarity, single-minded dedication, strength of character, hard-line intransigence—and Thiers realized this so well that he had him arrested on March 17 as he lay convalescing from illness at a friend's house in the country. Later, when offered a job lot of priests including Georges Darboy, Archbishop of Paris, in exchange for Blanqui's freedom, Thiers refused. The other Commune members presented an array of qualities and deficiencies. There was, most of all, a surplus of idealism, along with a corresponding deficit of realpolitik. Revolutions always seem to tilt the scale in one direction or the other; the opposite tilt is, if anything,

Louis-Auguste Blanqui

worse. Charles Delescluze, a veteran of most of the previous uprisings, was loved and respected by all, but his health was too poor to allow him to seize the reins. He was the one who, as minister of war, proclaimed on May 22, when the Versaillais entered the city, "Enough of militarism! No more gilded officer class! Make way for the people, for the bare-armed fighters! . . . The people know nothing of strategy, but with gun in hand and pavement underfoot, they fear no strategists." However, as the historian Lissagaray remarks, "When the minister casts off all discipline, who will ever want to obey? When he scorns all method, who will ever want to reason?" In the end, on May 25, Delescluze climbed unarmed atop the barricade at Château d'Eau and allowed himself to be shot dead.

Raoul Rigault

The Commune membership represented an array of political persuasions; there were hard-line Blanquists, Jacobins nostalgic for 1789, Montagnards nostalgic for 1848, even complacent Radical-Liberals, since the election, after all, took in the entire city, including Auteuil and Passy. Their leading personalities present us with novelistic characters, burning with passion, rife with contradictions, riddled with weaknesses. Raoul Rigault, named police commissioner and later attorney general at the tender age of twenty-five, was youthfully hotheaded and given to violent speeches. He was the one who debaptized the streets, changing Boulevard Saint-Germain to Boulevard Germain, for example, or Faubourg Saint-Antoine to Faubourg Antoine. He showed real promise, pending the fullness of maturity, although no one had a chance to find out. He was killed by the Versaillais while fighting in the Latin Quarter, in full uniform, on May 24. Théophile Ferré, a legal clerk, took charge of the Montmartre cannons on March 18 and afterward proposed marching on Versailles, but was voted down. In the frenzy of the last days he gave the order to execute the ecclesiastical hostages, which accomplished little other than handing the Church a clutch of ready-made martyrs. Nothing in life became Ferré like the leaving of it. Arrested and tried at Versailles, he gave a speech worthy of seventeenth-century theater, one that was constantly interrupted by catcalls, and concluded, "Fortune is capricious. I leave it to the future to guard my memory and achieve my revenge," while Colonel François-Xavier Merlin, presiding over the tribunal,

The fall of the Vendôme column, May 16, 1871

Félix Pyat

shouted, "The memory of a killer!" Ferré was shot by a firing squad at the Satory prison camp.

Léo Frankel, a jeweler, was a Hungarian immigrant, one of a number of foreigners active in the Commune who were permitted to hold office because "the flag of the Commune is the flag of the world republic." The only bona fide Marxist aboard, he was responsible for some of the most useful measures passed, such as the law ending night work in bakeries. He was an adept politician, although not one to step into the spotlight. The future novelist Jules Vallès, who put out the newspaper *Le Cri du Peuple*, seems perhaps closest to the liberal-left viewpoint of our own day. He took the unpopular stance of advocating for total freedom of the press—unpopular because of the damage done, before their suppression in late March, by such Versaillais disinformation sheets as *Le Figaro* and *Le Gaulois*. Along with Gustave Courbet, he was one of the members of the minority, which opposed the Committee for Public Safety that was elected in mid-May, with its ominous echoes of Thermidor. Félix Pyat, a successful if not exactly deathless playwright in the Boulevard du Crime days, ran the newspaper *Le Combat*, which was suppressed a month before the Commune; almost immediately he began putting out *Le Vengeur*. He was given to grand gestures—he was the one who proposed the demolition of the Vendôme column. He was inclined to rants and threats of resignation, implacable in his grudges—according to Lissagaray, "he would rather have seen the Commune dead than saved by his enemies"—and probably half-mad.

Émile Eudes was an upright and intelligent revolutionary who, because he led the capture of the Hôtel de Ville on March 18, was named a general. His lack of real military experience was an unfortunately decisive factor in the incompetent defense of the city when the Versaillais invaded the week of May 21. Then again, military training was no guarantee of strategic success. Gustave Cluseret, who among other things had fought as a general for the Union in the American Civil War, was unable to adapt to the circumstances of urban warfare, was accused of treason for his bad decisions, and spent most of the last month of the Commune locked up in Mazas. Louis Rossel, the only high-ranking French military officer in the Commune, was unable to impose discipline on the ranks. He refused Thiers's offer of exile and was shot with Ferré at Satory. Jaroslaw Dombrowski, a Pole who had received a superior education in Russian military academies and had planned an abortive uprising in Warsaw in 1862, was sufficiently formidable that Thiers tried to lure him to the other side with a bounty of a million and a half francs; Dombrowski had the emissary shot. He did the best he could, from a military standpoint, with ragged troops that took commands poorly if at all. He fought valiantly during the Bloody Week, leading a battalion that included women, one with a babe in arms. He died on the Rue Myrha barricade.

There were no female members of the Commune because women did not yet have the right to vote, also because one of the principal political models then, the peasant socialism of Pierre-Joseph Proudhon (1809–1865), was profoundly misogynistic, relegating women strictly to the kitchen and nursery. From our vantage it necessarily appears strange that these combatants for social progress were unable to recognize the equality of genders, although women did not have the right to vote anywhere in the world at the time and did not obtain suffrage in France until 1944. These factors did not, however, prevent quite a few women from acting almost as though there were no inequality; certainly the role of women in the Commune was unprecedented. Louise Michel might actually have led the Commune had the times been different. The illegitimate daughter of a wealthy landowner and his servant, she was raised in the manor and given a good education. She worked as a teacher, wrote poetry, and began moving in Parisian revolutionary circles sometime prior to 1869. She was elected president of a women's vigilance society in Montmartre, and attended Victor Noir's funeral dressed like a man and with a knife concealed on her person, just in case. On March 18 she was guarding the Montmartre cannons, rifle in hand. During the Commune she did everything. Like many women she was an *ambulancière* (a volunteer nurse), but she was also enrolled in the Sixty-First Battalion and fought on the front lines, worked on the Commune's proposed educational reforms, and led the Club of the Revolution, one of the active and influential debating societies that functioned as the Commune's outlets for direct democracy. During the Bloody Week, she managed to flee the city

Louise Michel

after fighting on the Clignancourt barricade, but gave herself up when she heard her mother had been arrested in her stead. At her trial she demanded to be shot in the field at Satory. Her stance inspired Victor Hugo's poem "Viro Major":

> Having seen the immense massacre, the combat,
> The people on their cross, Paris on its sickbed,
> Formidable pity was in your words;
> You did what the great mad souls do,
> And tired of fighting, of dreaming, of suffering,
> You said: I have killed! Because you wanted to die.
> Lying against yourself, you were terrible, superhuman.

She was sent to New Caledonia instead, and came back from it after the 1880 amnesty to become a pillar of the anarchist surge. In 1882 she was the first to fly the black flag—the color of mourning rather than the color of blood, in her words. She risked everything over and over again and spent many years in prison. Her enemies and her followers alike called her the Red Virgin because she was married to the revolution; you could almost say she was led by a mystical vision, like Joan of Arc. She possessed a moral grandeur no one during her lifetime could match.

The Union of Women for the Defense of Paris and Aid to the Wounded was founded on April 11 by Nathalie Le Mel and Élisabeth Dmitrieff, two intellectuals. Le Mel was a bookbinder and bookseller, and Dmitrieff, a Russian active in the International, was in Paris on a fact-finding mission for Marx. She cultivated an air of mystery and was noted for the elegance of her turnout: riding habits always, with a red feather in her hat and a red silk scarf trimmed with gold. The union organized labor for women, obtaining commissions and filling work crews, and agitated for women's rights: to vote, to enjoy full legal rights, to choose jobs, to receive pay equal to men. André Léo was a professional writer (her real name was Léodile Béra; her pseudonym came from the names of her two sons), well known before the Commune for her novels. She worked for the Union of Women and ran a newspaper, *The Workers' Republic*. She wrote:

> Later on, they'll be studied as models of illogic, those democrats who, right after proclaiming their famous dec-

A meeting of a debating society. Illustration by Honoré Daumier, from *Le Charivari*, 1848

laration . . . have the gall to sacrifice half of humanity to a dogmatic concept, to dissolve women into the family and construct yet another fiction atop that pretext beloved of all despots: order. Eighty years have passed since the launch of human rights, and it still seems like a bizarre novelty to claim justice for women, bowed since the beginning of the world under a double yoke, in slavery doubly a slave, eternally a slave in the bosom of the free family, and even now, in our civilizations, deprived of all initiative, of all vigor, abandoned to either the corruption of idleness or the corruption of misery, and everywhere subject to the demoralizing effects of the shameful mix of dependency and love.

These women and a few others whose names we know—Paule Mink, Maria Deraismes, Noémie Reclus, Marie Ferré, Élisa Gagneur, Maria Verdure, Sophie Poirier, Anna Jaclard, Béatrix Excoffon—were both well educated and involved with the social movement, a reasonably unusual combination in the mid-nineteenth century. But there were thousands of other women active during the Commune, many of them illiterate, some of them factory workers, some wives and mothers, some prostitutes.* They worked as *ambulancières* and *cantinières*, built barricades and fought and died on them, died in great numbers during the Bloody Week, filled the prison camp at Versailles (1,058 women and 651 children), and were executed or shipped off to New Caledonia. Still, as André Léo wrote:

> Once more, women have nothing to gain from the immediate effects of this revolution, since its present goal is the emancipation of men, not of women . . . You could write a history of the inconsequences of the revolutionary party going back to 1789. The woman question would form the longest chapter, and it would illustrate how that party found a way to drive over to the enemy half of its troops, which asked for nothing more than to march alongside.

* Prostitution all but vanished during the Commune, although there were strong conflicting opinions on the subject. Some of the clubs wanted to arrest whores (and drunks), whereas Louise Michel, for one, always made a point of refusing to judge the profession as different from any other.

A Versaillais shell explodes in the street, May 1871

The final battle between Communards and Versaillais, Père-Lachaise cemetery, on the evening of May 27, 1871

But over in that enemy camp, the notorious quip by Alexandre Dumas *fils* can be taken as a representative opinion: "We will say nothing about their females, out of respect for the women they resemble—when they are dead."

The Commune was so rich in ideas, initiatives, debates, and grand plans that it is easy to forget that it lasted only seventy-two days. The Versaillais army entered Paris on the morning of May 21 by the Point-du-Jour gate, which was left undefended—inexplicably, since it was the one closest to Versailles. The army also cut a deal with the Prussians, allowing them to attack from the north. Because the Germans occupied the northern suburbs, the Commune had given those gates only token support. Moreover, there was no strategy in place for how to repel an invasion. The Communards apparently hadn't read Blanqui, who advised, "Above all, don't shut yourselves up in your own neighborhoods, as republicans have never yet failed to do." But that is exactly what happened. And many of the barricades, built hastily when the enemy was just blocks away, were more symbolic than strategic—piles of rubble, irregularly defended, that ground troops could easily walk over. Barricades were erected on a whim, guarding corners of local significance that did not necessarily figure in any broader plan. The army sliced through the city from the southwest and across, then down from the north via the Batignolles, gradually closing in on the northeast, where they met the strongest resistance and where the fighting finally ended on May 28, in the Père-Lachaise cemetery.

Along the way, the troops executed on the spot anyone captured whose hands showed traces of gunpowder; many of the rest were judged by courts-martial in the Luxembourg Gardens or at the Lobau barracks near the Hôtel de Ville, after which they were shot. On May 23 the National Guard detachment headquartered in the Tuileries palace, realizing that they were outgunned and about to be overwhelmed, set fire to the building. The following day, Communards torched the police prefecture, the Palais de Justice, and the Hôtel de Ville (which contained the city's historical archives and thus constituted the one truly irreparable material loss of that week). Many other government edifices went up in flames—among others the Ministry of State, the Ministry of Finance, the Court of Auditors, and the Palace of the

Legion of Honor—but it has never been determined who burned them. A rumor spread that the fires had been set by *pétroleuses* (women bearing buckets of fuel oil), which focused the army's contempt for the women of the Commune and gave license to shoot on sight any working-class woman carrying any sort of jug or pail.

But then, the troops hardly needed goads or justifications. Communards were shot in the Catacombs, in the cellars of the uncompleted Opéra, in the gypsum quarries in the Buttes-Chaumont. Tony Moilin, a doctor and the author of a book called *Paris in the Year 2000*, was shot for attending to wounded Communards. Dr. Faneau, running a field clinic at Saint-Sulpice, was shot along with all eighty of his patients. People who merely looked like Commune leaders were summarily executed, "and their understandable emotions allowed the newspapers to assert that the heads of the Commune had died as cowards, even denying their own names." There were mass executions at the mint, at the observatory, at the law school and the polytechnic institute, at the Panthéon, at Mazas and La Roquette, and in Parc Monceau. The Commune member Eugène Varlin was stoned and had his eyes put out by a mob before being shot in Montmartre. People who had nothing to do with the Commune were shot after being falsely denounced by their enemies or their concierges. In 1897 a mass grave was found in Charonne that contained some eight hundred corpses, apparently mowed down with primitive machine guns.

No one knows how many died. Maxime du Camp claimed there were six thousand dead, an insufficient number according to him. In a parliamentary inquiry that August, General Félix Antoine Appert cited the figure of seventeen thousand, which was taken up by most of the historians of the Commune, beginning with Lissagaray, although most also allowed for the many back-street murders and unofficial burials and raised the figure to twenty thousand. In 1880 the politician Camille Pelletan claimed thirty thousand. Revisionist historians of recent times seem to think the figure is closer to ten thousand, half of that number from combat and half from summary execution, which still represents a large percentage of the Parisian population, less than two million in the 1866 census. On May 31, Edmond de

Corpses in the courtyard of La Roquette prison, May 1871

Ruins of the Palais de Justice, May 1871. Photograph by the Pignolet brothers

The Mur des Fédérés in Père-Lachaise cemetery, the site of mass executions of Communards by the Versaillais

Goncourt wrote in his journals that the wound had been bled white, and that with the warring part of the population dead or in prison, society could look forward to twenty years of rest. Maxime du Camp claimed that the population of Paris during the Commune had been three-quarters provincials and foreigners, and that if there had been only Parisians, there would have been no uprising. On the other hand, Pierre-Auguste Renoir, not especially a friend of the people, told his son Jean about the Communards, "They were insane, but they had that little flame that never goes out."

The Commune member Jean-Baptiste Clément wrote "Le temps des cerises" (cherry blossom time), the song that because it was in the air in May 1871, became, for anyone who was there, forever associated with the Commune, both its triumphs and its disasters. (It's a lovely tune, but with a hint of a dirge already built in.) He also wrote a song about the Bloody Week, which has the refrain "Les mauvais jours finiront" (the bad days will end). He was, of course, both right and wrong. In the meantime, Paris had to rebuild, even while it was under heavy repression. Between the killings, the imprisonments and deportations, and the flights of people—to Belgium, England, Switzerland, the United States—industry suffered. Tailors were down by a third. Plumbers, roofers, smelters, carvers, gilders, drapers, printers, tanners, sculptors, jewelers, lithographers, decorators, makers of surgical, optical, and musical instruments—all were lacking. The city was hollow; life itself felt as if it were being enforced. A law was passed on December 28 that prohibited "the exhibition and sale of all drawings, portraits, lithographs, photographs, or emblems connected to recent political events and particularly the insurrection," including, needless to say, "the acts of repression of the legitimate authorities." The sole exception to the rule: "From a purely artistic perspective: fire or ruins." Rimbaud, who may or may not have been in the city during the Commune—accounts differ—wrote a poem called "The Parisian Orgy, or Paris Repopulates":

When your feet danced so hard in its rages,
Paris! when you bore so many thrusts of the knife,
When you lay there inert, preserving in your clear eyes
A bit of the goodness of tawny spring,

O woeful city, o city nearly dead,
Your head and two breasts thrust toward the Future
Which opens to your pallor its billions of gates,
City that the dark Past could bless.

. . .

Society, everything is restored—the orgies
Cry their old death rattle in the old whorehouses,
And the delirious gaslights, against reddened walls,
Point their sinister flames toward the pale blue skies!

"The anarchist." Illustration by Félix Vallotton, 1892

"Revolution has its classics and its romantics, just like literature," wrote Lucien Descaves. He explains that those of 1834 and '48 were classics, following Horace's brand of sacrificial fatalism, but "the Commune will stand forever in your heart as the next-to-last romantics, the anarchists surely being the last." The anarchists had long been a minority, their influence—via Proudhon, the first to apply the term to himself—rather subsumed among all the warring factions in the Commune, but in the wake of the split between Marx and Bakunin in the late 1860s, the schism in the International Workingmen's Association in September 1871, and the dissolution of that body after 1877, they began to come into their own, buoyed by a generalized disgust with parties, their platforms and protocols. By the mid-1880s there began to be signs of a palpable rage in the streets, with members of innocuous-sounding clubs adopting such aliases as Friend of Robespierre, Partisan of Dynamite, Chopper of Heads, Incendiary. Soon there were clubs that did not sound innocuous: The Insurgents, The Stateless, The League of Antipatriots, The Panther of the Batignolles. It was Clément Duval, a member of the last group, who in 1886 initiated the practice of what was called *la reprise individuelle* (individual repossession, you might say). He set two fires in an *hôtel particulier* on Rue Monceau in order to cover the theft of silver, jewels, and such. When captured, he cried, "Vive l'anarchie!"*

In 1883, Louise Michel and Émile Pouget had called for a rally of all those who were starving, to be held on the Esplanade of the

The editorial office of *La Révolte*, circa 1890

---

* His death sentence was commuted to life in the *bagne*; he escaped from Devil's Island in 1901 and fled to New York City, where he spent the rest of his days. His thousand-page memoir was published in Italian in Newark, New Jersey, in 1929.

Alexandre "Marius" Jacob's market stall, 1930s

Émile Pouget's *Almanach du Père Peinard*, 1898

Invalides, which the police forestalled by blocking all the streets leading there. The starving, instead, looted three bakeries; Michel and Pouget were indicted for theft and incitement to riot. That was one thing—it was generally agreed among the anarchists that everyone in need had the right to bread—but the theft of valuables from a private house presented a thornier problem, which divided opinion and remained a contentious issue for decades. There were moral authorities on both sides. The great geographer Élisée Reclus and Sébastien Faure, later a leading Dreyfusard and pacifist, approved of theft, considering it a revolutionary act, based on Proudhon's idea that property is purely a function of labor and that any other assertion of property itself constitutes theft.* On the other hand, the libertarian collectivist Jean Grave took a hard line on lying, cheating, and theft, ranking them as counterrevolutionary and a betrayal of the people.

The practice of individual repossession reached its apex with Alexandre "Marius" Jacob (1879–1954), an accomplished burglar who approached his task with a clear sense of ethics; he stole only from the rich, and among them only from business owners, investors, clergymen, judges, and the military, but never from, say, doctors or architects, because they did useful things. He always gave away a significant part of his take to the poor. Once, realizing that he'd broken into the house of the writer Pierre Loti, he left an apology and money for damages; another time, learning that an intended victim was choked by debts, he left her ten thousand gold francs. He was almost certainly a primary model for Maurice Leblanc's *gentleman-cambrioleur* Arsène Lupin. Among the many tricks he devised was one often seen in movies (Jules Dassin's *Rififi*, for example): breaking into an apartment from the floor above by poking an umbrella through the ceiling and using it to catch the plaster. At one point he bought a hardware store, where he could dismantle safes at his leisure. He wrote: "The right to live is not to be begged for, it's to be taken. Theft is restitution, the redistribution of ownership. Rather than be shut up in a factory as in a prison, rather than beg for what is

* Or as Paul Reclus, Élisée's brother, put it, "As producers, we seek to obtain the most possible for our work. As consumers, we pay the least possible. The consequence of these combined transactions is that every day of our lives we steal and are stolen from" (*La Révolte*, November 21, 1892).

my right, I preferred to revolt and fight my enemies tooth and nail by waging war on the rich, targeting their goods."

The anarchist spectrum was broad. All the anarchists hated and feared capitalism, the state, the military, and the church, but beyond that commonality there were a thousand shades of difference. Jacob was a redistributionist, but there were others practicing individual repossession who kept their booty for themselves. They were individualist anarchists, who had read Max Stirner's *The Ego and Its Own* (1845): "I decide whether it is the *right thing* in me; there is no right *outside* me. If it is right for me, it is right. Possibly this may not suffice to make it right for the rest; that is their care, not mine: let them defend themselves." Even among the individualists there was a range of stances, from lone wolves not averse to collective action when it suited them, all the way over to people whose views resembled the ice-cold egotism that passes for libertarianism today. And there were many more who tried variously to reconcile their distrust of the state with their redistributive ethics, and professed a variety of forms of antiauthoritarian communism. Sébastien Faure attempted to define the thread that linked the diverse range of anarchists: "The common point is the negation of the principle of Authority in social organization and a hatred of all the constraints imposed by the institutions that are based upon that principle."

An 1894 police report claimed there were about five hundred anarchists in Paris. Among these some belonged to those historically anarchist professions, typesetting and proofreading; there were journalists, cabinetmakers, tailors, barbers, cobblers, cooks, as well as one investor, one stockbroker, one architect, one insurance agent, and three grocers. But there were many *anarchisants* (fellow travelers, to borrow the Soviet locution). There were writers and artists who were engaged with the cause: Félix Fénéon, Laurent Tailhade, Octave Mirbeau, Henri de Regnier, Francis Viellé-Griffin, Émile Verhaeren, Camille and Lucien Pissarro, Félix Vallotton, Paul Signac, Maximilien Luce; and some who were disengaged but varyingly sympathetic, such as Stéphane Mallarmé, Paul Valéry, Remy de Gourmont. The subscribers to *La Révolte* included some prominent enemies of the Commune: Anatole France, Leconte de Lisle, J.-K. Huysmans. There were connections running both ways between a wing of the anarchists

A poster for Georges Darien's journal *L'Escarmouche*, by Henri-Gabriel Ibels, 1893

and the fanatical anti-Semite Édouard Drumont. The arch-Catholic Léon Bloy hated capitalism and the bourgeoisie enough that he sometimes made common cause. One test of intellectuals' sympathy was whether they agreed to let excerpts from their works be reprinted gratis in the anarchist sheets; Zola, Maupassant, Georges Courteline, François Coppée emphatically did not. There was the singular Jehan Rictus, who behaved like an anarchist, shared tables with the anarchists, sometimes published in the anarchist press and read at anarchist cafés, but always let it be known that he belonged to the party of order. There was a class division among the anarchists in which exclusion worked contrary to the norm: Fénéon, Tailhade, et al. were never invited to the workers' estaminets where the hard-liners drank and sang. And of course there were a thousand touchy situations in which shadings of dogma and degrees of commitment opened or closed doors. As the journalist Arthur Ranc observed, "Everyone is someone else's reactionary."

On May 1, 1891, the army opened fire on a crowd of strikers in the textile manufacturing town of Fourmies, near the Belgian border, killing ten, including two children, ages eleven and thirteen. The same day, a demonstration in Clichy turned into a shoot-out between anarchists and police; no one knew why, or who started it (though two of the anarchists were given long prison terms). To avenge both incidents, a man whose nom de guerre was Ravachol (né François Koenigstein) planted a bomb on March 11 of the following year at the home of a judge in the Clichy case, and then two weeks later another bomb at the residence of the other judge. In between the two, an anonymous bomb that everyone assumed Ravachol had planted went off in the Lobau barracks. There were no injuries from any of them, but forty thousand francs in damages. The evening of the Lobau bombing Ravachol dined at a restaurant on Boulevard Magenta and chatted with the waiter about the latest bomb, which hadn't yet been reported in the press. Two days later he came back; the waiter tipped off the cops; it took ten of them to subdue Ravachol. In court he was accused of a long list of unsolved crimes that included the robbery of the grave of a countess and the murder of a famous hermit who had amassed a fortune in alms—none of which could be realistically linked to him. Nevertheless, he was

François Koenigstein, a.k.a. Ravachol

sentenced to death. He was the least moved of all those in the courthouse when the sentence was pronounced; he shouted, "Vive l'anarchie!"

Octave Mirbeau wrote, "Ravachol doesn't scare me. He is transitory, like the terror he inspires, which is the thunderbolt that will be followed by a joyful sun and clear skies. After the dark business is finished, the dream of universal harmony beckons." Ravachol entered into myth even before his head was separated from his shoulders. He was compared to Christ, portrayed framed by the guillotine with the rising sun behind; people sang "Dansons la Ravachole" to the tune of "La Carmagnole," a famous song of 1792. In prison, Ravachol received flowers, requests for autographs, an expensive box of grapes from Algeria. A sign appeared in the window of a cheap hotel in the Épinettes: THERE ARE NO JUDGES IN THIS HOUSE. A story went around town about a man who enjoyed an expensive meal in a restaurant, after which he told the proprietor that he had no money, but that his friends were anarchists who would blow up the place in case there was trouble—so the owner treated him to a bottle of champagne. On July 11, on his way to the Widow, Ravachol told the chaplain, "I don't care about your Christ. Don't show him to me— I'll spit on him," and then sang "Le Père Duchêne," a song that had just appeared anonymously that year: "If you want to be happy / Hang your landlord / Chop the priests in half . . ." The sheet music sold on the streets like chestnuts in winter, the vendors just a beat ahead of the cops, who seized all they could find. An enterprising reporter went around asking vendors what kind of people had bought them, to which the reply was invariable: "We sold them only to the gentry."

That reporter (Charles Flor, a Belgian who wrote under the pseudonym Flor O'Squarr, as his father had before him) explained to his readers the rationale behind the bombings, "in vulgar French": "You don't have a rifle. And even if you had a rifle it wouldn't do you much good, since you have no bullets, since you don't know how a rifle works, since despite your courage you are hardly up to measuring your skills against those of the army . . . You are a combatant in the war of today, so prepare your dynamite. The time is not far off when you'll be called to the front."

Ravachol at his execution. Illustration by Charles Maurin, 1892

The massacre at Fourmies, 1891

A series of attempted reprisals followed Ravachol's execution, culminating in the bomb that Auguste Vaillant threw into the Chamber of Deputies on December 29, 1893. There were no injuries and hardly any damages; after the brief commotion ceased, the chairman intoned, "La séance continue." Vaillant, the son of a gendarme in Corsica, had left his family and lived alone in Paris from age twelve, was arrested for begging, emigrated to Argentina and came back three years later, and at the time of the bombing was secretary of the Philanthropic Library for the Study and Popularization of the Natural Sciences. At the guillotine, a mere month after the bombing, he predicted that his death would be avenged. And so it was, a week later, when a bomb went off in the Café Terminus outside the Gare Saint-Lazare.

Its author was Émile Henry, twenty-one years old, the son of Fortuné Henry, a Communard sentenced to death in absentia who died of lead poisoning from working in a mine in Spain during his exile. Émile was admitted to the Polytechnique but decided not to attend, instead making his way to the anarchist circuit. At first he repudiated Ravachol: "A true anarchist attacks his enemy; he doesn't bomb houses where there are women, children, workers, and servants." He changed his mind a few months later. In November 1892 he delivered a package containing a bomb to the offices of a mining company, but it looked sufficiently suspicious that it was taken to the police precinct house on Rue des Bons-Enfants, where it exploded, killing six. He disappeared for a year or so, then came back to town and rented a room under the name Dubois (i.e., Smith). He made a bomb using a cooking pot, a quantity of zinc, twenty-four bullets, dynamite, fulminate of mercury, and a miner's wick measured to burn for fifteen seconds. He left with the bomb fastened to his belt, and armed with a revolver loaded with dum-dum bullets and a knife the blade of which he had attempted to coat with poison. He made his way up Avenue de l'Opéra, but the fancy places—Café de la Paix, Café Américain, Restaurant Bignon—were insufficiently crowded. Café Terminus, not nearly as fancy, was crowded. He sat near the door, ordered a bock and a cigar and then another bock. At nine o'clock, while the orchestra played a piece by Vincent d'Indy, he lit the wick with his cigar, stepped to the door, turned around, and threw the bomb, which

The arrest of Émile Henry, 1894

witnesses described as looking like a tin can, in the direction of the orchestra. It hit the electric chandelier, broke a crystal tulip, and hit the ground, spreading thick, bitter smoke. A few seconds later it exploded, injuring twenty people and killing one. The action profoundly divided anarchist opinion. Octave Mirbeau declared that "a mortal enemy of anarchism could not have done better than Émile Henry," adding that police provocation was widely suspected. Laurent Tailhade, on the other hand, uttered his notorious *mot*: "Of what importance are a few vague people if the gesture is beautiful?"

Two bombs went off the following week with no significant damage, probably set by the Belgian anarchist Désiré-Joseph Pauwels, who died in the vestibule of the Madeleine church on March 15, the sole victim of his own bomb. On April 4 a bomb went off in the Foyot restaurant, across the street from the Palais de Luxembourg, meeting place of the Senate. Tailhade, with exquisite irony, was the sole victim. Although the clientele was made up primarily of politicians, financiers, and their mistresses, Tailhade, an inveterate gourmand, was there romancing his own mistress. He lost an eye in the blast while protecting his companion, Julie Mialhe. No one was ever formally accused, although rumors flew, especially fifty years or more later, when people took turns accusing the dead, including Fénéon and the veteran activists Louis Matha and Paul Delesalle, perhaps based on ancient grudges (the most persuasive case involves a certain "Julien," who has never been identified). On June 24 an Italian anarchist, Sante Geronimo Caserio, fatally stabbed the president of the republic, Sadi Carnot, during a ceremony in Nice, after which people all over France looted and burned businesses owned by Italians. A thematically related show trial was held two months later, at which the indicted included Fénéon, Faure, Grave, Paul Reclus, Émile Pouget (editor and publisher of the workers' journal *Le Père Peinard*, written entirely in slang; also noted for coining the word *sabotage*), a number of apolitical burglars, and a butcher's apprentice accused of stealing a cutlet. The anarchists were all acquitted. The era of bombings had ceased, although, until the war broke out twenty years later, bomb squads were kept busy attending to every lost suitcase or misplaced kitchen appliance that happened to turn up on the street.

The bombing of Chez Foyot, 1894

"The pallbearers." Illustration by Félix Vallotton

A room tossed by the police

Albert Libertad

The Dreyfus case opened sharp divisions among the anarchists. Many rallied to Drumont on the grounds of that tiresomely recurrent "socialism of fools"; many declared Dreyfus's guilt or innocence irrelevant, since treason was inculcated in the military; many would say, like Descaves's character Philémon, an old Communard, "We're with him provisionally, but he'll never be with us. If another popular uprising broke out, he'd be back in service gunning us down." Grave and Faure, figures of moral authority, took the side of Dreyfus, and they eventually convinced Pouget, not previously a friend of the Jews. Nevertheless, the internal sniping and doctrinal hairsplitting that resulted from the case hastened the demise of many alliances and the departure of numerous anarchists for socialist or anarcho-syndicalist configurations. The artists and intellectuals did not abandon the cause so much as drift away. The last act of the glamorous era occurred in 1899, when Zo d'Axa (né Alphonse Gallaud de La Pérouse), the flamboyant editor of *L'Endehors* and *La Feuille*, vigorously campaigned a donkey for public office. The animal wound up being seized by the cops.

In the early years of the twentieth century, the anarchists hunkered down. They only rarely put up posters anymore they claimed had been printed by the Imprimerie Nationale or the Ministry of State, but they still organized house moves *à la cloche de bois* (to skip out; literally "by the wooden bell"), still held their meetings on the cheap by walking in on meetings of other political groups and simply hijacking the podium. But now the anarchists were younger, more ragtag, more personally troubled, less in public view, less grounded in tradition. Until his early death in 1908, their most visible spokesman was a man who called himself Albert Libertad, an orphan whom early illness had left with withered legs and who propelled himself on two crutches, which he could use as formidable battering instruments. He was generally accompanied by the sisters Armandine and Anna Mahé, both of them his lovers, one or both of them the mothers of his sons, Minus and Diamant. He was a cynic, bitterly sarcastic, famous for haranguing a priest in the pulpit during a service at the Sacré-Coeur. Among his followers, according to Victor Méric, an early adherent, "you found every sort: very studious quasi-intellectuals, poets, and also—necessarily—informants and provocateurs. And then there were the 'scientific' types, confirmed in their ignorance, smart alecs always on the hunt for some scheme."

They were attempting to refashion the rules of life from its essential principles. Most were vegetarians, even vegans (*végétaliens*), and drank only water. They read Darwin and Huxley and sought a scientific rationale for an ideal existence freed from unthinking adherence to social norms.

The Romainville commune, headquarters of *L'Anarchie*, circa 1911

> The autonomous social cell bows to no law and no prejudice . . . The right to life justifies everything! The lives of others are no longer sacred for us; only what matters to our "I" can have any value in our eyes. If in order to survive I have to crush thousands of troglodytes, I'll do it with no remorse. If we have to cut down everything that surrounds us, let's not hesitate! As Émile Henry put it, there are no innocent victims. Let's hit hard! Let's be strong! That is the true moral law of life, as biology teaches us! That's how to be a real revolutionary—nothing to do with the mystical and redundant babble of the workerist charlatans. It's galling to think that, with no knowledge of anatomy or astronomy, nor psychology, nor zoology, nor embryology, idiots presume to address the social question!

There was always, on every issue, someone with a more radical stance. If it was agreed that marriage was legalized prostitution and the family an incubator of misery, someone might say, "Cohabitation—that's our worst enemy! It can't be engaged in without compromises and consequent servitude. Anarchism must give the social cell—the individual—complete autonomy. It would be idle to abolish marriage only to substitute for it a bond that is equally as servile, for all that it isn't legalized." At the communal house in suburban Romainville where the editorial offices of *L'Anarchie* were located, a sign on the door to the library read, IDLERS, CROOKS, DRUNKS, STINKERS, CLIMBERS, SNOBS, HYSTERICS, EGGHEADS, GASBAGS OF EVERY DESCRIPTION, DO NOT PASS THROUGH THIS DOOR. DEATH AWAITS YOU! Painted on the library wall was a motto: IF YOU WANT TO LIVE, BE YOUR OWN BEST FRIEND.

It was from this milieu that the Bonnot Gang emerged. It

Left to right, top to bottom: Édouard Carouy; Raymond Callemin, a.k.a. Raymond-la-Science; Élie Monier, a.k.a. Simentoff; Octave Garnier

Bonnot Gang exhibits in the courtroom, 1912

Chez les loups: Moeurs anarchistes (Among the wolves); a roman à clef about the Bonnot Gang, by André Lorulot, 1922

was a misnomer from the start. Jules Bonnot was an excellent driver—he was a professional chauffeur, who had driven Arthur Conan Doyle and the prolific true-crime hack H. Ashton-Wolfe, among others, so he was a known quantity the press could latch on to, and he was also, at thirty-five, by far the oldest—but he was really only a driver. The rest were all young working-class autodidacts, quite a number of them orphans, all of them laboring since age twelve or thirteen. Édouard Carouy, twenty-eight, a Belgian, had worked in a sugar refinery. Octave Garnier, twenty-two, from Fontainebleau, was a baker. René Valet, twenty-one, from Verdun, was a locksmith and typesetter. André Soudy, nineteen, from near Orléans, was a grocery clerk. Eugène Dieudonné, twenty-seven, was a carpenter's apprentice from Nancy. Raymond Callemin, twenty-one, called Raymond-la-Science, was a typesetter from Brussels. Élie Monier, twenty-two, called Simentoff, was a peasant from the Pyrénées-Orientales. On December 11, 1911, a bank messenger was making his way down Rue Ordener, in Montmartre north of the hill, to the local branch of the Société Générale, carrying a bag containing 318,772 francs in securities and another bag with 5,266 francs in coins, while in an inner pocket of his coat a wallet held 20,000 francs in banknotes and a bit of gold. He wore the uniform of his trade: a sky-blue frock coat and a Napoleon hat. A car stopped and a man got out. Without a word he shot the messenger twice and grabbed his bags, while a second man went through the messenger's pockets. The automobile took off. It was the world's first getaway car.

The car was found abandoned the following day in Dieppe, on the coast. As soon as the news hit the press, the bandits were seen everywhere in Europe, but at first nobody thought of the anarchists, although many lived just up the hill from the robbery. Two days after the New Year, a ninety-one-year-old *rentier* and his housekeeper were found murdered in the southeastern suburbs; around 20,000 francs in securities and gold pieces were missing. Witnesses in the neighborhood who were shown photographs identified Garnier, and after his name appeared in the newspapers, the bank messenger, who had survived, also pegged him. In addition he claimed to identify Dieudonné, who was irrefutably in Nancy on December 21. The police tossed the Romainville house and arrested everyone there, then let everybody go except Rirette Maîtrejean, twenty-four, and Viktor Lvovitch Kibaltchiche, twenty-one, despite the fact that they had no demonstrable connection with the case. Meanwhile, a crime wave had broken out: there were car thefts and robberies of stores, post offices, factories, and armories all over France and Belgium. The police were objects of widespread ridicule.

On February 28 a car running down Rue d'Amsterdam almost hit a bus, knocked over a woman, then was blocked by the bus and had to stop. A traffic cop who happened to be named Garnier started writing a ticket, but the car took off with him clinging to the running board; he was shot three times from inside the car, and died soon after. The police, in hot pursuit, hit a pedestrian and had to stop; the car vanished. Eyewitnesses identified the shooter as Garnier and the driver as Bonnot, with Callemin in the back. A wave of arrests swept up Dieudonné; Garnier wrote an open letter to the newspapers, taking responsibility and clearing him. A month later, six of the gang stole a car and killed the driver, then drove to Chantilly and raided the Société Générale. The employees resisted; one was killed. The bandits emptied the coffers to the tune of 47,555 francs. A witness pegged Soudy. Hysteria ensued, with denunciations and false leads galore—the prosecutor received as many as seven hundred letters a day. Thirteen associates of the gang were indicted. Soudy was arrested in a coastal town, Carouy in the suburbs, Callemin in Paris, loaded down with three Brownings.

Bonnot got away from the cops once and then, on April 22, was tracked down to a garage in Choisy-le-Roi, in the southeastern suburbs. The police, who didn't know he was alone, called in reinforcements: firemen, two companies of the Garde Républicaine, a cordon of volunteer sharpshooters. Taking in the scene were the attorney general, a party of judges and VIPs, and a film crew from Pathé. The house was soon riddled with bullets, but Bonnot kept firing, so the police dragged in a cart loaded with explosives. After an initial misfire, there followed two explosions. Somehow the house was still standing, although there was no sign of life from within. The cops broke in, shielding themselves with mattresses, and found the mortally wounded Bonnot, also wrapped in mattresses. According to legend, he shot at them, although by that time he had put two bullets in his head. He died

Police dragging the nearly dead Bonnot down the stairs, Choisy-le-Roi, 1911

Léo Malet's *Trilogie noire*, of which *La vie est dégueulasse* is the first part (1969 edition). Illustration by René Magritte

on his way to the hospital. A piece of paper was found in which he exonerated Dieudonné and four other people; it is said that he died exclaiming, "Dieudonné is innocent!" Newspapers pointed out that Bonnot alone, equipped with just one revolver with a fifty-foot range, his other arm paralyzed from a wound received in a previous encounter with the police, had managed to hold at bay an army equipped with Lebel rifles and dynamite. Léon Bloy wrote, "The newspapers are full of heroes. Everybody was heroic except Bonnot. The entire population, flouting laws, took up arms and fired away while shielding themselves . . . I confess that all my sympathy goes to the desperado giving his life in order to scare them, and I think that God will judge them more harshly."

A few days later, Garnier and Valet were tracked to the eastern suburb of Nogent-sur-Marne, to a house in a densely populated area. Gendarmes, firemen, and Republican Guards surrounded the house, while Zouaves stood on the viaduct above and rolled boulders down, aiming at the house. As riflemen fired from surrounding rooftops and bombs were thrown to no effect, spectators showed up, some in evening dress, some with picnic baskets. The gun battle went on for hours. Sometime after midnight a huge explosion shook the house, and when the wall of smoke cleared, Garnier and Valet were found dead in a pool of blood. In 1947, Léo Malet wrote a novel, *La vie est dégueulasse* (Life sucks), that featured a character loosely modeled on Garnier. As a teenage runaway, Malet had been taken in by veterans of the Romainville commune, acquaintances of the gang, who in the 1920s ran a vegan cooperative on Rue de Tolbiac. His character, Jean Fraiger, a member of a revolutionary gang inspired by the teachings of a sinister oracle called Christ, is on the run from the police following a motorized caper. Along the way he has met and fallen in love with Gloria, who doesn't know his true identity. He is itchy and paranoid, as well as jealous; disturbed by Gloria's periodic absences, he follows her to the house of friends. The husband of the couple is a psychoanalyst, who notes Fraiger's anxieties and persuades him to unburden himself, serially. During their second session, the women rush in from an adjoining room: the newspapers have reported that one of Fraiger's comrades has given him up. Fraiger takes out his revolver and holds the three captive, while the analyst coolly continues the session. "There's your penis," he says, pointing to the gun. "Like Lacenaire, your life has been nothing but a long, artful suicide." Twitching, unsure if he will kill the others or kill himself, Fraiger says, "I would so much have liked to live," and rushes out. Two weeks later he bursts into a precinct house, on the point of death from starvation, but waving his gun and begging the cops to shoot him in the crotch. They oblige.

Eight months elapsed before the surviving gang members went on trial. Carouy, Callemin, Soudy, Monier, Dieudonné, Maîtrejean, Kibaltchiche, and seven other people faced charges ranging from murder to receiving stolen property and harboring fugitives. During their time in the Santé, seven of the bandits were examined by Émile Michon, the prison psychologist, who questioned them on every possible topic. In the resulting book, with its improbably lovely title, *A Little of the Bandits' Soul*, he never identifies them by name—with the sole exception of Kibaltchiche, "because I will never be able to consider him an evildoer"—the result being that they become a blurry mass, bugs in a jar. Still, Michon's ambivalences add up to a convincing group portrait. They intellectualized their emotions; they were so invested in their "I" that they were often ignorant of the most basic facts about others; they were ascetics even in matters of the heart; they had excellent memories. Most of them could lecture endlessly on Spinoza, Lamarck, Schopenhauer, the sciences. They were slobs.

> They seem to want to attach themselves to nothing, and they dread all discipline, even that of habit. They are inconstant in every sense of the word: they come and go, move, travel, are always leaving someone; when they arrive somewhere they go away again almost immediately. They settle nowhere. Since they are always wanted for some infraction or violation they change names as easily as they change addresses, and they sleep with one eye open.

Extrapolating a bit from his account, you can figure that Monier, from the Midi, was the warmest and most passionate, Raymond-la-Science cold and pedantic. Carouy was stolid and

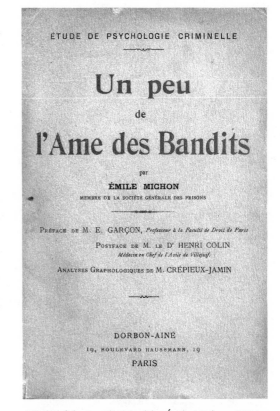

A Little of the Bandits' Soul, by Émile Michon, 1914

André Soudy takes aim, 1911

slow, Dieudonné earnest and deliberate. Jean De Boë, who got ten years, was poetic and a gifted artist. Michon refers to only one of them as a psychopath. By process of elimination that would leave Soudy, who had himself photographed aiming a rifle at the camera.

Before even being sentenced Carouy had bit down on a cyanide capsule he'd obtained somehow. Seven, including Rirette Maîtrejean and the two other women, were acquitted. Three were sentenced to prison terms, including Kibaltchiche, who served his five years, then changed his name to Victor Serge—he fought in revolutions in Spain and Russia, was among the first to warn the West about Stalin, wrote extraordinary books. Dieudonné, despite all the efforts to exonerate him, was sentenced to death, and then the sentence was commuted to life in the *bagne*. Soudy, Callemin, and Monier all married the Widow. On his way, Monier said, "Farewell to you all, gentlemen, and to society as well"; Callemin said, "It's a beautiful sight, isn't it, a man who's about to die"; Soudy said, "Brr . . . it's cold." Callemin and Monier left their bodies to science: Monier to surgical anatomy, Callemin to biochemical research—his disembodied hands remain preserved in formaldehyde at the Medico-Legal Institute in Lille. Soudy left his brain to the dean of the medical faculty at the University of Paris, his burglary tools to the Ministry of War, his skull to the Museum of Anthropology—that it be exhibited and the profits given to soup kitchens—his hair for the barbers' union to sell to benefit the cause, and his autograph to *L'Anarchie*, so that "priests and apostles of philosophy can use it to further their cynical individualism." Instead he was buried in Ivry.

12

The Game

The flâneur, exemplar of this book, was notable for making use of the whole city. For centuries, hardly anyone else did. When Louis-Sébastien Mercier and Restif de La Bretonne began plying the streets of Paris in the eighteenth century, and even when Privat d'Anglemont and Alfred Delvau took their strides in the mid-nineteenth, the city was still a collection of villages arrayed around a narrow band of common use, of fairs and executions and ten-day wonders. Even after public transport and the centralization of jobs began to take people out of their neighborhood villages, most people carved ruts from home to work, with only the occasional weekend ventures to parks and attractions, usually the same ones again and again. If you lived in Grenelle, you might know of Montmartre more from hearsay than from experience, and vice versa.

That wasn't due to lack of imagination or even force of habit as much as to lack of time. The ninety-six- or eighty-two- or sixty- or forty- or even thirty-five-hour workweek keeps people from straying far from their rotation around one pole. The enforcement of the constraint was one in which employers and the ostensible liberators of the working class were equally complicit. "A strange delusion possesses the working classes in nations where capitalist civilization dominates. This madness entails individual and social sufferings that over the last two centuries have tortured poor humanity. This madness is the love of work,

Monumental map of Paris, 1920

An American edition of *The Right to Be Lazy*, by Paul Lafargue (1907/1977)

the raging passion for work, which pushes to the limits of exhaustion the vital forces of people and their progeny." Those are the words of Paul Lafargue, Karl Marx's son-in-law, about whom Marx once said something like: If he's a Marxist, then count me out. Lafargue, who wrote his manifesto, *The Right to Be Lazy*, while incarcerated in Sainte-Pélagie in 1883, called laziness the "mother of the arts and noble virtues." He looked forward to the day when machines would relieve humans of drudgery, not suspecting that the rise of machines would remove many people's ability to make a living, while "laziness" could be advanced as a reason to let them rot.

The use of the whole city could not be a function of work. It just wasn't practical for colporteurs to try to work every single corner, floor by floor, the way they could elsewhere traipse from farm to farm; census takers and religious zealots and vendors of Épinal prints were bound to territories as firmly as laborers and typists. The city—compact and curled within itself, a labyrinth—had to be played like a game. Many of the flâneurs were compulsively garrulous types who played the city the way they'd work a party (or perhaps, in the case of Restif, like a pervert at an orgy). If they had constraints or ground rules, they didn't leave descriptions. The first to consciously engage the game were the

Dadas, whose ventures to overlooked parts of Paris were feeble if not touristic. On their excursion to Saint-Julien-le-Pauvre in 1921, for example, it rained; they shouted vaguely provocative slogans to no reaction and handed out printed statements that people threw in the gutter. They were far less interested in seeing than in being seen.

Their successors, the Surrealists, did a bit better, on the evidence of Louis Aragon's 1926 *Paris Peasant*, a poetic account of their investigations of the Passage de l'Opéra, one of the earliest arcades, built in 1822 and demolished a bit over a century later as part of the extension of Boulevard Haussmann; and of the Buttes-Chaumont, which, "seen from on high, has the shape of a nightcap," and which at the time, being located squarely in the middle of a *quartier populaire*, was seldom visited by the intelligentsia. "The fauna of the imagination and its oceanic vegetation, as through a mane of shadow, lose and perpetuate themselves in the badly lit areas of human activity. It is there that appear the great spiritual lighthouses, formal neighbors of less pure signs. The door to mystery is opened by human exhaustion, and we find ourselves in the kingdoms of shadow." That was the protocol: to move through the city as if in a dream, interpreting artifacts along the way as clues to an unresolvable mystery. The Surrealists regularly met for drinks at the Café Certa in the Passage de l'Opéra, initially because it was neither Montmartre nor Montparnasse, which were fashionable hence hateful, but they came to appreciate that "human aquarium" for its own sake. Aragon's text, which combines exhaustive inventory with regular flights into the ether, was by way of an obituary for the arcade, a found object of the highest magnitude, a three-dimensional counterpart to those nineteenth-century steel engravings that Max Ernst cut up and recombined in *The Hundred Headless Woman*. As Walter Benjamin expressed it, "The nineteenth century is the set of noises that invades our dream, and which we interpret on awaking." The inventory of images he and the Surrealists had experienced in earliest childhood was now impossibly remote, could scarcely be reconciled with the roar and flash of their present, and yet there it was, preserved in amber.

Contemplating the Buttes-Chaumont, Aragon writes, "Night in our cities no longer resembles the racket of dogs of the Latin

The Dadas at Saint-Julien-le-Pauvre, 1921

The Mazda billboard on the boulevard, from *Nadja*, by André Breton, 1928

twilight, nor the bat of the Middle Ages, nor that image of sorrows which is the night of the Renaissance. It's an immense monster made of sheet metal, pierced by a thousand eyes." The *noctambule,* or nightwalker, is a subset of the category of flâneurs. Restif, the speleologist of a city plunged in darkness, was the undisputed pioneer. Chance encounters are dramatic in his accounts; people emerge from the night as from out of a dense fog. Restif swims from rock to rock, searching for humans. After him, curiously, night ceases to be a subject of inquiry for a very long time, unless it is the night in the *Mysteries of Paris* or, for that matter, the *Chants de Maldoror,* a vast trench of dangers. Privat is out in the night, for example, but for him it seems to be a landscape mostly of bars, while the streets are seldom evoked, and so it is for most of his successors. Out of nowhere, the earliest night photographs appear in the late 1880s—although they were unknown until fairly recently—the work of Gabriel Loppé (1825–1913), a genre painter of mountain scenes who left behind more canvases than biographical details. He is mostly famous for his photographs of the Eiffel Tower struck by lightning, made around 1905, but his earlier pictures are like photographs of celestial bodies taken with a telescope: very long exposures that focus on commercial lighting and the objects caught or suggested relative to its glow. An illuminated Morris column sets trees in relief; the department store Belle Jardinière sets the whole Right Bank ablaze—and you remember that those are gas lamps—or the same store is seen from the opposite bank, its lights silhouetting the statue of Henri IV on the Vert-Galant.

That last picture in particular makes it impossible not to think of Brassaï, who pursued similar effects in the age of electric lighting forty or more years later. The milky, fogbound glow of lights in a park sketches the outline of Marshal Michel Ney, brandishing his saber at a derisory neon HOTEL. Brassaï owned the night—to some extent he still does—and he rang all its changes. His nocturnal interiors of bars, dance halls, and whorehouses are best known; he also made documentary pictures of prostitutes on the beat and sewer workers and road repair crews, staged photos of lovers and criminals in action, and created a great variety of streetscapes that have ever since colored everyone's expectations of the Paris night: parks, alleys, industrial sites,

A view of the statue of Henri IV on the Vert-Galant, with the Belle Jardinière department store behind it. Photograph by Gabriel Loppé, circa 1889

canals, honky-tonk streets full of signs, and his magnificent views of the Tour Saint-Jacques, a trembling Gothic skyscraper. Brassaï is so definitive that his pictures have been absorbed into the sort of tourist nostalgia imagery that precludes thought or experience—you could once buy, and perhaps still can, poster-size reproductions of his photo of car lights in the fog (circa 1934) with tiny embedded piezoelectric bulbs, a kitsch effect that actually succeeds in making the scene even more oneiric. That Brassaï profoundly understood the city game—much better than his contemporaries; his friends the Surrealists look even more like dilettantes and poetasters in comparison—is demonstrated by the absolute seamlessness of his transitions between fact and fiction. He knows, that is, that threat and corruption are actual and at the same time playacting, that the most daunting dark alley is equally a stage set, and that the flesh trade routinely blurs the line between passion and contempt.

The time of Brassaï's world ran from the *années folles* (the 1920s) through the Popular Front, and they blend together democratically in his pictures: *bals-musette* and drag balls and Folies Bergère and opium dens and streetwalkers and vegetable displays at Les Halles all one continuous tableau. The curtain came down on that world in 1940. After the war came something else. The first decade after the Liberation distilled Paris. People were lean; rations and privations were still in place; nobody had any money except a few black marketeers who rode out the purges. People made a meager living, in driblets, begging, bartering, stealing, doing odd jobs, collecting paper—of which there was a shortage for years—or metal or rags, selling each other trash at the flea markets. It was a bit like the Siege of eighty years earlier, in that the only staple in bottomless supply was wine. The frozen past came out of the attics and into the street. Those were the last years of bicycles vastly outnumbering cars, of significant numbers of horse-drawn vehicles, of numerous houseboats on the Seine, of coal-and-wine shops, of gypsy encampments in the Zone, of nearly rural pockets within the city—of styles of life that were very little removed from the time of François Villon. It was a time of historical regurgitation, when all the ghosts came out maybe for a last dance.

"Time works for those who place themselves outside of time.

Instantané
JEAN-PAUL CLÉBERT

A press item on Jean-Paul Clébert upon the publication of *Paris insolite*, 1952

No one can be *of Paris*, can know that city, who has not made the acquaintance of its ghosts," wrote Jacques Yonnet, a writer and artist who, beginning in the Occupation, accumulated encounters with the uncanny in the Maubert–Mouffetard corridor. His sole book is *Rue des Maléfices* (1954); the title refers to a map of the neighborhood drawn up around 1600 by students of the Irish College at the Sorbonne, in which Rue Zacharie (now Rue Xavier-Privas) is identified in English as "Witchcraft Street." The narrative alternates between accounts of activities in wartime (forging papers; concealing Jews, Roma, and American paratroopers) and after (making ends meet, persuading Fréhel to perform one last time), with tales of curses, disappearances, revenants, and the inevitability of Fate with a capital *F*. What makes it so disquieting is how deeply the uncanny is embedded in the quotidian, in the meagerness of rations and the toll of drink and routine, not to mention that scenes and characters are unequivocally documented in photographs by Doisneau. Its historical and personal specificity underscores the idea that time is fluid, that the same characters have always been around, that the Middle Ages never ceased but merely moved to a back court.

Jean-Paul Clébert hung around that same orbit for a while. Born to an apparently indifferent bourgeois family—he changed his name very early, and never said what it had been—Clébert dropped out of Jesuit boarding school at sixteen and joined the Resistance. After the war and some peregrinations in Asia, he came back to Paris and spent a few years living nowhere and everywhere. He got a job, one of those peculiarly French bureaucratic undertakings, that involved measuring the area of seemingly random apartments all over the city. It was thus that he met—besides bored housewives who answered the door in négligées—a man who lived in his vestibule and raised snails in his rooms, an artist whose studio was filled with hundreds of birds at large, a man whose mania for efficiency had led him to connect his doorbell to the flushing mechanism of his toilet, not to mention the people whose collections had taken over the lion's share of their lodgings and those who earned a respectable living from mail-order fraud.

He went on from there to live the life of a wide-ranging clochard, earning small coin by hawking *L'Intran* or unpacking at

Les Halles or selling tourists artfully packaged "filthy postcards" that would turn out to be views of marble nudes at the Louvre. Along the way he inventoried every possible way to live for no money in the open Paris of that time: sleeping in warm weather in the Buttes-Chaumont or vacant lots or construction sites or behind the wine casks at Bercy or in nooks along the Petite-Ceinture railway, abandoned since 1934. In cold weather the problem was tougher but not irresolvable; there were various shacks and sheds in industrial parts of the city, ragpickers' storerooms, the rescuers' cabins (*secours aux noyés*) along the Seine, or, for that matter, a number of ancient but officially uninhabitable houses along Rue Xavier-Privas that had been turned into clandestine dormitories for clochards. Or, with a bit of extra contrivance, there were the houses surrounding Les Halles, "the whole neighborhood as bottomless as a vast perforated basket, each house concealing in its flanks a mysterious labyrinth leading who knows where, toward underground passages, sewers, catacombs, no storefront an ordinary cul-de-sac but every one an antechamber . . ." Clébert's book *Paris insolite* (1952; "unexpected" or "uncanny" or "fantastic" or "bizarre" Paris—*insolite* is a very hard word to translate adequately) is a road novel, for all that it is entirely contained within the city limits, but then, "It takes longer to traverse Paris than to cross a *département*." It is also, for that matter, a road novel in which the only mode of transport is shoe leather. Weirdly, its long, jangling, cascading sentences sound very much like spontaneous bop prosody, although it was written years before Jack Kerouac found his own voice. It is also a memorial to a city that even sixty-plus years ago was disappearing quickly.

An illustration by Théophile Steinlen for *Barabbas*, by Lucien Descaves, 1914

> What an awakening, silent but alive, happens when this city—its streets, houses, sidewalks, lampposts, trees, urinals—is no longer covered like a skin, like a crust, by that grublike swarm of humans rushing to the job machine, but at night comes back to life, swims back to the surface, washes off its filth, stands back on its feet, scratches itself, sings to break the silence, makes light to rend the darkness. It stretches, relaxes, spreads itself out before me, the solitary walker, the unknown strider, stranding me

Ed van der Elsken's *Love on the Left Bank*, 1956.

"If you think you are a genius, or merely possess a superior intelligence, get in touch with the Lettrist International." Circa 1955

among its scattered limbs, a vast labyrinth in which I rapturously lose myself, turning every corner, leaving every boulevard at the first left, catching up with the stream once again or passing it by, hopping on one foot, whistling with a butt in the corner of my mouth.

Clébert sometimes hung out with Yonnet, Giraud, and Doisneau at Chez Fraysse on Rue de Seine, and sometimes he wandered a couple of blocks over to Rue du Four, to Chez Moineau, where a younger and even more motley crowd gathered. It's where you would find, for example, the beautiful and mysterious Vali Myers, an artist and dancer from Australia; an enormous guy called Fred (Auguste Hommel, actually) and his smaller friend Jean-Michel Mension, both of whose clothes were sometimes covered with slogans; Jean-Claude Guilbert, who appears in *Paris insolite* as "the Shepherd" and who went on to act in Robert Bresson's *Mouchette* and *Au hasard Balthazar*; Joël Berlé, an accomplished thief who ended up a soldier of fortune in the Katanga in the mid-1960s—they and their friends can be seen in pictures by the Dutch photographer Ed van der Elsken, whose *Love on the Left Bank* (1956) stitches them into a chronicle that is somewhat fictionalized, although you can't call it romanticized, since their actual daily life stood at the very limit of romance. An emblematic image is the one of Mension, head down on a café table, next to a couple of hundred-franc notes crumpled at the bottom of a note that reads: "To go make love I seek 450 francs. All donations accepted. Don't wake me." They drank, fucked, begged, stole, smoked hash and kif, occasionally danced, ate and slept where and when they could; some of them also made art of some kind. Also at Chez Moineau, although much more shy of the camera, were Patrick Straram, Ivan Chtcheglov, Jean-Louis Brau, Serge Berna, Michèle Bernstein, Mohamed Dahou, Jacques Fillon, Gil J. Wolman, and Guy Debord—the members of the Lettrist International.

They were "Lettrists" because they had been briefly involved with Isidore Isou, deranged and ambitious, who wanted to replicate the success of fellow Romanian Tristan Tzara with Dada, in his case, breaking poetry down to unanchored lexemes and vocables; "international" because of Dahou, who was Algerian.

They lived the same way as the other Moineau regulars, but Debord devoted his enormous intellectual energy to finding a way to convert their daily existence into a program for the transformation of life, or at least the beginnings of one. He borrowed from Surrealism and Marxism, but that life of serious dissipation, seriously intended and seriously pursued, which combined pleasure, poverty, chance, sex, disputation, wandering, and the self-conscious theater of youth, stood at the core of his work for the next forty years. As Benjamin wrote of the Surrealists, he wanted "to win the energies of intoxication for the revolution."

Paris (as setting and landscape and self-renewing source) was central, and its proper employment an exemplary act. Hence his theory of the drift (*dérive*), which was "a technique of forward movement through a variety of ambiances . . . One or several persons, giving themselves over to the drift for a period of variable length, dispense with the usual reasons for moving about, and with their relationships, jobs, and leisure activities, in order to let themselves follow the pull of the landscape and the encounters that come from it." Debord gave credit for the germ of the theory to Thomas De Quincey's descriptions of his rambles in *Confessions of an English Opium Eater*, with his boasts of having discovered terrae incognitae and his search for an elusive "northwest passage" homeward when he'd gone too far afield. But a much more obvious source, in every way, was Clébert's book, just as that book was surely also the source of the Lettrists' fascination with the generally obscure and unvisited Rue Sauvage. Clébert had mapped the territory, and his drifts beggared theirs. The only two accounts of Lettrist drifts, which appear in the November 1956 issue of the Belgian Surrealist journal *Les Lèvres Nues*, are pretty small beer. The first takes place over the course of a week and does not, until the very end, stray from one Algerian bar on Rue Xavier-Privas, while the other sees Debord and Wolman tacking resolutely north-northeast from Rue des Jardins-Paul up to the town of Denis—like the Communards, the Lettrists dispensed with canonical titles—pausing briefly to admire Ledoux's rotunda on Place de Stalingrad and establish it as a psychogeographic "turntable." Perhaps closer to the point is Jacques Fillon's "Rational Description of Paris," in the December 1955 issue of the same journal:

Sheet music for "À la dérive," by Germaine Lix, 1927

The center of Paris is the region of the Contrescarpe, oval in shape, which can be circumambulated in about three hours. Its northern part consists of the Montagne-Geneviève; the terrain falls in a gentle slope toward the south. The inhabitants are very poor, and generally of North African origin. There can be met emissaries of various little-known powers.

An hour's walk toward the south brings one to the Butte-aux-Cailles, of mild and temperate climate. The inhabitants are very poor, but the layout of the streets has a labyrinthine sumptuousness.

And so on. Those stated distances are, of course, notional; like Clébert's description of Paris as bigger than a province, they are a measure of exploratory psychogeographic time rather than of pedestrian efficiency.

In 1958, Debord recast the group as the Situationist International, by which time only he and Bernstein, who were married, as well as Dahou (briefly), remained of the original grouping. Debord, who enjoyed playing commissar, had excluded everyone else, including Ivan Chtcheglov, the brilliant if wayward son of an exiled Ukrainian family, tossed for "mythomania, interpretative delirium, and lack of revolutionary consciousness." Nevertheless, in the first issue of the journal *Internationale Situationniste,* Debord published a text Chtcheglov had written in 1953, "Formula for a New City," under the nom de guerre Gilles Ivain.

A marker for Rue Neuve-[Sainte]-Geneviève (now Rue Tournefort), with the *Sainte* gouged out during the revolution

All cities are geological; you can't go three steps without meeting ghosts fortified with the aura of their legends. We move through a *closed* landscape where the landmarks draw us unceasingly toward the past. Certain *shifting* angles, certain *receding* perspectives allow us to catch glimpses of original spatial concepts, but this vision remains fragmentary. It must be sought in the magical sites of folk tales or surrealist writings: castles, endless walls, small forgotten bars, mammoth caves, casino mirrors.

Chtcheglov proposes the construction of a kind of ultra-Paris. It is a utopia, sure enough—he wastes some time on a very *Jetsons* conception of the ideal house: rotating, mounted on rails, with a glass ceiling—but when he gets to the nub of what he wants, it turns out to be a *dirty* utopia. Its primary architectural inspiration will be the paintings of de Chirico—those shifting angles, those vanishing perspectives—and more important, "the wards of this city could correspond to the various sensations encountered *by chance* in the modern city." These will include neighborhoods designated as Bizarre, Happy (residential), Noble and Tragic ("for well-behaved children"), Historic (museums and schools), Useful (hospitals and equipment storage), and Sinister. This latter "would not need to contain real dangers . . . It would have a complicated entry, be hideously decorated (piercing whistles, alarm bells, intermittent sirens with an irregular cadence, monstrous sculptures . . .) and both poorly lighted at night and violently lit during the day through the extreme use of reflection . . . Children and adults alike would learn by exploring the Sinister ward not to fear the painful occurrences of life, but to be amused by them." Naturally, "the principal occupation of the citizenry would be a CONTINUOUS DRIFT." It would be a city of play, comparable to Las Vegas and Monte Carlo in its contrast with a normal city, but unlike them it would not be founded upon the sadly banal institution of the skin game.

Ivan Chtcheglov

But then: "Now it's finished. You'll never see the hacienda. It doesn't exist. *The hacienda must be built.*" A year after the publication of the "Formula," Chtcheglov suffered a mental and emotional breakdown; he remained institutionalized until his death in 1998. The Situationist project was the last hand in the Paris game, and it coincided brutally with the end game played by money and power. In the second issue of their journal, Abdelhafid Khatib's "Attempt at a Psychogeographical Description of Les Halles" now appears drenched in morbid irony. "The Situationists, thanks to their current methods and to anticipated developments of those methods, feel themselves capable not only of changing the urban milieu, but of changing it almost at will," he wrote on the cusp of 1959, little more than a year before the fate of Les Halles was decided by fiat in the Palais de l'Élysée. Two years and four issues later, Raoul Vaneigem could see what was coming:

Bulle Ogier and Pascale Ogier in Jacques Rivette's *Le Pont du Nord*, 1981

The industrialization of private life: "Run your life like a business"—that will be the new slogan . . . It seems that the working class no longer exists. Large numbers of former proletarians now have access to the comforts once reserved for a small elite—you know the tune. But isn't it rather that an increasing amount of comfort usurps their needs and creates an itch for consumer demands?

The fever dream of May '68 dissipated quickly; the future had by then already been set. Revolution may have existed in a million minds, perhaps well-furnished minds equipped with erudite slogans, perhaps with appendant hands clutching paving stones or Molotov cocktails, but that was not enough. A nineteenth-century insurrection cut no ice with the new consumers, including those who still held Communist Party cards. Soon enough, many of the revolutionaries changed teams. Being a former *soixante-huitard* carried a worldly cachet not unlike claiming to have been in the Resistance; boards of directors are lousy with them.

The Paris game was given a final representation in Jacques Rivette's film *Le Pont du Nord* (1981). Marie (Bulle Ogier) has just gotten out of prison, where she has been incarcerated for unspecified radical activities, and as a consequence she is profoundly claustrophobic, unable to enter a shop or even a phone booth. She meets Baptiste (Pascale Ogier, her daughter in real life), young, brave, and foolhardy, who rides around the city on her motor scooter, thinking of herself as an urban warrior, and who appoints herself Marie's protector. They encounter Marie's shifty ex-boyfriend Julien (Pierre Clémenti) and nab his briefcase. All it contains are newspaper clippings and a map of Paris overlaid with a spiral that has been cut up into segments—a labyrinth that suggests but doesn't correspond to the spiral of the arrondissements. It is in fact the Jeu de l'Oie, an ancient game controlled by dice, the object of which is to move from the periphery to the center (square 63) while avoiding the traps set along the way. They decide to play the city, following the indications on the map. But as they repeatedly encounter traps, they never get beyond the periphery. At every turn there are construction cranes that loom like monsters. Even as they are unable to get anywhere near the center, the outer edges are being eaten away. The movie trails off, but the point has been made.

The game may not be over, but its rules have irrevocably changed. The small has been consumed by the big, the poor have been evicted by the rich, the drifters are behind glass in museums. Everything that was once directly lived has moved away into representation. If the game is ever to resume, it will have to take on hitherto unimagined forms. It will have much larger walls to undermine, will be able to thrive only in the cracks that form in the ordered surfaces of the future. It is to be hoped, of course, that the surface is shattered by buffoonery and overreaching rather than by war or disease, but there can be no guarantee. It may be that whatever escape routes the future offers will be shadowed by imminent extinction. Life, in any case, will flourish under threat. Utopias last five minutes, to the extent that they happen at all. There will never be a time when the wish for security does not lead to unconditional surrender. The history of Paris teaches us that beauty is a by-product of danger, that liberty is at best a consequence of neglect, that wisdom is entwined with decay. Any Paris of the future that is neither a frozen artifact nor an inhabited holding company will perforce involve fear, dirt, sloth, ruin, and accident. It will entail the continual experience of uncertainty, because the only certainty is death.

The Jeu de l'Oie in *Le Pont du Nord*

Notes

1. Capital

4   *"Communists, get your bags"*: Vladimir Jankélévitch, *Les Temps Modernes*, June 1948, cited in Eric Hazan, *L'invention de Paris* (Éditions du Seuil, 2002), p. 303.

5   *"Tumbledown hovels sheltering"*: Georges Cain, *Nouvelles promenades dans Paris* (Flammarion, 1908), p. 27.

5   *"A shoelace vendor"*: Eugène Dabit, *Faubourgs de Paris* (Gallimard, 1933), p. 157.

8   *"The noise of the bars"*: Paul Verlaine, *La bonne chanson* (Alphonse Lemerre, 1869–70).

8   *"I walked as far as the Pacra"*: *La rue* (1930), in *Romans*, ed. Jean-Jacques Bedu and Gilles Freyssinet (Robert Laffont, 2004), pp. 776, 815.

9   *"a strange city"*: Émile Zola, *Le ventre de Paris,* in *Les Rougon-Macquart* (Bibliothèque de la Pléiade, 1963), vol. 1, p. 621.

9   *"river of greenery"*: Ibid., p. 627.

9   *"The splendid horses of Paris"*: From Sherwood Anderson, *Paris Notebook, 1921*, excerpted in Adam Gopnik, ed., *Americans in Paris: A Literary Anthology* (New York: Library of America, 2004), pp. 257–58.

11   *"Civilization has acted here"*: Alexandre Privat d'Anglemont, *Paris anecdote* (Les Éditions de Paris, 1984 [1854]), p. 186.

11   *"an ardent plebeian capital"*: Victor Serge, *Mémoires d'un révolutionnaire* (Éditions du Seuil, 1951), p. 29.

11   *"high citadel of l'esprit parisien"*: Richard Cobb, *Paris and Elsewhere* (New York: New York Review Books, 2004), p. 146.

12   *"This kingdom, one of the richest"*: Léon-Paul Fargue, *Le piéton de Paris* (Gallimard, 1993 [1939]), p. 20.

13   *"As a result of the transformation"*: Edmond Texier, *De la décentralisation des Halles* (1850), cited in T. J. Clark, *The Painting of Modern Life: Paris in the Art of Manet and His Followers* (Princeton, NJ: Princeton University Press, 1984), p. 33.

13   *"located between Faubourg Saint-Antoine"*: Victor Hugo, *Les misérables* (Pléiade, 1951), p. 468.

14 *"I understand very well"*: Privat d'Anglemont, *Paris anecdote*, p. 202.

14 *"My Paris, where I was born"*: Edmond and Jules de Goncourt, *Mémoires de la vie littéraire*, vol. 1: 1851–1861 (Bibliothèque Charpentier, 1891), p. 346.

15 *"The ruins of the bourgeoisie"*: Honoré de Balzac, *Le diable à Paris: Paris et les Parisiens* (1845), cited in Walter Benjamin, *The Arcades Project* (Cambridge, MA: Belknap Press/Harvard University Press, 1999), p. 87.

15 *"our time is hard"*: Dabit, *Faubourgs de Paris*, p. 47.

16 *"Not one of these places"*: Louis Chevalier, *L'assassinat de Paris* (Éditions Ivréa, 1997 [1977]), pp. 300–301.

16 *"Paris, a city then so beautiful"*: *In girum imus nocte et consumimur igni*, in Guy Debord, *Oeuvres cinématographiques complètes, 1952–1978* (Gallimard, 1994), p. 222.

17 *"We were, more than anybody"*: Ibid., pp. 278–79.

2. Ghosts

19 *Paris contains some 3,195*: Jacques Hillairet, *Dictionnaire historique des rues de Paris* (Éditions de Minuit, 1963).

22 *"Couldn't an exciting film"*: Walter Benjamin, *The Arcades Project*, p. 83.

24 *"The crowd is his domain"*: Charles Baudelaire, *Oeuvres complètes* (Bibliothèque de la Pléiade, 1954), p. 889.

24 *"into the streets"*: Cobb, *Paris and Elsewhere*, p. 187.

24 *"to dawdle, to stop"*: Ibid., pp. 142–43.

26 *"Each of those casements"*: G. Lenotre, *Paris et ses fantômes* (Grasset, 1933), p. 8.

27 *"the most confounding"*: *Potlatch*, no. 7, August 3, 1954 (Éditions Gérard Lebovici, 1984).

28 *"inclines toward atheism"*: Guy Debord, "Introduction à une critique de la géographie urbaine," in *Les Lèvres Nues* 6 (Brussels, September 1955): 11 (Plasma, 1978).

28 *"There is always a certain"*: Taxil Delort, in *Les rues de Paris*, ed. Louis Lurine (G. Kugelmann, 1844), vol. 1, p. 69.

29 *"a particularly criminal district"*: Louis Chevalier, *Classes laborieuses et classes dangereuses à Paris pendant la première moitié du XIXe siècle* (Hachette, 1984 [1976]), pp. 503–504.

30 *For that matter, excavations*: Jean-Louis Brau, in *Guide de Paris mystérieux*, ed. François Caradec and Jean-Robert Masson (Tchou, 1976), pp. 38–39.

32 *"He bore to the right"*: Francis Carco, *Jésus-la-Caille* (1914), in *Romans* (Robert Laffont, 2004) pp. 61–62.

3. Pantruche

34 *"When I asked him"*: A. J. Liebling, *The Road Back to Paris* (Garden City, NY: Doubleday, Doran and Co., 1944), p. 37.

35 *These include Grenelle*: Éric Hazan, *L'invention de Paris* (Éditions du Seuil, 2002), passim.

36   *"you turn a corner"*: Privat d'Anglemont, *Paris anecdote*, p. 15.

36   *"the Parisian of Faubourg Saint-Antoine"*: Privat d'Anglemont, *Paris inconnu* (Adolphe Delahaye, 1875), p. 71.

36   *"the city is only apparently homogeneous"*: Benjamin, *Arcades Project*, p. 88.

37   *"almost all the courtyards"*: Victor Fournel, *Paris nouveau et Paris futur* (1868), quoted in ibid., p. 146.

37   *"A kind of solidarity developed"*: Quoted by Chevalier, *Classes*, p. 342.

38   *"a sewer and the emptying point"*: Quoted by Benjamin, *Arcades Project*, p. 98.

38   *"If from the heights"*: Henri Lecouturier, *Paris incompatible avec la République* (1848), quoted by Chevalier, *Classes*, p. 279.

38   *"There is no such thing as"*: Ibid., p. 602.

39   *"Paris belongs to France"*: Georges-Eugène Haussmann, *Mémoires* (Victor-Havard, 1890), vol. 2, p. 177.

42   *"Wretched houses, with scarcely"*: Eugène Sue, *The Mysteries of Paris*, anonymous nineteenth-century translation (London: Stanley Paul and Co., n.d.), p. 9.

42   *"these dark, muddy, pestilential streets"*: Paul L. Jacob, in *Rues de Paris*, vol. 1, p. 142.

42   *"hideous, filthy, squalid misery"*: Privat d'Anglemont, *Paris anecdote*, p. 241.

42   *"the widest part of which"*: Honoré de Balzac, *Une double famille*, in *La comédie humaine* (Pléiade, 1951), vol. 1, pp. 925–26.

43   *Not far away, around*: Recollected by Victorien Sardou, in Georges Cain, *Nouvelles promenades dans Paris* (Flammarion, 1908), pp. 192–97.

44   *"Bismarck finished what"*: Victor Hugo, *Actes et paroles: Avant l'exil, 1841–1851* (Michel Lévy, 1875), p. x.

46   *"women in camisoles"*: Georges Cain, *Promenades dans Paris* (Flammarion, 1907), p. 222.

46   *"a strange spiderweb"*: Ibid., pp. 268–70.

47   *"After climbing a rotting"*: Ibid., pp. 84–86.

48   *At the start of the eighteenth*: As noticed by Hazan, *L'invention de Paris*, p. 92.

48   *"what historical interest"*: Cobb, *Paris and Elsewhere*, p. 167.

49   *"Listen: every seven years"*: Jacques Yonnet, *Rue des Maléfices* [originally published as *Enchantements sur Paris*, 1954] (Phébus, 1987), p. 98.

50   *"whenever the municipal hammer"*: Privat d'Anglemont, *Paris inconnu*, p. 62.

50   *"The saloons of the Maubert"*: Jean-Paul Clébert, *Paris insolite* (Denoël, 1952), pp. 184–85.

52   *"Most of the traffic"*: Elliot Paul, *The Last Time I Saw Paris* (New York: Random House, 1942), p. 14.

4. Zone

54   *"Forty years ago"*: Hugo, *Les misérables*, p. 445.

55   *"expedient of philanthropists"*: Ibid., p. 449.

56   *"Some twenty-five hundred cubic feet"*: Alexandre Parent-Duchâtelet, *Les chantiers d'équarrissage de la ville de Paris* (1832), quoted by Chevalier, *Classes*, p. 363.

56   *"in such numbers"*: Chevalier, *Classes*, p. 364.

58   *It was documented more by painters*: For these examples I am indebted to T. J. Clark, in his *The Painting of Modern Life* (Princeton, NJ: Princeton University Press, 1984).

60   *The titular heroine*: Quoted in Jean Bedel, *Les puces ont cent ans* (no imprint, 1985), p. 30.

61   *"surrounded by an attentive audience"*: André Warnod, *Les "fortifs": Promenades sur les anciennes fortifications et la zone* (Éditions de l'Épi, 1927), unpaginated.

61   *"I took a path that zigzagged"*: Blaise Cendrars, *L'homme foudroyé* (Denoël/ Folio, 1973 [1945]), pp. 201–202.

63   *" fugitive personalities whose eyes"*: In Carco, *Romans*, pp. 215, 220.

63   *"a filthy ribbon of grass"*: Clébert, *Paris insolite,* p. 50.

63   *Its fame endured*: A portion of the film, detailing the work cycle of the ragpickers, can be viewed at http://www.mheu.org/en/ragpickers/ragpickers -territory.aspx.

64   *"Gone are the fortifications"*: G. Van Parys and M. Vaucaire, "La chanson des fortifs." Recorded by Fréhel. Columbia DF 2434, 1938.

66   *"She walked toward"*: Didier Daeninckx, *Meurtres pour mémoire* (Gallimard/ Folio, 1988 [1984]), p. 24.

67   *"now an entire population aspires"*: Jean Follain, *Paris* (Phébus, 1978 [1935]), p. 93.

67   *"a circle of buildings"*: Dabit, *Faubourgs de Paris,* p. 98.

68   *"Everything is a sham"*: In Robert Doisneau, *La banlieue de Paris* (Denoël, 1983 [1949]), p. 8.

69   *"The landscape being generally"*: The full text of the narration is available (in French) at http://www.passant-ordinaire.com/revue/44-522.asp.

5. La Canaille

72   *"One of the most distressing"*: Honoré de Balzac, *La fille aux yeux d'or* (Pléiade, 1952), vol. 5, p. 255.

73   *"A swarm of ordinary folk"*: In Doisneau, *La banlieue de Paris*, pp. 17–18.

74   *". . . all those carved stones"*: Ibid., p. 18.

75   *Louis Chevalier insisted*: Louis Chevalier, *Les Parisiens* (Hachette, 1967), passim.

75   *"When it comes to the people"*: Hugo, *Les misérables*, p. 608.

77   *"For all the book's shortcomings*: Chevalier, *Classes*, p. 41.

77   *Readers thought that Rodolphe*: Ibid., pp. 656–57.

78   *"Popular culture provided"*: Clark, *The Painting of Modern Life*, p. 205.

79   *"It is above all* collectivity": Ibid., p. 236.

80   *"the first Auvergnat"*: Privat d'Anglemont, *Paris anecdote*, p. 18.

81   *"the poorest creatures"*: Anon., *Le journal d'un bourgeois de Paris* (1427), quoted in Jean-Paul Clébert, *The Gypsies* (Harmondsworth, UK: Penguin, 1967 [1961]), p. 61.

83 *"Among the workers"*: Maurice and Léon Bonneff, *La vie tragique des travailleurs* (Études et Documentation Internationales, 1984 [1908]), p. 249.

83 *"He had been completely"*: In Georges Darien, *Voleurs!* (Omnibus, 2005), p. 934.

83 *By the late 1890s*: Bruno Fuligni, ed., *Dans les archives secrètes de la police* (L'Iconoclaste, 2009), p. 240.

84 *"lice, plague, and typhus"*: André Kaspi and Antoine Marès, eds., *Le Paris des étrangers* (Imprimerie Nationale, 1989), p. 29.

84 *"shot by firing squad"*: Fuligni, ed., *Dans les archives*, p. 250.

84 *"The undesirables must be"*: Kaspi and Marès, eds., *Le Paris des étrangers*, p. 29.

87 *"200,000 Algerians"*: Jan Brusse, *Nights in Paris* (London: André Deutsch, 1958 [1954]), pp. 57–58.

88 *"France is the only country"*: Kaspi and Marès, eds., *Le Paris des étrangers*, p. 162.

88 *Meanwhile, at that very same*: Ibid., p. 158.

89 *"There is deep anger"*: Anderson, *Paris Notebook*, p. 261.

89 *"One of the gentlemen"*: Cited in Louis Chevalier, *Montmartre du plaisir et du crime* (Payot, 1995 [1980]), p. 323.

90 *A census in 1889*: Kaspi and Marès, eds., *Le Paris des étrangers*, p. 14.

90 *"He turned the corner"*: Carco, *Romans*, p. 653.

6. Archipelago

91 *"a long series of walls"*: Lucien Descaves, *Philémon vieux de la vieille* (Ollendorff, 1913), pp. 1–2.

93 *"Not only did the murder rate"*: In Chevalier, *Classes*, p. 55.

93 *A worker was quoted*: Eugène Roch, *Paris malade, esquisses du jour* (1832–33), cited by Chevalier, *Classes*, p. 53.

94 *". . . suddenly, in the middle"*: Enid Starkie, *Petrus Borel the Lycanthrope* (Norfolk, CT: New Directions, 1954), pp. 57–58.

96 *"far away, at the end"*: Privat d'Anglemont, *Paris anecdote*, p. 173.

96 *Sophie Foucault, cousin*: *Le Petit Parisien*, July 28, 1892.

96 *"a sewer from which"*: In Victor Hugo, *L'intégrale: Romans* (Éditions du Seuil, 1963), vol. 1, p. 268.

97 *its earliest vocabulary*: Alice Becker-Ho, *Les princes du jargon* (Éditions Gérard Lebovici, 1990), passim.

97 *The intricate social structure*: Robert Giraud, *Le royaume de l'argot* (Denoël, 1965), pp. 252–55.

98 *"a mud house"*: Henri Sauval, *Histoires et antiquités de Paris* (1724; written 1670s), quoted by Élie Bertret in *Rues de Paris*, vol. 1, p. 241.

98 *"innumerable quantity of houses"*: Privat d'Anglemont, *Paris inconnu*, p. 37.

98 *"much more to the Kingdom"*: Ibid., p. 38.

101 *"Look at mine"*: In Privat d'Anglemont, *Paris anecdote*, pp. 115–16.

101 *"but even when they"*: Adolphe Gronfier, *Dictionnaire de la racaille* (Horay, 2010), p. 294.

103 *"by turns a pickpocket"*: Ibid., p. 78.

103 *"Generally that sort"*: Chevalier, *Montmartre*, pp. 251–52.

103 *"He doesn't eat every day"*: Hugo, *Les misérables*, pp. 591–92.

104 *"Little hands wanted"*: Cain, *Promenades dans Paris*, p. 33.

104 *The makers of silk flowers*: Frères Bonneff, *La vie tragique*, p. 240.

104 *At least until the middle*: Chevalier, *Classes*, p. 371.

105 *"In the eyes of Parisians"*: Chevalier, *Montmartre*, p. 96.

105 *"Steam rose from"*: In Émile Zola, *Les Rougon-Macquart* (Pléiade, 1961), vol. 2, pp. 386–87.

106 *"huts encrusted on"*: Cobb, *Paris and Elsewhere*, p. 176.

107 *"Colored in every hue"*: Cain, *Nouvelles promenades*, pp. 68–71.

107 *"No eyes . . . could locate"*: Honoré de Balzac, *La femme de trente ans*, in *La comédie humaine*, vol. 2, p. 780.

107 *"in the air, thousands"*: J.-K. Huysmans, *La Bièvre et Saint-Séverin* (Brionne: Gérard Montfort, 1986 [1890/1898]), pp. 26–27.

109 *"stinking from the exhalations"*: Léon Bonneff, *Aubervilliers* (Saint-Vaast-la-Hougue: L'Amitié par le Livre, 1949), pp. 13–14.

109 *"They work over rectangular"*: Frères Bonneff, *Les métiers qui tuent* (Bibliographie Sociale, 1906), pp. 105–108.

110 *"Restaurant kitchens are like"*: Frères Bonneff, *La classe ouvrière* (Publications de la "Guerre Sociale," 1910), pp. 100–101.

7. Le Business

111 *"His pocket empty"*: *Bel-Ami,* in *Contes et Nouvelles, 1884–1890* (Robert Laffont, 1988 [1885]), vol. 2, p. 270.

112 *"It wasn't so much"*: Francis Carco, *De Montmartre au Quartier Latin* (Albin Michel, 1927), p. 187.

112 *"In the 1850s"*: Theodore Zeldin, *Ambition and Love* (Oxford: Oxford University Press, 1979 [1973]), p. 307.

113 *"the first thing that assaulted"*: Quoted in Chevalier, *Montmartre*, p. 62.

114 *"On the sidewalks"*: Émile Zola, *Nana*, in *Les Rougon-Macquart*, vol. 2, p. 1312.

115 *"For almost twenty minutes"*: Émile Zola, *Paris* (Bibliothèque Charpentier, 1898), pp. 284–85.

115 *"every skin disease"*: Marius Boisson, *Coins et recoins de Paris* (Éditions Bossard, 1927), p. 93.

116 *"which the proprietor"*: Zola, *Nana*, p. 1122.

116 *"A hundred meters"*: Ibid., pp. 1312–13.

116 *"as tall and beautiful"*: Ibid., p. 1269.

117 *"a party girl"*: Ibid., p. 1253.

117 *"I have made a pact"*: Comte de Lautréamont, *Les chants de Maldoror*, in *Oeuvres complètes* (Au Sans Pareil, 1927), p. 67.

117 *"I've often wondered"*: Maxime du Camp, *Salon de 1861*, quoted by Clark, *The Painting of Modern Life*, p. 113.

117 *"We find in the"*: Flévy d'Urville, *Les ordures de Paris*, quoted by Clark, *The Painting of Modern Life*, p. 105.

117 *"But certain connoisseurs"*: Chevalier, *Montmartre*, p. 243.

118 *the physical and mental deterioration*: *In the Land of Pain*, edited and translated by Julian Barnes (London: Jonathan Cape, 2002).

118 *"hang out on a corner"*: Gustave Geffroy, *L'apprentie* (1904), quoted in Chevalier, *Montmartre*, p. 205.

119 *A reporter in the 1930s*: *Le Crapouillot*, May 1939, pp. 12–13.

120 *Chevalier relates a* fait-divers: Chevalier, *Montmartre*, p. 251.

120 *A 1930 study alleged*: Henri Drouin, *La Vénus des Carrefours* (Gallimard, 1930), passim.

120 *An American writer*: Sam Boal, "The Pros of Paris," in *Fille de Joie* (New York: Grove Press, 1967), pp. 342–54.

123 *Of the twelve such houses*: *Le Crapouillot*, May 1939, pp. 4–7.

123 *"All day long"*: Quoted in Chevalier, *Montmartre*, pp. 255–56n.

124 *A police raid*: Ibid., p. 257n.

125 *One-Two-Two*: Véronique Willemin, *La mondaine: Histoire et archives de la police des moeurs* (Hoëbeke, 2009), p. 97.

127 *"the collapsed foundation"*: Quoted in Ibid., p. 119.

127 *"It's worse than"*: Bruno Fuligni, ed., *Dans les archives secrètes de la police* (L'Iconoclaste, 2009), p. 512.

128 *"restaurant porters, hotel"*: Laurent Tailhade, *Les reflêts de Paris, 1918–1919* (Coeuvres-et-Valsery: Ressouvenances, 1997), p. 79.

128 *But the facilities*: Cited in Chevalier, *Montmartre*, p. 239n.

131 *The police inspector noted*: Fuligni, ed., *Dans les archives*, pp. 551–54.

131 *In Pigalle there were*: Ibid., p. 555.

131 *"Sailors wearing sashes"*: In Carco, *Romans*, p. 950.

132 *"On Rue de Lappe"*: Cited in Claude Dubois, *La Bastoche* (Perrin, 2007 [1997]), p. 210.

133 *"every type came"*: Brassaï, *The Secret Paris of the 30s*, translated by Richard Miller (New York: Pantheon, 1976), unpaginated.

133 *"once in a while"*: Ibid.

8. Saint Monday

137 *"a smoky, dark, low"*: Privat d'Anglemont, *Paris anecdote*, p. 252.

138 *Fights were frequent*: Gérard de Nerval, "Les Nuits d'Octobre," in *Le rêve et la vie* (Calmann-Lévy, 1895), p. 348.

138 *"Their life is one"*: Privat d'Anglemont, *Paris anecdote*, p. 168.

138 *"Our generation . . . is bored"*: Ibid., p. 192.

138 *"the toxic powers"*: Anon., *Annales d'hygiène publique*, quoted in Chevalier, *Montmartre*, p. 277n.

138 *"Michelet said that you"*: Descaves, *Philémon vieux de la vieille*, p. 56.

139 *The Bonneff brothers*: *Marchands de folie* (Marcel Rivière, 1912), passim.

139 *"a notorious bistro"*: Cain, *Promenades*, pp. 305–308.

140 *"Dirty, stinking Rue des Anglais"*: Ibid., pp. 88–93.

141 *"a meeting place for"*: Huysmans, *La Bièvre*, p. 148.

141 *"In Paris there are"*: Richard Harding Davis, "The Show-Places of Paris," in *Americans in Paris*, pp. 174, 177.

141 *"In 1925, many"*: Follain, *Paris*, pp. 85–86.

142 *The Bonneffs explain*: Frères Bonneff, *Marchands de folie*, pp. 76–77.

142 *"All night long"*: Quoted in Chevalier, *Montmartre*, p. 234.

144 *"cafés for unemployed"*: Fargue, *Le piéton de Paris*, p. 40.

144 *"when the night . . . le père la Tulipe"*: Cobb, *Paris and Elsewhere*, p. 182.

145 *"it's easy to become"*: Robert Giraud, *Le vin des rues* (Denoël, 1983 [1955]), p. 36.

146 *"All those hideouts"*: Clébert, *Paris insolite*, pp. 125–26.

146 *"a sleeping clochard"*: Giraud, *Le vin des rues*, p. 36.

147 *"descended in a direct line"*: Serge, *Mémoires d'un révolutionnaire*, pp. 32–33.

148 *". . . vagabonds, discharged soldiers"*: Karl Marx, *The Eighteenth Brumaire of Louis Bonaparte* (New York: International Publishers, 1963), p. 75.

150 *"crusade against beauty"*: Privat d'Anglemont, *Paris anecdote*, p. 143.

150 *"A great anxiety haunted them"*: Ibid., p. 146.

151 *"clocks in the shape"*: Anatole Jakovsky, *Paris mes puces* (Les Quatre Jeudis, 1957), p. 188.

151 *Enid Starkie maintained*: Starkie, *Petrus Borel the Lycanthrope*, p. 89.

151 *Most famously, he had a pet lobster*: Scott Horton, "Nerval: A Man and His Lobster," *Harper's*, October 12, 2008.

152 *"Like [Louis-Sébastien] Mercier"*: Preface to Privat d'Anglemont, *Paris inconnu*, p. 9.

152 *After Privat's death*: Willy Alante-Lima, *Alexandre Privat d'Anglemont: Le funambule* (Éditions du Parc, 2011), p. 35.

152 *"Yes, our literature"*: Quoted in Chevalier, *Classes*, p. 68n.

154 *"Upon one panel"*: Davis, "The Show-Places of Paris," p. 180.

155 *"The Chat Noir"*: Daniel Halévy, "Pays parisiens," *La Revue Hebdomadaire*, May 1929, p. 36.

156 *"Blond, laughing Pierrot"*: Roland Dorgelès, *Bouquet de bohème* (Albin Michel, 1947), p. 61.

158 *"You could do everything"*: Blaise Cendrars, *Trop c'est trop* (Denoël, 1957), pp. 27–28.

158 *"Paris was a city"*: Debord, *In girum imus nocte et consumimur igni*, pp. 222, 227–29, 235.

9. Show People

162 *"Fashionable people go"*: Cited in Chevalier, *Montmartre*, p. 61.

162 *"He's a loafer"*: Honoré de Balzac, *La Cousine Bette,* in *La comédie humaine* (Pléiade), vol. 6, p. 456.

163 *"pale, slender, in colorless"*: Cited in Pierre Gascar, *Le Boulevard du Crime* (Atelier Hachette/Masson, 1980), p. 156.

165 *"covered them from"*: Victor Hugo, *Choses vues* (Nelson, n.d. [1887]), pp. 345–46.

168 *"The whores and hoodlums"*: Carco, *Jésus-la-Caille,* pp. 29–30.

169 *"Before 1848"*: Victor Rozier, *Les bals publics de Paris* (1855), cited in Chevalier, *Montmartre*, p. 98n.

169 *"the most incredible jumble"*: Privat d'Anglemont, *Paris anecdote*, p. 219.

170 *"she was burned"*: André Warnod, *Les bals de Paris* (G. Crès, 1922), p. 60.

171 *From inhabiting the* hôtel: Janet Flanner, *Paris Was Yesterday, 1925–1939* (New York: Popular Library, 1972), pp. 49–50.

171 *"persuaded of their superiority"*: Warnod, *Les bals de Paris*, pp. 95, 97.

171 *"where the dances were nothing"*: Ibid., p. 133.

171 *The area around the Contrescarpe*: Ibid., p. 151.

172 *"to the musette"*: Émile de la Bédollière, *Les industriels* (1842), cited in Chevalier, *Classes*, p. 494.

172 *"where the accordion"*: Dubois, *La Bastoche*, p. 142.

172 *"It's free to enter"*: Warnod, *Les bals de Paris*, pp. 89–90.

173 *The java seems*: Dubois, *La Bastoche*, p. 173.

174 *It was at La Java*: Ibid., pp. 343–44.

174 *"It's nothing but a banal"*: Ibid., p. 306.

176 *"To live at home"*: Alfred Delvau, *Les plaisirs de Paris* (1867), cited in Clark, *The Painting of Modern Life*, p. 304n.

176 *"The audience is divided"*: J.-K. Huysmans, "Autour des fortifications," in *Revue Illustrée*, December 1885, p. 58.

176 *"an agreement to listen"*: Clark, *The Painting of Modern Life*, p. 212.

176 *"A big circular room"*: Cited in François Caradec and Alain Weill, *Le café-concert* (Atelier Hachette/Massin, 1980), p. 42.

178 *"After every revolution"*: Ibid., pp. 63–64.

179 *" 'The other day' "*: Cited in Chevalier, *Montmartre*, pp. 130–31.

180 *"Every third number"*: Davis, *The Show-Places of Paris*, p. 179.

183 *"a stallholder at"*: Cited in Éric Rémy, liner notes to *Fréhel, 1930–1939* (Frémeaux et Associés).

184 *"One afternoon in 1938"*: Cited in Nicole and Alain Lacombe, *Fréhel* (Pierre Belfond, 1990), p. 301.

184 *"She scared me"*: Cited in Chevalier, *Montmartre*, p. 353.

185 *"She was ephemeral"*: Flanner, *Paris Was Yesterday*, p. 67.

186 *"Her face and arms"*: Francesco Rapazzini, *Damia: Une diva française* (Perrin, 2010), p. 147.

189 *"I'll tell you what"*: Simone Berteaut, *Piaf* (Robert Laffont, 1969), p. 152.

189 *"The subject of"*: Cited in Éric Rémy, liner notes to *Édith Piaf, 1935–1947* (Frémeaux et Associés).

10. Mort aux Vaches

193 *"On the whole"*: Chevalier, *Classes*, p. 119.

193 *"Those who have"*: Guillaume-Tell Doin and Édouard Charton, *Lettres sur Paris* (1830), cited in ibid., pp. 278–79.

193 *"There are no"*: George Sand, *Le diable à Paris*, cited in ibid., p. 122.

194 *"In Paris there are"*: *Ferragus*, in Balzac, *La comédie humaine* (Pléiade), vol. 5, p. 17.

194 *"a sort of drain"*: Taxil Delort, *Les rues de Paris*, p. 72.

194 *"In the summer the gardens"*: *Le Matin*, September 28, 1907, cited in Cain, *Nouvelles promenades*, p. 160.

195 *"it is not so much"*: Chevalier, *Classes*, p. 500.

195 *"the greatest number"*: Chevalier, *Montmartre*, p. 195.

195 *"most of the dives"*: Georges Cain, *Le long des rues* (Flammarion, 1913), p. 80.

195 *"thieves are a separate"*: Honoré de Balzac, *Code des gens honnêtes* (J.-N. Barba, 1825), pp. ii, xvii.

196 *"One day I saw"*: Jules Janin, *L'âne mort et la femme guillotinée*, cited in Chevalier, *Classes*, p. 125.

201 *"A man uses"*: Chevalier, *Montmartre*, p. 298.

201 *"The Hearts of Steel?"*: Ibid., p. 286

202 *"By 1925 the hard"*: Foreword to *L'homme traqué*, in Carco, *Romans*, p. 575.

206 *"the Prix Goncourt"*: Cited in René Fallet, *Carnets de jeunesse*, vol. 2 (Denoël, 1992), p. 273.

207 *"I sat on"*: [Hippolyte Bonnelier and Jacques Arago], *Lacenaire après sa condamnation* (Marchant, 1836), p. 11.

208 *"an illustration of"*: André Breton, "Projet pour la bibliothèque de Jacques Doucet," in *Oeuvres complètes*, edited by Marguerite Bonnet (Pléiade, 1988), vol. 1, p. 634.

208 *"the simplest Surrealist"*: "Second manifeste du surréalisme," in ibid., pp. 782–83.

208 *a law clerk in Tours*: Jacques Simonelli, introduction to Lacenaire, *Mémoires* (José Corti, 1991), pp. 14–15.

209 *"the Dreyfus Affair"*: "Un sans patrie," "Liabeuf . . . & Caserio," *La Guerre Sociale*, June 29, 1910.

209 *"a lesson in energy"*: Gustave Hervé, "L'exemple de l'apache," *La Guerre Sociale*, January 12, 1910.

209 *"Excited couples came straight"*: Serge, *Mémoires d'un révolutionnaire*, pp. 37–38.

211 *"I have chosen"*: Jacques Mesrine, *L'instinct de mort* (Flammarion, 2008 [1977]), p. 468.

212 *"It would be less evil"*: Cited by Noël Arnaud in *Guide de Paris mystérieux* (Tchou, 1976), p. 379.

214 *"one the antechamber"*: Delvau, *Les plaisirs de Paris*, p. 174.

217 *"Take a murder"*: Roland Barthes, "Structure du fait-divers," in *Essais critiques* (Seuil, 1964), p. 190.

11. Insurgents

222 *"join, as no other"*: Friedrich Engels, *Travel Journal, Paris to Bern, October–November 1848*, cited in Chevalier, *Montmartre*, p. 129.

222 *"Paris is a counterpart"*: Benjamin, *The Arcades Project*, p. 83.

223 *"In Paris under"*: Preface to *Histoire des treize*, in Balzac, *La comédie humaine* (Pléiade), vol. 5, p. 11.

225 *"the 4,054 barricades"*: Exhibition catalog to *Le romantisme*, Bibliothèque Nationale, 1930, cited in Benjamin, *The Arcades Project*, p. 139.

225 *"Fewer were felled"*: Friedrich von Reumer, *Briefe aus Paris* (1831), cited in Benjamin, *The Arcades Project*, p. 138.

225 *"In less than an hour"*: Hugo, *Les misérables*, p. 1089.

226 *"The Saint-Antoine barricade"*: Ibid., p. 1195.

227 *"young, beautiful, wild-haired"*: Hugo, *Choses vues* (augmented edition; Arvansa, n.d.), p. 120.

227 *Among other things, he*: Auguste Blanqui, *Instructions pour une prise d'armes* (Cent Pages/Cosaques, 2009 [1866]), p. 48.

228 *"perfectly constructed"*; Prosper-Olivier Lissagaray, *Histoire de la Commune de 1871* (La Découverte, 2000 [1896]), p. 324.

228 *"The statues were made"*: Louise Michel, *La Commune, histoire et souvenirs* (La Découverte, 1999 [1898]), pp. 301–302.

228 *"Outside the insurgent neighborhoods"*: Hugo, *Les misérables,* pp. 1092–93.

233 *"Pustules had swarmed"*: Zola, *Nana*, p. 1485.

234 *"It was a paste"*: Victorine B., *Souvenirs d'une morte vivante* (François Maspéro, 1976 [1909]), p. 114.

236 *"the central committee"*: Pierre Vésinier, *Comment a péri la Commune* (1892), cited in Maurice Choury, ed., *1871: Les damnés de la terre* (Tchou, 1969), p. 78.

237 *"Enough of militarism!"*: Lissagaray, *Histoire de la Commune*, pp. 315–16.

237 *"When the minister"*: Ibid., p. 316.

237 *"Fortune is capricious"*: Ibid., p. 405.

238 *"the flag of the Commune"*: "Rapport de la commission des élections," in *Journal officiel de la Commune de Paris*, March 31, 1871, p. 207.

238 *"he would rather have seen"*: Lissagaray, *Histoire de la Commune*, p. 253.

240 *"Having seen the"*: Victor Hugo, *Oeuvres posthumes: Toute la lyre* (Hetzel, 1897), p. 77.

240 *"Later on, they'll be"*: André Léo, *La femme et les moeurs* (Tusson: Le Lérot, 1990 [1869]), p. 109.

241 *"Once more, women have"*: André Léo, "La révolution sans la femme," in *La Sociale*, May 8, 1871.

242 *"We will say nothing"*: Cited in Descaves, *Philémon vieux de la vieille*, p. 84.

242 *"Above all, don't shut"*: Blanqui, *Instructions pour une prise*, p. 30.

243 *"and their understandable emotions"*: Descaves, *Philémon vieux de la vieille*, p. 255.

244 *"They were insane"*: Cited in Chevalier, *Montmartre*, p. 112.

244 *"the exhibition and sale"*: Gronfier, *Dictionnaire de la racaille*, pp. 93–94.

244 *"When your feet danced"*: Arthur Rimbaud, *Oeuvres complètes* (Pléiade, 1972), pp. 48–49.

245 *"the Commune will stand"*: Descaves, *Philémon vieux de la vieille*, p. 158.

246 *"The right to live"*: Alexandre Marius Jacob, *Les travailleurs de la nuit* (L'Insomniaque, 1999), pp. 10–11.

247 *"I decide whether"*: Max Stirner, *The Ego and His Own*, translated by Steven T. Byington (Sun City, CA: Western World Press, 1982 [1845]), p. 190.

247 *"The common point"*: Sébastien Faure, *Encyclopédie anarchiste* (1934), cited in Jean Maitron, *Ravachol et les anarchistes* (Gallimard, 1964), p. 7.

249 *"Ravachol doesn't scare me"*: Quoted in André Salmon, *La terreur noire* (Jean-Jacques Pauvert, 1959), p. 204.

249 *"I don't care about"*: Maitron, *Ravachol et les anarchistes*, p. 201.

249 *"We sold them only"*: Flor O'Squarr, *Les coulisses de l'anarchie* (Nuits Rouges, 2000 [1892]), p. 213.

249 *"You don't have"*: Ibid., p. 87.

250 *"A true anarchist"*: Maitron, *Ravachol et les anarchistes*, p. 221.

251 *"a mortal enemy"*: Quoted in ibid., p. 227.

252 *"We're with him provisionally"*: Descaves, *Philémon vieux de la vieille*, p. 295.

252 *"you found every sort"*: Victor Méric, *Les bandits tragiques* (Simon Kra, 1926), p. 141.

253 *"The autonomous social cell"*: André Lorulot, *Chez les loups: Moeurs anarchistes* (Conflans-[Sainte]-Honorine: Éditions de l'Idée Libre, 1922), pp. 41–42.

253 *"Cohabitation—that's our"*: Ibid., p. 27.

253 IDLERS, CROOKS, DRUNKS: Méric, *Les bandits*, p. 109.

256 *"The newspapers are full"*: Léon Bloy, *Le pèlerin de l'absolu, 1910–1912* (Mercure de France, 1914), pp. 267–68.

257 *"I would so much"*: Léo Malet, *La vie est dégueulasse,* in *Trilogie noire* (Éric Losfeld, 1969), pp. 147, 148, 150.

257 *"because I will never"*: Émile Michon, *Un peu de l'âme des bandits* (Dorbon-Ainé, 1914), p. 104.

257 *"They seem to want"*: Ibid., pp. 208–209.

258 *"Farewell to you all"*: Léon Daudet, *Paris vécu*, 2e série: *Rive Gauche* (Gallimard, 1930), p. 247.

258 *"priests and apostles"*: Méric, *Les bandits*, p. 205.

12. The Game

259 *"A strange delusion"*: Paul Lafargue, *Le droit à la paresse* (Henry Oriol, 1883), p. 8.

261 *"seen from on high"*: Louis Aragon, *Le paysan de Paris* (Gallimard, 1953 [1926]), p. 169.

261 *"The fauna of the imagination"*: Ibid., p. 20.

261 *"The nineteenth century"*: Benjamin, *The Arcades Project*, p. 831.

261 *"Night in our cities"*: Aragon, *Le paysan*, p. 173.

263 *"Time works for those"*: Yonnet, *Rue des maléfices*, p. 13.

265 *"the whole neighborhood"*: Clébert, *Paris insolite*, p. 110.

265 *"It takes longer"*: Ibid., p. 40.

265 *"What an awakening"*: Ibid., pp. 252–53.

267 *"to win the energies"*: Walter Benjamin, "Surrealism: The Last Snapshot of the European Intelligentsia" (1929), in *Selected Writings* (Cambridge, MA: Belknap Press/Harvard University Press, 1999), vol. 2, p. 216.

267 *"a technique of forward movement"*: Guy Debord, "Théorie de la dérive," *Les Lèvres Nues* 9 (November 1956): 6.

268 *"The center of Paris"*: Jacques Fillon, "Description raisonnée de Paris," *Les Lèvres Nues* 7 (December 1955): 39.

268 *"mythomania, interpretive delirium"*: Gil J. Wolman, "À la porte," *Potlatch* 2 (June 29, 1954).

268 *"All cities are geological"*: Gilles Ivain, "Formulaire pour un urbanisme nouveau," *Internationale Situationniste* 1 (June 1958): 15.

269 *"the wards of this city"*: Ibid., p. 19.

269 *"Now it's finished"*: Ibid., p. 15.

269 *"The Situationists, thanks"*: Abdelhafid Khatib, "Essai de description psychogéographique des Halles," *Internationale Situationniste* 2 (December 1958): 13.

270 *"The industrialization of private life"*: Raoul Vaneigem, "Commentaires contre l'urbanisme," *Internationale Situationniste* 6 (August 1961): 36, 37.

Acknowledgments

Thanks go, first of all, to Philippe Bordaz, who started feeding me books and pamphlets as far back as 1976, and more recently acted as my guide to places in Paris I would never have found on my own. Thanks to Lilith Jaywalker and her friends James and Badia and Philippe for the life-changing *dépucelage* (figuratively speaking) they administered in and around Rue de l'Ourcq a bit more than thirty years ago. Thanks to Jenny Turner for putting a flea in my ear twenty-odd years ago, for all that she may have forgotten the occasion. Thanks to Catherine Temerson and Israel Rosenfield for their hospitality and kindness and memorable after-hours tour of the august institutions along Rue d'Ulm. Thanks to Marina van Zuylen for being my first reader and a fount of good counsel, and for having more than once saved my hide.

Thanks to Peter Hutton, Olivier Verschueren (at the Livre au Trésors in Liège), Richard Devereaux, Michael Atkinson, David Schwartz (then of the American Museum of the Moving Image), Brent Kite, Alex Abramovich, Lance Ledbetter, Eric Mitchell, and the phenomenal Brian Berger for supplying crucial information and documents. Thanks to my two favorite Parisian bookstores: L'Oeil du Silence, long on the corner of Rue Yvonne le Tac and Rue des Martyrs but now sadly gone, and the Librairie du Patrimoine, which happily remains in the Hôtel de Sully on Rue Saint-Antoine. Neither place ever allowed me to leave empty-handed. A shout-out, too, to the venerable Delamain, a bedrock institution on Rue Saint-Honoré for more than three hundred years—here's hoping for at least a few more. I could not have carried out my research without the assistance, grudging and otherwise, of the stallholders at the Porte de Vanves flea market or those at the book market on Rue Brancion, where the mark-ups forcibly recall the fact that the place once dealt in livestock.

Major thanks to the wonderful Jean Strouse and Marie d'Origny at the Cullman Center of the New York Public Library, which hosted and financed a utopian final year of research, and thanks to my fellow Fellows for being such a good-humored and tolerant gang. Thanks to Lyall Bush and Adam Sekuler at the Northwest Film Forum in Seattle for hiring me to put together a film program that proved invaluable to the course of the work, and for supplying me with the title for this book. Thanks to Robert Silvers, Edwin Frank, Liz Helfgott, and Josh Glenn for assigning me topics to write about that helped clarify what I was doing here. For miscellaneous imponderables, thanks to Régine le Meur, Angelika Becker, Joseph Mullender, Diane Dufour, Alexandre Civico, Bruce Goldstein, Hannah Jablonski, Odile Chilton, and above all Jem Cohen. Thanks to Mike McGonigal and Steve Connell for publishing me during my years in the desert of self-doubt. Thanks to my son, Raphael, for being a good sport through it all. And thanks to "Mr. Chrysler" for underwriting the homestretch.

This book would not exist without the wisdom, foresight, generosity, and incredible patience of my agent, Joy Harris, and my editor, Jonathan Galassi. They set the ball rolling, and watched as it disappeared over the horizon for an unsettling length of time. Even more fundamentally, the book would not exist without the example of my late father, Lucien Sante, even if he might not sign off on the entirety of its contents. I owe my dad for his love of Paris and the French language and the well-turned phrase, for throwing me whatever crime novels turned up in the packages sent by his sister the village news vendor, for bequeathing me his dictionaries and the collected works of G. Lenotre, for educating me as he had educated himself. And finally, thanks to Mimi Lipson, who lived through the infernal process, for being my best friend, confidante, and resident golden ear.

Index

Page numbers in *italics* refer to illustrations.

62, 139, 155, 171–73, *193*, 198–202, *198–201*, 218; *barrières* and, 54–55, *55*; Bonnot Gang, 254–55; capital punishment, 205–10, 214; Corsican, 204; Fantômas novels, 197, *197*, 198; immigrant, 204; milieu, *195*, 202–203; press, 217–20, *218–20*; prison, 206–16, *211–16*; underworld, 119 and *n*, 123, 195–97, 202, 216; women, 199–201, *199–200*, 213; Zone, 54–55, 62–63, *63*; *see also specific criminals*
crippled, 97, *97*
Cros, Charles, 154
Croulebarbe, 7, 35
cult of morbidity, 94–95

Dabit, Eugène, 5, 15, 67
Dada, 261, *261*, 266
Daeninckx, Didier, *Meurtres pour mémoire*, 67
Dahou, Mohamed, 266–67, 268
Damia, 174, 186–87, *187*, 188–89; "En maison," 121, *122*
dance halls, 7, 79, 80, 120, 123, 132, 169–74, *169–72*, 262
dancers, 113, 133, 142, 169–74, *169–72*
Darcier, Joseph, 76, 177–78
Darien, Georges, 215, 247; *Biribi*, 215, *216*; *Les Pharisiens*, 83
Daudet, Alphonse, 118
Daumier, Honoré, 23, 44, 105, 164, 213, 229; illustrations by, *39*, *57*, *98*, *163*, *194*, *213*, *225*, *229*, *240*
David, Jacques-Louis, 44*n*, 149
Davis, Richard Harding, 141, 154, 180
Death, *see* cemeteries; cult of morbidity; guillotine; murder; public execution
Debord, Guy, 16–17, 23, 26–28, 158, 266–68; *Guide psychogéographique de Paris*, 27, *27*; *The Naked City*, 27
Deburau, Charles, *162*, 163
Deburau, Jean-Gaspard, 162–63
Degas, Edgar, 24, 105, 175
de Gaulle, Charles, 15, 85, 210
Delacroix, Eugène, 113, 149, 224

Delannoy, Aristide, illustration by, *129*
Delaunay-Belleville, *108*
Delescluze, Charles, 237
Delvau, Alfred, 23, 176, 214, 259
Dépôt, 113, 121, 213
Deprince, Adolphe, 174
Desbordes-Valmore, Marceline, 153
Descaves, Lucien, 91, 108, 138, 245, 252; *Barabbas*, 24, 265
Descente de la Courtille, 166, *166*
Desnos, Robert, 185, 197
Detaille, Édouard, 60
Détective, 203, 219 and *n*, 220, *220*
Dieudonné, Eugène, 219, 254–58
Dignimont, André, 24, 156
disabled veterans, *223*
disease, 38, 42, 45, 68, 75, 84, 87, 91–94, 96, 107, 109, 110, 165, 225; prison, 212, 213; prostitutes, 115, 118, 126, 181, 213; *see also specific diseases*
dishwashers, 109–10
Dmitrieff, Élisabeth, 240
dogs, 29, *63*, *98*, 102, *121*, 233, 234
Doisneau, Robert, 24, 65, 68, 264, 266
Don't Touch the White Woman! (film), 10–11, *11*
Dreyfus, Alfred, 82–84, 146, 215, 252
drift (*dérive*), 27, 267
drinking, 49–50, 59, 68, 95, 96, 100, 135–58, *136–44*, *157*, 166, 168, 182, *195*, 203; bohemia, 148–58; clochards, 144–48; terminology, 135–36; types of establishments, 135–38
drugs, 119, 128–29, *129*, 182–83, 185, 203, 204, 263
Drumont, Édouard, 83, 248, 252; *La France juive*, 83
Dubus, Édouard, 154 and *n*
du Camp, Maxine, 113, 117, 178, 243, 244
Ducasse, Isidore, *see* Lautréamont
Dumas, Alexandre, 66*n*, 77, 78, 152; *Count of Monte Cristo*, 78; *The Duchess of Salisbury*, 77; *Les Mohicans de Paris*, 199
dumps, 56, 66

University of Paris, 25, 113
upper class, 47–48, 78, 117, 142, 161, 176, 191, 193, 223–24
urban planning, 26, 34–52, 53, 57; Haussmann and, 39–52; pre-Haussmann, 34–39
urban renewal, 26, 44, 47
urinals, public, 58, 130

vagrants, 20, 29–30 and *n*, 32, 49–50, 65, 96, 144
Vaillant, Auguste, 250
Val d'Amour, 114
Valéry, Paul, 247
Valet, René, 254, 256
Vallès, Jules, 213, 238
Vallotton, Félix, 24, 247; illustrations by, *4, 209, 217, 245, 251*
van der Elsken, Ed, 24, 266; *Love on the Left Bank*, 266, *266*
Vaneigem, Raoul, 269
Van Gogh, Vincent, 118; *The Outskirts of Paris*, 58, *58*
Vanves, 60
Varlin, Eugène, 243
Vaucanson, Jacques de, 47
Vaugirard, 35
vegetables, 101, 184, 234, 253; market, *9, 10*; sellers, *36*
Vendôme column, fall of, 238, *238*
vendors, 9–11, *36*, 58–60, 100–104, *102–104*, 146, *146*, 147, *159*, 164, 234
Verlaine, Paul, 8, 147, *147*, 148, 153, 154
Vermersch, Eugène, 234
Versailles, 30, 193, 235–37, 241, 242
Vichy government, 84, 85, 155*n*
Vidocq, Eugène François, 77, 195–97, 213; *Memoirs*, 77, 196
Vigo, Jean, 129, 185, 209
Villon, François, 33, 42, 44, 97, 137, 191, *191*, 263
Villon, Jacques, 147
Viseur, Gus, 174
Voilà, 142
Voltaire, 212
Volvic, Gilbert Chabrol de, 39

Vouillemont, Paul, photographs by, *21, 42, 45, 46*
Vuillaume, Maxime, 234

walking, 7, 19–32; flâneurs, 23–32, 44, 111, 259–71
walls, 7, 34, 35, 49, 53 and *n*, 56–59, 62; military, 53, 56–57; tax, *53*, 54–55, *56*
Warnod, André, 23, 61, 128, 142, 171, 172
water, 40, 58, 65, 101, 106–107; canals, 106–107, *107*; carriers, 80; infected, 93
weavers, 106, 110
Weill, Kurt, 184, 185, 197
Wely, Jacques, drawing by, *209*
Wilde, Oscar, 141, 212*n*
Willette, Adolphe, illustrations by, *93*, *155*
wine, *15*, 16, 25, 53, 60–61, 68, 135–42, 151, 166, 192, 234, 263; jug, 139
Wolman, Gil J., 266, 267
women, 23*n*, 46, 68; anarchists, 240; bohemian, 153; Commune and, 239–41, *239–41*; criminals, 199–201, *199–200*, 213; dancers, 169–74; insurgents, 226–28, 239–41, *239–40*; labor, 96, 104–106, 109, 240; laundresses, 104–105, *105*, 106; lesbians, 133–34, 186 and *n*; in prison, 118, *118*, 200, 213, 214, *214*, 240, 241; public letter-writers, *99*; Roma, 80; sex trade, 111–34, *112–33*; singers, 177, *177*, 181–90, *182–90*; Zone, 62, 63, *63*, 64
working class, 11, 30, 34, 68, 78–79, 117, 148; industry, 106–10; Jewish, 83; street trades, 99–110
World War I, 24, 46, 66, 67, 89, 110, 115, 168, 184, 219
World War II, 70, 84, 85, 125–26, 134, 204–205, 263–64
writers, 23, 76–78, *99*, 108–10, 147–48, 208, 219, 244, 264; anarchists, 247–48; bohemia, 148–58; ghostwriters, 152; of serial novels, 77–78; *see also specific writers*